Cut in Stone

Cut in Stone

Confederate Monuments and Theological Disruption

Ryan Andrew Newson

BAYLOR UNIVERSITY PRESS

Cover design by Kasey McBeath
Cover image: The Robert E. Lee Monument, Richmond, Va. Photograph
by the author.
Book design by Kasey McBeath

Library of Congress Cataloging-in-Publication Data

Names: Newson, Ryan Andrew, author.
Title: Cut in stone : Confederate monuments and theological disruption /
    Ryan Andrew Newson.
Description: Waco : Baylor University Press, 2020. | Includes
    bibliographical references and index. | Summary: "Theological analysis
    of the meaning of Confederate monuments, arguing for their
    recontextualization through a counternarrative about whiteness, memory,
    and the goal of humanity"-- Provided by publisher.
Identifiers: LCCN 2020008633 (print) | LCCN 2020008634 (ebook) | ISBN
    9781481312165 (hardcover) | ISBN 9781481312202 (adobe pdf) | ISBN
    9781481312196 (kindle edition) | ISBN 9781481312189 (epub)
Subjects: LCSH: United States--History--Civil War, 1861-1865--
    Monuments. | United States--History--Civil War, 1861-1865--
    Moral and ethical aspects.
Classification: LCC E468.9 .N485 2020 (print) | LCC E468.9 (ebook) |
    DDC 973.7/6--dc23
LC record available at https://lccn.loc.gov/2020008633
LC ebook record available at https://lccn.loc.gov/2020008634

Printed in the United States of America on acid-free paper with a
minimum of thirty percent recycled content.

Their land is filled with idols; they bow down to the work of their hands, to what their own fingers have made.

—Isaiah 2:8

Not everything that is faced can be changed, but nothing can be changed until it is faced.

—James Baldwin, "As Much Truth as One Can Bear" (1962), in *The Cross of Redemption* (ed. Kenan), 34

Contents

List of Images

Unless otherwise stated, all photos are by the author.

Preface

"In the name of Jesus, this flag has to come down. You come against me with hatred and oppression and violence. I come against you in the name of God. This flag comes down today." It was June of 2015, and the nation was preoccupied with how to respond to the murder of nine worshippers at Mother Emanuel Church in Charleston, South Carolina. Rightly, attention soon shifted from Dylann Roof himself to the ways his white supremacist views were reinforced by symbols and narratives that are embedded within Southern culture. Indeed, following this church shooting, momentum quickly gathered to remove the Confederate flag that waved on the capitol grounds of South Carolina. The legislature shuffled its feet, and the conversation proceeded at the usual pace and with the repetition of familiar talking points.

Until Bree Newsome.[1] For me, these words spoken by an activist from Charlotte cut through the noise. On June 27, Newsome climbed the flagpole and removed the Confederate flag as a sign of defiance, invoking the name of Jesus as she did so. Something about this action shook me to my core, especially when coupled with the reality of black worshippers welcoming a young white man for Bible study, and for their hospitality receiving an act of violence and cruelty beyond measure. At that moment, I began to think seriously about Confederate iconography and Confederate monuments, and the way these structures are bolstered by

Christian theology. I have not really stopped thinking about these matters since that summer in 2015.

At first, I kept these thoughts to myself. After all, I had but a few intuitions that I could not shake: that removing or somehow disrupting Confederate symbols was long overdue; that the stubbornness or willful ignorance of the many defenders of Confederate images was inexcusable; and, crucially, that uprooting the underlying narratives that gave both Dylann Roof and these symbols their power was much harder work than some seemed to realize. I felt that dealing with these statues was the *beginning* of the work that needed to be done, but some seemed to think it was the end—or worse, that dealing with it was strictly a Southern matter, of little concern to people in other parts of the country. Also, I now had a young son. I knew that when I looked at these statues, my stomach turned at this thought: "What if he grows up to be one of these angry young white men? What if he is taken in by this philosophy, this theology, this narrative, this aesthetic?"

I knew deep in my bones that this ideology needed to be faced and uprooted. I knew that Confederate monuments served as a flashpoint for this investigation. And I knew that doing this work would not be easy.

And so, I wrote. Close friends and colleagues encouraged me as I wrote an op-ed (never published), which grew into a presentation, then into an article, and that article the seeds of this book. The line of thinking I have traced over these past four years has evolved and changed—indeed, I myself have changed as I have walked this road, and current events have outpaced my ability to write on the subject—but my central purpose has remained the same: to uncover and understand the theology behind Confederate monuments. These statues hold great meaning for people. Why? Where is that power coming from? My purpose in writing this book is to lay bare the theological roots of Confederate monuments, in the hopes of disrupting narratives that have been told and retold for generations.

Of course, in attempting to write about Confederate monuments in the contemporary United States, I recognize my limitations. I am a white man. What right do I have to speak on theology, memory, and white supremacy? It is important to name this from the outset. I write from my own social location, and my goal is to describe what I see from this particular vantage point, rather than to write "the book" on theology and Confederate monuments, the last and universal word on this matter for all times and places. Without patronizingly dictating what I think should be done or felt about these statues, I have come to consider it important to deconstruct statues that are built ostensibly for and about me.

Indeed, in some ways I am precisely the kind of person who should be thinking through these issues. This is because Confederate monuments are products of white culture and white theology, and as such it is the charge of white theologians to deconstruct these symbols. Philosopher George Yancy brought this point home for me in his reflections following the revelation that Virginia Governor Ralph Northam is pictured in his 1984 medical school yearbook with one student wearing Ku Klux Klan robes and another wearing blackface. (Whether Northam himself is one of these two students remains inconclusive.) Rather than limiting one's focus to this specific incident, Yancy notes that the very existence of blackface reveals something about the structural reality that could give rise to this practice in the first place. The only way for white people to face the scandal of blackface is to recognize what blackface says about ourselves, for blackface does not tell us anything about black people. Rather, the phenomenon tells us something about whiteness—about the ideological soil that could produce such a thing. "Blackface is not a black problem," Yancy concludes. "It is a white one, and fixing it is the job of white America."[2] These words apply as much to Confederate monuments as to blackface: as the monuments are the constructions of white people, the task of facing and fixing what these statues represent is also the job of white people. The burden is on those of us who benefit from the racialized space these statues create to push against them, recognizing that when it comes to the power and allure of whiteness, Confederate monuments are only the tip of the iceberg.

Faced with such a daunting task, the temptation might be to run. As James Baldwin writes, when a person sees the difference between who one thought one was and who one really is, there are two options: "You can meet the collision head-on and try and become what you really are or you can retreat and try to remain what you thought you were, which is a fantasy, in which you will certainly perish."[3] This book is written in the hope that such a reckoning can yet occur, that some of us will not run. It is a central conviction of mine that this kind of reckoning can happen. Even so, I must admit that lately I have despaired of this possibility becoming an actuality, and when it does happen it seems miraculous. But even if such a reckoning is unlikely, I remain convinced that criticizing the narratives behind Confederate monuments—including narratives that may appear innocuous—is important; at the very least, it reveals the more quotidian forms of violence these statues help normalize. One might succeed in getting Confederate monuments removed without doing the hard work of facing the past and the present. However, skipping that hard work will almost surely leave the underlying narratives that gave these statues their power untouched, thus allowing them a pernicious afterlife that will take forms that are hard to predict.[4] As such, I have attempted to face this collision in myself and society, come what may.

In the time it has taken to complete this book, the list of people to whom I am indebted has grown long. I am deeply thankful for the privilege of teaching and working at Campbell University. Campbell has provided me with an institutional home to do theological work, and afforded me the blessed opportunity to teach students about God, theology, and ethics. Campbell is a place where investigations of this sort are not merely tolerated but supported and empowered. This support was spiritual and psychological as well as material, including a summer research grant and access to the treasure trove that is Wiggins Memorial Library. When resources were not in Campbell's library—and this was rare—they were granted to me thanks to Anna Grace Fitzgerald, who checked out books for me from North Carolina State University. Thank you for this case of nerdy rule breaking; it allowed me the ability to read books outside the lonely confines of an eighth-floor library desk.

Many thanks to the wonderful people at Baylor University Press, who saw the value of this project when it was little more than an idea and helped craft it into what it is now. This book is better for the insights and advice given by the editorial staff all along the way.

Several friends and colleagues warrant special thanks for listening to me at varying stages of writing, pointing me toward resources and critiquing my claims in ways that honed what I try to say here. Tommy Givens helped reframe the questions I was asking on this subject early in the process. Mikeal Broadway thought through ways churches could respond to Confederate monuments in their local communities; I am happy that our initial conversations some four years ago have blossomed into a friendship that I treasure. Karen Guth read an early article on this topic, encouraging me and pointing me to resources to consider as I continued to write. E. Harold Breitenberg was also encouraging early in the process. Conversations with Kris Norris helped and encouraged me along the way. Andrew Wright and Eric Schnitger walked with me through New Orleans several years ago, visiting several of these monuments and thinking aloud with me about their theological weightiness. Scott Looney helped clarify the connections I was making between speech-act theory and monumental performance. Kolby Knight introduced me to Michel-Rolph Trouillot, who became a central conversation partner. Tracey Stout and Rebecca Todd Peters offered invaluable feedback during a session of the Southeastern Commission for the Study of Religion. Indeed, questions and feedback offered by colleagues at the Society of Christian Ethics and the National Association of Baptist Professors of Religion were immensely helpful. Obviously, by mentioning these people I do not mean to suggest that they endorse the work done here; it is simply to say that they made what does appear here better, saving me from several misstatements and generalizations.

I have now been in the academy long enough to know that not every department is as collegial and encouraging as mine. I count myself lucky to work with people who cheer each other on, who are excited to discuss these topics during work and after, and who generously offer their time reading essays and articles for one another. Truly and deeply, thank you—Jen, Thomas, Adam, Glenn, Kathy, and Ken.

Rarer still is having a spouse who is willing and able to provide feedback on a piece of writing like this—who is truly called "partner." But I am exceptionally lucky, beyond my deserving. Before anyone else, Rebecca saw that I should write this book, and encouraged me to follow the argument wherever it took me. She gave me space to read and think, and thought aloud with me about monuments and race and Christology. More than this, she read through the entire manuscript (twice), editing for clarity and providing substantive feedback. Thank you for your patience and erudition over these past four years. More than I can say, you know.

As always, I am thankful to my family, my children and brothers and sisters and parents and in-laws. I see all that you all do for us, and it means the world.

Finally, I dedicate this book to my dad. My dad is not a theologian. At least, he wouldn't say that he is. But he is an able writer and a careful thinker, and someone who is willing to read an entire manuscript to offer his insights and copyedits and critiques. And perhaps that is what is owed, since it was my dad who piqued my interest in American history and the Civil War a long time ago, and who would always dismiss what I now know were "Lost Cause" talking points. ("My teacher says that the South fought for states' rights, not slavery." "Well, your teacher is wrong.") There are few people I would lay this burden on in this world, but to him I think it is fair: what's written here, for good and ill, is in large measure your fault.

And so, I dedicate this book to my father, in hope that another world may yet emerge, for him and for his grandchildren. Despite everything, I still believe it is possible.

Introduction

> The true focus of revolutionary change is never merely the oppressive situations which we seek to escape, but that piece of the oppressor which is planted deep within each of us.
>
> Audre Lorde[1]

The debate over Confederate monuments was forever changed on August 12, 2017, when several thousand white nationalists, neo-Confederates, and members of the alt-right descended on Charlottesville, Virginia. The previous evening, about three hundred attendees of the "Unite the Right" rally gathered on the campus of the University of Virginia, carrying torches and chanting "White Lives Matter," "Blood and Soil," "You will not replace us," and "Jews will not replace us." The throng of white nationalists marched to the Rotunda on UVA's campus, which sits across the street from and in view of St. Paul's Memorial Church. On this night, about six hundred protesters, local clergy, and other organizers who opposed the Unite the Right rally were gathering for prayer and training. The people in the church were concerned for their safety with this group of white nationalists headed their way, and so a makeshift security team was put together, made up of professors and clergy.[2] But the marchers did not bother the people

1

anxiously preparing for a day of nonviolent protest; instead, they continued toward the statue of Thomas Jefferson, where a small group of unarmed and unprotected students were protesting at the base of the statue, holding a single sign that read: "VA Students Act Against White Supremacy." The marchers stopped and surrounded the students—thirty students trapped by three hundred white nationalists—who were yelled at, intimidated, and finally attacked. People in both groups used pepper spray. It is possible that the violence might have escalated, but it was at this moment that the police arrived and dispersed the crowd. During the entire haunting scene, the marbleized form of Thomas Jefferson stood in the background, watching in silence.

This march through campus was only a preview of things to come. The next day, white nationalists gathered once more for their planned rally. Thirty clergy members sang "This Little Light of Mine," while white nationalists responded with chants of "Our blood, our soil!", a clear reference to Nazi ideology.[3] The ranks of protesters and counter-protesters swelled, and clashes between the two occurred for hours. DeAndre Harris, a counter-protester, was beaten by six men within feet of the police headquarters. Finally, unlawful assembly was declared, and the crowd was again dispersed. People continued to march and gather, however, and in the early afternoon a twenty-year-old white nationalist from Ohio drove his car into a crowd of counter-protesters, injuring nineteen people and killing Heather Heyer.

What was it that prompted these forces of the Right to gather on this particular weekend and in this particular town? At least on the surface, the protesters were not gathered for an abstract idea or a politician; they gathered because of a monument. The Unite the Right rally was planned in order to defend a statue of Robert E. Lee (erected in 1924), which had been slated for removal from Emancipation Park by the city council. In making this decision, Charlottesville was following the lead of dozens of cities across the country. On June 17, 2015—the day after Donald Trump announced his candidacy for the presidency—a white supremacist entered the iconic Mother Emanuel Church in Charleston, South Carolina and killed nine black church members during a Bible study. Following this heinous act committed by Dylann Roof, a twenty-one-year-old from South Carolina, many Confederate flags and monuments were removed from places of public prominence and governmental property.[4]

The act of removing Confederate imagery and iconography reenergized the debate about the appropriateness of Confederate symbols in public. Some people supported the act of profoundly disrupting and removing Confederate statues and flags. While such actions might be long overdue and symbolic, removing Confederate imagery would at least signal a desire and willingness to move forward as a society. However, embarking on this path made it clear that Confederate symbols were far more ubiquitous and embedded within the structure of American society than previously imagined.[5] Confederate images seemed to be hiding around every corner, smuggled into every cultural nook and cranny. Even Mother Emanuel's address spoke to this phenomenon: the church sits on Calhoun Street, which is named after John C. Calhoun (d. 1850), a former vice president of the United States who refused to say that slavery was a necessary economic practice or the lesser of two evils. Instead, Calhoun defended slavery as a positive good, rooting his argument in paternalism and white supremacy.[6] One of the most iconic and important African American churches in the South has an address named after a perfect embodiment of its ideological enemy. The work of removing Confederate symbols from public view would be difficult, it turned out; some could easily be removed—such as a flag—but others would take more time to remove, like street names and monuments. Regardless of whether or not these symbols were changed, the poison these Confederate symbols represented continued to flow through the veins of the body politic. For some activists, Charlottesville revealed that there could be no more waiting with Confederate monuments; the statues represented a sickness at the heart of the nation and must be toppled, by whatever means necessary. This attitude was well represented by a group of protesters in Durham, North Carolina, who pulled down the Confederate monument in town (also erected in 1924) two days after Charlottesville. And of course, other people perceived the removal of Confederate imagery as a threat to their heritage and identity, much like the white nationalists in Charlottesville. In public, a version of white grievance politics reemerged as a national force, wherein people argued that removing Confederate statues presaged a wider erasure of white identity.[7]

At Charlottesville, something about Confederate monuments was laid bare, reframing the debate about their place in society from then on. Confederate monuments served as physical objects toward which people could direct their anxieties about the present and the future: fear of the other that feeds a neo-authoritarian impulse, fear of being forgotten by future generations, and fear about the return of white supremacy in a way that some people had believed (or hoped) was long gone. Wounds that had been ignored or hidden were revealed once more. An American apocalypse was happening, and Confederate monuments sat at the center of the unveiling. To be sure, the events in Charlottesville were not *just* about a monument; deeper forces were at play. But the Confederate monument had something to do with the forces that were conjured on that day—both the forces of evil and the forces resisting the return of white supremacy. The Robert E. Lee statue stood in the background of the entire murderous weekend. The events in Charlottesville could not be divorced from the monument. Some connection existed between the Confederate statue and the teeming collection of people that was at once powerful and subtle, evoking issues of race, memory, power, justice, and societal ideals. A response was now required, for Confederate monuments would no longer go unnoticed or hide in plain sight.

Monumental Parallels and Types of Response

The crisis represented by Confederate monuments—how a society should face its past, and particularly injustices from its past, without valorizing these events—is not relegated to the United States or the American South. It is a constant challenge for cultures to think through how to remember complex or unjust legacies that enable their present existence. Debates similar to the ones surrounding Confederate monuments have happened elsewhere in the world, particularly in countries marked by settler colonialism.

For instance, in 2015 a global campaign was waged to take down statues to Cecil Rhodes, a British imperialist and racist.

The campaign began at the University of Cape Town in South Africa, and it was successful: the statue to Rhodes was eventually removed from that campus. From there, the movement spread to other universities in South Africa with monuments to Rhodes. Attention eventually focused on the Rhodes statue at Oxford University itself, and a heated debate unfolded that Oriel College administrators were taking seriously. However, the debate ended when prominent alumni threatened to withdraw donations to the school if the statue was removed. Some estimate that the school was set to lose up to £100 million.[8] In Swakopmund, Namibia, a statue memorializing German soldiers who committed genocide against rebelling native populations came under fire. So offensive was this monument that it was repeatedly splattered with fake blood. Residents asked for the monument to be put in a museum or destroyed, but to leave a statue glorifying such events was said to be a disgrace and an insult.[9] In Budapest, following the fall of the Soviet Union, Hungarians seeking to remember and educate about the Stalinist dictatorship moved statues of Communist leaders out of the cityscape and to a special "monument park" in 1993. The idea was that rather than destroying these monuments or leaving them undisturbed, they should be placed in a context in which lessons from the past could be taught with less danger of glorification.[10] And in the United States, Confederate monuments are not alone in attracting controversy. Even in Charlottesville, the statue of Thomas Jefferson has drawn criticism, and it has periodically been covered with a shroud or marked for removal. In April of 2018, it was spray-painted with the words "Racist + Rapist."[11] Some activists have suggested that monuments to any slaveholder should be removed, including George Washington.[12]

While every struggle over the appropriateness of a given monument is distinct, they also tend to evoke similar questions that are as complicated as they are controversial and important. Inheriting or forgetting problematic features of the past is tricky business, and something as innocuous as a statue suddenly serves as the grounds of a cultural proxy war. Debates over monuments inevitably involve questions of power—who gets to narrate the past, and whose narration is privileged in the present articulation of things—which usually dovetails into questions about who has the resources to make one's version of the past heard.[13] Debates about statues concern whether and how a society should learn from or forget the "mistakes" of the past, and in many cases they concern questions about the danger of remembering the past. People contesting a monument tend to point to the absence of other versions of history in the public landscape, particularly stories issuing from subaltern members of the society in question. And in disputes over controversial monuments, the question arises as to why societies remember the past through public symbols at all. In short, to think through issues that are brought up by Confederate monuments is not an isolated investigation: it opens onto challenges of collective memory, past sins, contested space, and the values of a pluralist society.[14]

Calls for a statue to be removed are usually what get controversies about monuments off the ground in the first place, as they spark the debate about a monument's appropriateness, usefulness, or offensiveness. The motive behind the call for removal is twofold: to avoid public valorization of something like a rebellion fought to continue enslaving other humans, and to undermine coded messages monuments always contain in their placement and design. The call to remove monuments notices that something is wrong with the way the past is being remembered and seeks to destroy the offending symbol. Of course, the mirror opposite response is to protect monuments from destruction or alteration. Whenever a monument is criticized, there will be people who rise up to defend it against attack. Descriptively speaking, such defenses can only come from people who are comfortable with the status quo and who find very little fault with the way the past is narrated. One type of defense is couched in the language of neutrality, claiming that monuments are just monuments after all, and are only meant to help people remember the past. As such, any desire to change monuments must be motivated by political or ideological commitments, as opposed to the monuments themselves, which are seen as simple markers of remembrance. On this view, monuments are neutral; calls to remove them are not. Often accompanying such a call is the reminder that one cannot simply rewrite the past in order to avoid events that people now recognize to be wrong. Best to let sleeping dogs lie and to look forward, not back. This argument suggests objectivity on the part of the one making it—they, unlike others, are not driven by passions or desires. However, this argument can also be made without this kind of performative detachment. In the latter case, defenders of monuments will argue that the problematic events in question are actually good and should be remembered for that reason; they do not grant that the monuments are problematic. Those who publicly defend Confederate monuments against what they call "white genocide" would fall into this category.[15]

For others, the proper response to monuments that are offensive is not to deny the problematic nature of the monument in question, but to alter the way it functions in the public landscape. This response seeks to move beyond either total removal or neutral defense as the only two options of monumental disruption. The motives for taking this more complicated and controversial path can vary. Some societies will be motivated to remember and educate future generations, as in the case of the Budapest removal of statues to Monument Park. This type of response may also be a physical necessity for some monuments, given their design or size. For instance, if Americans one day decided to take down every single statue to Thomas Jefferson, they would still have to be rather creative with Mount Rushmore! The goal of this response is to alter the monument such that its performative power is disrupted, altered, or shifted.[16] In any case, no response to a monument is neutral; each is "valued" and embodies a particular point of view about the world and the nature of ultimate reality.[17] Even to do nothing is to make a choice.

Theological Description and Disruption

The response to monuments one instinctively prefers depends on one's social location and background, the vision of the good life that one wishes to impart to future generations, the value one places on public memory in general, and where one locates oneself in the culture wars that continue to mark American politics.[18] But there is a sense in which to restrict analysis of Confederate monuments to matters of politics, culture, or history is to neglect deeper issues of theology that are prompted by the statues themselves, and this can lead to superficial responses to the challenge at hand. Historical analysis can only go so far in untangling the power of Confederate monuments, for that power is wrapped up in the theological convictions these statues already manifest but that are only sometimes made explicit.[19] Confederate monuments are not ideologically neutral, and arguments that present them as such should be dismissed. Nonetheless, given the deep, intergenerational convictions that gave rise to these statues, the quick and simple removal of monuments may not go deep enough into the soil that produced them in the first place. Cries of "This is not us!" clash with the continued prevalence of policies that negatively and specifically impact African Americans and other people of color, to the degree that they can be described as a kind of new Jim Crow.[20] The sad truth is that this *is* the United States—and not just the South—much as one may wish it were not.[21] Something seems off, even dangerous, about insisting that this is not the present reality of the United States; it rings like a signal that one is not really a part of this history, that one could sidestep a confession of one's complicity, ignorance, or laziness.

To pay attention to the theology evoked by Confederate monuments is to deepen one's criticism of these statues without neglecting sociopolitical, historical, and philosophical modes of analysis. Viewed through a theological lens, the spiritual and explicitly Christian imagery utilized on Confederate monuments becomes much more obvious. Even on a surface level this has always been true: Confederate monuments employ Christian language and symbols in a way that is sincere—that is, their employment is not a cynical attempt at controlling the population but is a genuine expression of a type of religiosity, indeed theology, that produced these structures. But at a deeper level, in their performativity, Confederate monuments unquestionably conjure forces and attitudes that cry out for theological analysis: questions about where a society should be headed, the nature of remembrance, and constant evocations of the language of sacrifice. Confederate monuments clearly produce attitudes and beliefs in their defenders that are quasi-religious, and thus it is vital to produce theological reflections about the monuments that challenge these beliefs head-on—even if such reflections expand and destabilize the conversation as it is normally conducted. Undermining Confederate monuments at their most fundamental level must include undermining the theology that they assume and reinforce for future generations; anything less is to ignore a huge part of their performative power.

Any theological analysis of Confederate monuments must attend to the complex relationship monuments have with time: their stance toward the past, their hopes for the future, and their performativity in the present. Monuments purport to remember some aspect of the past, necessarily implying that this event or person is more worthy of remembrance than others. Monuments always do this remembering in service to some future end, in the hope that in remembering this event the future will be affected in ways it would not be otherwise. And monuments always function in some historical present, with and for people who can maintain or alter them based on circumstances that change the aspect under which a monument appears. Each element of monuments—past, present, future—is intimately related to and even implies the other, which is precisely what gives monuments their performative power. Unlike a piece of art that is safely relegated to a museum or a collector's house, a monument does not privilege the past over the present, but leverages the past to make claims about the future.[22]

Happily, Confederate monuments' relationship to the past, present, and future dovetails with theological convictions. Christians have always had a stake in remembering well. For Christians, history is not autonomous, but exists in relation to the God of all time. A theological assessment of the quality or non-quality of an object's stance toward the past, then, should be intimately informed by the Christian conviction that God remembers every past in order to judge and redeem creation. Put differently, Christians have a stake in avoiding theories about the past that reinforce a way of remembering that acts as if God does not exist.[23] Regarding the future, Christian theology clearly has much to say about the goal humanity should be aiming toward, and which ideals should be named as idolatrous. Indeed, when it comes to the gods of blood and soil that were explicitly conjured at Charlottesville, Christians must once again declare themselves to be atheists. And

Christians have a stake in creating a society marked by justice and which is capable, to whatever limited extent, of facing the injustices of the past in order to achieve a good that is truly common. In proceeding in this way, Christian theology might be able to help Americans—including Americans of other faiths or no faith—to face the past in order to act differently in the present and the future.

Charlottesville revealed that the challenges represented by Confederate monuments are of immediate importance and must be addressed with urgency and care. The central problem with Confederate monuments is not so much the events they remember or fail to remember, but the way these events are pieced together. It is the framing of these events that makes them untruthful, and the particular frame employed here is the myth of white supremacy. Given that one cannot totally erase the elements of memory with which one has to work, the task is to put these events together differently, in such a way that Americans, and particularly white Americans, begin to recognize how deep the sin of white supremacy really goes. White supremacy is in the DNA of this country, North and South alike, and until this is recognized and repented of, the ills signaled by Confederate monuments will continue to wreak havoc on the present, unnoticed and unabated.

1

History

Monuments' Shifting Contexts

The most terrible thing about War, I am convinced, is its
monuments—the awful things we are compelled to build in order to remember the victims. In the South, particularly, human ingenuity has been
put to it to explain on its war monuments, the Confederacy. Of course,
the plain truth of the matter would be an inscription something like
this: "Sacred to the memory of those who fought to Perpetuate Human
Slavery." But that reads with increasing difficulty as time goes on. It does,
however, seem to be overdoing the matter to read on a North Carolina
Confederate monument: "Died Fighting for Liberty!"

W. E. B. Du Bois[1]

Confederate monuments are not neutral. The statues did not fall
from the sky, they did not emerge from nothingness, and they
were not erected free from the ideologies of their day. Quite the
opposite, Confederate monuments embody the often uninterrogated values of the cities, states, and country within which they
sit. But monuments tend to hide this fact about themselves, going
overlooked and unseen for long stretches of time. Monuments can
stand in a city square for years, as prominent as any street sign,

11

and serve as little more than a marker for locals to use in giving directions or a place for people experiencing homelessness to find rest. And yet it only takes a person looking at the monument from a slightly different angle, by virtue of their being from out of town or being raised under different circumstances, to thrust a monument into painful obviousness. Even a single event can change the way a monument appears, moving it from something one cannot see to something one cannot avoid seeing, for good or ill. Human attention is funny that way: a phenomenon, a historical narrative, a set of facts about the world becomes more or less obvious depending on if attention is directed toward it. What people see depends upon what they look for.[2]

The famous "gorilla experiment" illustrates this fact about human attention well. In the experiment, subjects are directed to watch a video of people playing basketball and told to count the number of passes between people wearing white shirts. While the subject's attention is focused on counting passes, a person in a gorilla suit walks on the court. The experiment found that a majority of subjects did not notice the gorilla.[3] The conclusion to draw from this experiment is not that humans are blind to obvious things, per se; it is rather that what humans seek, they tend to find. While this experiment does suggest that human attention is capable of being directed rather easily, the good news is that it also suggests that people's attention can be redirected if they are given a different set of things to look for. After all, everyone notices the gorilla once they watch the video a second time and are told to keep an eye out for it. Only the most willfully ignorant, stubborn, or delusional person would say otherwise. Until recently, Confederate monuments were gorillas in the cityscape, at least for white Southerners. These statues to the Confederacy embodied the values of American Southern society with such subtlety that they were often ignored, both revealing and hiding truths about the South and the United States. But then the Dylann Roof shooting happened, followed by the Charlottesville disaster, and rather quickly the gorillas became noticeable. The historians and activists who had been decrying Confederate monuments for decades could now be heard; the story they had been telling about these monuments suddenly seemed much more plausible, even obvious.

Of course, from time immemorial humans have memorialized the dead, battles, and other significant events, whether through paintings on walls or rocks drawn from rivers that remind one to tell a story to one's children. Humans are story-telling animals, including stories which are remembered and passed down to the next generation. Confederate monuments themselves are stories that are passed down and that orient a people toward the past. But monuments face the past in a particular way and for a particular reason: in order to shape the future, assuming and projecting a particular vision of the future onto the past, for future generations to receive. What is more, the way monuments face the past is rooted in the power struggles and arguments of the present. Confederate monuments thus tend to be haunted spaces where time collapses onto a structure in a way that is highly contested.

The Southerners who erected Confederate monuments were often quite explicit about how they thought right remembrance of the Civil War was vital to the society they were constructing as well as the shape they hoped that society would take in the future. Consider these words from John B. Gordon, issued in 1895:

> To cherish such memories and recall such a past whether crowned with success or consecrated in defeat, is to idealize principle and strengthen character, intensify love of country and convert defeat and disaster into pillars of support for future manhood and womanhood. Whether the Southern people under their changed conditions may ever hope to witness another civilization which shall equal that which began with their Washington and ended with their Lee, it is certainly true that devotion to their glorious past is not only the surest guarantee of future progress and holiest bond of unity, but also the strongest claim they can present to the conscience and respect of the other sections of the Union.[4]

Confederate memory was never simply about the past. It was also wrapped up in an idealized version of this past that, if proper "devotion" was paid to it, would forge a "holy bond" of solidarity in the present and guarantee success in the future. Confederate monuments were constructed and utilized to reinforce a narrative in the South that was built on explicitly Christian themes. What is more, the sacred canopy created by Confederate monuments is not simply a mask for a broader will to power. It is genuine in its deployment of theological imagery. As such, making the theology of Confederate monuments explicit is important to critiquing them at the deepest possible level; it uncovers the theological soil from which Confederate monuments spring, and in which they flourish. Attending to the theology within and behind Confederate monuments is thus important to understanding these monuments in their full complexity, and because for Christians what is at stake with these monuments is the faithful use of theological language in public.

In order to understand Confederate monuments and dismantle the underlying theological, racist convictions that they assume, it is imperative to begin with a thick description of their history in the United States. After all, one cannot debate the significance of any historical product without considering the context of its contemporary consumption as well as the context within which it was produced in the first place.[5] Any honest assessment of the historical context of Confederate monuments reveals twin ideological commitments that can sometimes be explicitly found on the monuments themselves, but more often are implicit in the monument's design, placement, and date of construction. These commitments are the "Lost Cause" narrative, which attempted to whitewash the history of the Civil War, and the belief in white supremacy that necessitated this historical renarration. The often-assumed function of Confederate monuments as sites of mourning that were constructed immediately following the Civil War is complicated, if not belied, by attending to this history.

First Wave: Grief and Lost Honor

The historical backdrop of Confederate monuments is complicated. Layers of meaning and encoded symbols have accrued over time, forming a tapestry that stone monoliths both reveal and hide insofar as they appear simple and unmoving. What any honest assessment of the history of Confederate monuments reveals is the contested nature of these structures, not just today but from their inception. In order to understand these monuments, then, one must understand their aesthetic, geographical, and chronological diversity. A major source of confusion in arguments about Confederate monuments is their being treated as though they are homogenous. But not all Confederate monuments are alike or perform in the same way, and getting clear about the distinctions between Confederate monuments allows one to specify precisely what makes them problematic.

The initial wave of Confederate monuments came after the Civil War ended in 1865. The Civil War was devastating, and in the South the land itself bore the scars of battle. Whole towns were destroyed, whole generations of young men gone. Reporting the raw number of casualties itself tells a gruesome story. About as many died during the Civil War as died in all other American wars combined; further, the number of casualties in the Battle of Gettysburg alone nearly doubled the total number of battle casualties from all previous American wars.[6] But these numbers do not begin to describe the psychological damage the war had on people in the United States. The fighting was brutal and protracted. The fighting was in one's backyard. The fighting was with neighbors and friends. Even for those who came to see the war as the righteous struggle for the abolition of slavery, the trauma of it was no less real.

Initial efforts to memorialize the Confederate dead were slow, not only because everyone was still getting over the shock of the war, but also because the postbellum South was economically devastated. The infrastructure, political will, and funds were not readily available for such projects. The earliest memorial to Confederate soldiers was dedicated in Romney, West Virginia in 1867. It was placed, appropriately enough, in a cemetery, and its muted aesthetic came to reflect many Confederate monuments erected during this time throughout the South. The form the monument took was an obelisk—a tall, narrow monument reaching to the sky, similar to the Washington Monument—with names inscribed on the side. And yet the complicated process of historical interpretation is already present in this first Confederate monument. Its inscription—"The Daughters of Old Hampshire Erect This Tribute of Affection to Her Heroic Sons Who Fell in Defence of Southern Rights"—is mute about which rights these heroic sons fought to defend. Interestingly, the town of Cheraw,

South Carolina disputes Romney's claim to having the earliest Confederate monument, and the monument there is similar in tone and placement. Located in a cemetery and dedicated in 1867, its inscription reads: "To the memory of our heroic dead who fell at Cheraw during the war 1861–1865. Loved and honored though unknown. Stranger, bold champion of the South, revere and view these tombs with love; Brave heroes slumber here, Loved, and Honored, though unknown." The underlying cause of the war that evoked such martial bravery is not mentioned; a pregnant silence marks these inscriptions. Nonetheless, the tone of both monuments is mournfulness rather than triumph or defiance, which was evident in the ceremony marking the latter monument's dedication. Speaking at the monument's unveiling, J. H. Hudson remarked: "Darkness has come upon us—poverty is our lot, and a sigh our song, . . . The land that once blossomed as a garden, and flowed with milk and honey, is now draped in sorrow and desolation."[7]

In their own ways, both monuments exemplify twin concerns that show up in early Confederate monuments: grief and the recovery of honor. From these starting points people tended either toward escapism or pining to somehow recover that lost world. On the one hand, understandable grief at the sheer loss of life—including one's family members, neighbors, and friends—is on display in these monuments. Memorial markers are never only about grief, particularly if they are prominently displayed in public space, but they can *also* be about grief, especially early in the process of memorialization. Almost immediately at the close of the Civil War, plans were made to gather Confederate dead, as well as to memorialize fallen soldiers—an important task given that a great many men and boys died anonymously. Memorial associations sprung up across the South, often with names like the Ladies' Memorial Association (LMA), under the belief that "sentimental" matters were better handled by women.[8] While markers were sometimes placed in local battlefields, the preference was to have cemeteries erected in local communities and for markers to go in these cemeteries.[9] Monuments erected in the first two decades after the Civil War overwhelmingly served to grieve the dead. Indeed, over 90 percent of the monuments erected in this time had some "funereal aspect" in placement or design, and 70 percent were placed directly in cemeteries, which came to be known as "cities of the dead."[10]

On the other hand, the process of memorialization is complicated, even if it is ostensibly motivated by and expressive of grief. Monuments always purport to be about some past event, but they are never only about the past. Because someone has to build them, because the people with financial resources (or the ear of those with resources) are the ones who will be able to do the building, and because this kind of work is bound to spark argumentation, monuments are inexorably rooted in the political needs of the moment.[11] Motives are always mixed. As a case in point, the other major concern among white people during the earliest period of Confederate monument construction was a loss of honor, and even early monuments served to assure white people that this honor would not be defamed. The war had already challenged traditional conceptions of masculinity and femininity. In some cases, women agitated against elements of the war effort, although these efforts were largely forgotten in subsequent years.[12] But even supportive women presented a challenge to traditional gender roles insofar as many performed "masculine" roles while the men were away, and insofar as the men had failed in their task of "protecting the women and children." Furthermore, the loss of the war itself was seen as emasculating. Exemplifying this fear is the rumor of Jefferson Davis being caught by the Union trying to escape capture by dressing as a woman, which the North picked on mercilessly.[13] A loss of white male honor, and the visceral need to reassert it, was a major concern. It was one thing to imagine one's loved one dying in battle for an honorable cause or for their country. But as one woman wrote in her diary, "now to know that those glad, bright spirits suffered and toiled in vain, that the end is overwhelming defeat, the thought is unendurable."[14]

Some Southerners could not face this reality, and withdrew into alcohol and opiate abuse, religious piety, or (in rare cases) dreamt of leaving the United States altogether. Beginning in 1865, groups of Southerners variously attempted to emigrate to other countries—most prominently Brazil and Mexico—in order to recreate a slave society. These projects were not successful. The past was gone, and attempts to recreate it in other lands proved quixotic. But for some Southerners, apparently, it was better to attempt a society with slaves elsewhere than brave a homeland with freed blacks. While these emigrants constituted a tiny minority (ten thousand people), they represented the general mood even for people who stayed home. The goal had to be to reclaim honor, which (in many white Southerners' minds) was further wounded by the imposition of Reconstruction, the requirement to swear an oath of loyalty to the United States, and the mere presence of black people in seats of power.[15]

The emergence of Confederate monuments as objects of cultural significance was bolstered by the creation of Confederate Memorial Day or "Decoration Day." These celebrations, which were at once marked by lament and latent hope, had as their goal the decoration of Confederate graves and likely had multiple independent origins beginning in 1866. Celebrated on various days in the spring, towns would close as people gathered to sing hymns, listen to speeches from veterans and politicians, and hear an address by a local minister. Speeches typically despaired of Southern defeat, mourned the dead, and vaguely defended the purity of the motives of those who fought. Immensely popular, the gatherings would express grief as well as bring the community together in a show of solidarity to face the present and the future; it allowed white Southerners to face the fact of their defeat without disparaging those who were defeated.[16] Put differently, it offered a vague sense of hope for some future vindication, and through that process created a powerful set of cultural symbols that would decorate the "New South."[17] These celebrations served as the beginnings of a civil religion in that they were ritualized, they brought together elements of the past, present, and future, they strengthened the bonds of the community, and they invoked the transcendent.[18] Decoration Day became something of a holy day, and Southern women would compare those decorating the graves to Mary and Martha who attended the tomb of Christ. Other contemporary voices compared the aroma of flowers on Memorial Day to "incense burning in golden censers to the memory of the saints."[19] The combination of non-deistic Christianity and Confederate ritual was intimately tied not just to ideology, but items—physical artifacts and symbols that gathered people together and held special significance.[20] Monuments and memorials in particular were central to the ritualistic process. The use of devotional objects, despite the usual aversion Southern Protestants had to "outward signs," continued even after Decoration Day waned in popularity. The entire process of mourning offered relief to white Southerners longing for escape, who lamented both dead soldiers and a dead cause by incorporating these feelings into a memorial movement that transcended their individual attitudes.[21]

Confederate Memorial Day also reveals the one-sided nature of this mourning, and how the events were geared toward white people's sense of grief. The very presence of black people in the South complicated the processes of mourning and "honor-claiming" that were going on. Clearly, reception of the South's defeat in former slave communities would be different than in the majority of white communities, but the contested nature of this reception is not represented in the official process of memorialization, even of these early "grieving" monuments. In reality, Memorial Day betrayed a contest between three divergent, sometimes overlapping, groups: black people and their abolitionist allies, white Northerners, and white Southerners.[22] Each group represented deep fissures within the newly recreated United States—different civil religions with different understandings of the American story and different views of where the American experiment should go.[23] Black communities mourned the dead and remembered the war in early rituals at battlefields and cemeteries as well.[24] But freed slaves did not have the political, cultural, or material power to influence a wider audience. Black communities did not remember in the same way as many of their white neighbors, and as such they used Memorial Day for different purposes. The struggle over Civil War memory had begun.[25]

And so in the South, a predominant use of Memorial Days and the monuments they gathered around was resistance to Reconstruction and the fear of "black domination," of radical ideology taken too far—a view eventually echoed by some Northern commentators as well.[26] Even early monuments were erected in a context of intransigent resistance to and resentment of Northern rule, and the association with black empowerment assumed by such rule. One of the oldest monuments in North Carolina illustrates the complex mix of mourning and resentment found within Confederate monuments constructed during this period: the monument in Historic Oakwood Cemetery in Raleigh, dedicated in 1870. An obelisk erected in the years immediately following the war, the early date of its dedication as well as its placement in and among the dead would suggest that it is, in part, about mourning a societal loss. And yet the message that would become more amplified and coded in future monuments is inscribed directly on the monument, which shades into something besides mourning: "Sleep warrior, sleep the struggle, The battle-cry is hushed, our standards have been lowered, our blooming hopes been crushed." The precise nature of these crushed hopes is left unstated, although one can guess: the hope of an independent nation-state is what has been crushed. But in the midst of Reconstruction, this expression of crushed hope cannot be separated from the sense that the

Fig. 1.1 The Oakwood Cemetery Obelisk, Raleigh, N.C.

South was enduring a lowering of Southern honor and valor at the hands of Northern aggressors, rulers, and scalawags (Southern cooperators).

Over time, grief morphed into anger and active resistance to these seismic societal changes, as is evidenced by instances of mob violence in the years following the war, typically utilized to suppress the vote. The height of such violence was during the second wave of monument building, but it began in earnest during this early period. Already in 1868, the Democratic strategy in the presidential election was to openly express white supremacist views in order to resist "Republican oppression" of the South as well as rule by a "semi-barbarous race of blacks," as vice presidential candidate Frank Blair put it.[27] With the passage of the Fifteenth Amendment in 1870, many commentators declared an end to the "negro problem," as it was often called, even though words of warning about a growing white counterrevolution were being issued by black voices in the South.[28] And indeed, at least 10 percent of black members of constitutional conventions were victims of Klan violence in 1867–1868. During elections, white mobs would not infrequently use vigilante violence to terrorize the black community and assure a low voter turnout, or to celebrate an electoral victory, as in 1870. Around four hundred lynchings were committed by the Klan between 1868–1871 alone.[29] While these lynchings did not take place in the majority of counties, their purpose was to send a message far past one's local town: acquiesce to white Democratic power, or else.

Congress investigated the Klan and these instances of violence, culminating in a report that provides thousands of pages of testimonies of the violence suffered by victims who usually feared returning to their homes. And when black homes were abandoned for fear of further vigilante violence, white people did not hesitate to seize the vacated land. Generally, Democratic Southern presses claimed that these charges were either not real, were exaggerated, or were the product of Republican propaganda, and counterclaimed that Southern whites were the real victims of Reconstruction-era policies. More often, Southern white folks simply remained silent about lynching.[30] The silence exhibited in early Confederate monuments and by the speakers at these ritualized gatherings—as well as the growing silence about slavery even being partly related to the reasons the South fought in the Civil War—portended a coming wave of reaction against the war's result. The path to preservation of honor through mourning would be to accept the abolition of slavery as providential while retaining the white supremacy that had been used to justify its retention. As to guilt over slavery and secession, few Southerners showed any expression of the like. One reason for this could be that the guilt was so deep that it could not be acknowledged even to oneself. But another, haunting possibility is that no guilt was expressed because no guilt was felt.[31]

Second Wave: The Lost Cause, Lynching, and Jim Crow

If the first wave of Confederate monuments was generally marked by mourning, silence, and a coded nostalgia for an age gone by, the second wave moved toward a more explicit form of triumphalism, apologetics, and blatant expressions of white superiority while retaining a silence on the racialized causes of the war itself. The majority of Confederate monuments were dedicated not in the years immediately following the Civil War but decades later, peaking in the 1910s. As such, most Confederate monuments reflect a time period when white people across the country were reclaiming power that was threatened by Republican black and Populist white political movements through the passage of Jim Crow laws and the horrific practice of lynching. In short, the majority of Confederate monuments were erected during the struggle to reestablish America as a white nation and reinforce the belief that black people are inherently subordinate and therefore unfit for governing.[32]

There is no bright line separating the first and second waves of monument building, but there is also no question that a major shift occurred as the country moved further away from the war itself. Confederate monuments completed after 1885 are markedly different from the ones that came before, both in placement and design.[33] Instead of cemetery markers and monuments containing a funerary design mourning the dead, by the 1890s the main wave of Confederate monuments began. These monuments tended to be placed not in cemeteries and battlefields but in places of public prominence, active government property, and spaces of political power—legislative buildings and courthouses. Simultaneous to this explosion of Confederate monuments was the emergence of the "common soldier" statue—containing a single white man with a gun resting at his side—with 192 documented examples placed in towns between 1900 and 1912 alone, by far the biggest increase in monument construction.[34] As such, the main jump in the number of Confederate monuments began two decades after the war and continued well into the twentieth century, which correlated with a shift in monuments' aesthetic and placement. Common soldiers and generals replaced obelisks; courthouses and legislative buildings replaced cemeteries.[35]

This later period in U.S. history is quite different from what came before, and monuments constructed during this time reflect these shifts. Second-wave monuments were constructed after the demise of Reconstruction, and "radical" Republican beliefs about the continued urgency of racial justice were becoming passé. Amendments had been made to the Constitution and slaves had been emancipated. What more was to be done? What use was there in continuing the fights of the past?[36] Gone was any place for the radicalism of a Thaddeus Stevens or Frederick Douglass, who continued to insist that the South, and as such the country as a whole, had put off a full reckoning with the Civil War and slavery. In this context, the monuments that arose, and even the ones already in place, performed differently. The three major markers of this historical moment, which Confederate monuments and monument dedication ceremonies increasingly served to bolster, are the spread of the Lost Cause tradition, the increase of lynching, and the passage of Jim Crow laws.

As the Civil War came to a close, a new struggle emerged in its wake: a struggle over how to properly interpret the trauma that had just occurred. A very self-conscious fight commenced to justify the events of the Confederacy's rebellion as noble, and to re-member the South around a new vision of the past. The main vehicle for this interpretive shift was the Lost Cause myth. The basic tenets of this ideology are that the South had not fought the

Civil War about slavery, but about states' rights; that in fact most Southerners would have supported emancipation anyway, in due time; that the South, particularly its leadership as represented by Robert E. Lee and Stonewall Jackson, exemplified the virtues of honor, valor, and decency; and that the Confederacy had only lost the war because they were overwhelmed by superior numbers and resources, rather than outwitted on the battlefield.[37] One preacher in 1909 put the main idea of the Lost Cause this way: the South's real cause was not lost, since a fight for "right and truth and honor" can never be lost. "The spirit of the men of '61 goes marching on!"[38] No one could deny that the South had lost the war, but Southerners were determined not to lose the war over opinions.[39] The Lost Cause was the afterlife of the Confederacy, the birth of a Southern civil religion marked by a particular religious-moral identity as a chosen people.[40]

Begun almost immediately at the end of the Civil War, the Lost Cause offered a particular interpretation of the past and the future: the South as virtuous in defeat, the South as a people that God would still use to bless the nation, the South as justified in their previous actions. It was a war of ideas, as Edward Pollard put it in his seminal manifesto, *The Lost Cause* (1866), and the South aimed to win.[41] Whereas before and during the war, Southerners had been adamant that they fought the war for slavery—slavery being a natural, biblical, God-ordained practice[42]—afterwards Southerners justified secession with little mention of slavery or even black persons generally. Most notable were Pollard's *Lost Cause*, Albert Taylor Bledsoe's *Is Davis a Traitor?* (1866), Alexander Stephenson's (former vice president of the Confederacy) *Constitutional View of the Late War between the States* (1870), and the many writings of Jubal Early. The Lost Cause was an ideology born out of grief as well as the desire to win control of the nation's memory of the Civil War.[43] These early books and other magazines about the Lost Cause laid the groundwork for the ideology of the South, but as a narrative about history the Lost Cause was not codified until the tail end of the nineteenth century.[44]

What truly cemented the legacy of the Lost Cause was the ritualized activity that spread its message in the decades after the war, giving it "must be" status. The Lost Cause was organized around various rituals and practices, including the dedication and celebration of Confederate monuments. The influence of the Lost Cause began to take hold in the 1870s, first with Robert E. Lee's death on October 12, 1870, and even more so as other generals followed suit. As each general died, he took his place in a canon of heroes, and in some cases generals were almost deified—especially Lee and Stonewall Jackson.[45] Ironically, these men proved more useful to the Lost Cause after their deaths, for a dead hero can more easily be made into a perfect and unchanging hero.[46] The tenets of this emerging civil religion were reinforced at ever-more-frequent monument dedications.[47] Whereas earlier, it had been relatively easy to raise money for local funerary monuments to local war dead but nearly impossible for more "national," celebratory monuments—even for as venerated a figure as Lee[48]—a new kind of monument emerged in this time period which functioned differently than before, marked by the impulse toward celebration

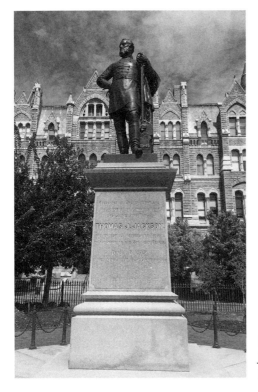

FIG. 1.2 The Stonewall Jackson Monument, Richmond, Va.

and defense of the Southern cause.[49] Monuments featured either the heroic saints of the cause (the generals) or ordinary devotees ("common soldier" statues), and their dedications were marked by speeches, fanfare, and celebration. If the Lost Cause was an intellectual attitude, then the Confederate monument was its marble embodiment.[50]

The 1875 dedication of the first monument in the South to Stonewall Jackson in Richmond, Virginia did much to reinforce the Lost Cause in popular imagination. The events of its dedication and the tone of the celebration are representative of the many public dedications of Confederate monuments that followed. Richmond, the de facto capital of the Lost Cause, held a ceremony marked by both joy and lament—death and resurrection—that included fifty thousand attendees. Veterans, along with representatives from local universities, churches, and governments, spoke of Jackson's Christian witness and nobility, and saw the monument as an inspiration to future generations to instill similar virtues. Most prominently, Moses Drury Hoge, pastor of Richmond's Second Presbyterian Church and a chaplain to the Confederacy during the war, frequently and explicitly referred to the day as inaugurating a new era of hero-making and mythmaking, at one point opining, "We lay the counter-stone of a new Pantheon in commemoration of our country's fame."[51] The monument was then unveiled by Jackson's daughter, to great fanfare and tears of joy. This presaged a larger monument-making boom in the South that peaked between 1890 and 1910.[52] Over and over, the same moves showed up in the monuments and their unveilings. People from across the South come to participate, with towns sending representatives; there is a parade featuring militias and veterans, school groups and Farmers' Alliances, churches and the KKK, which ends at the monument; there are a series of orations claiming that the South did not fight for slavery, and promoting the virtues and courage of the Confederacy generally and the generals in particular; and finally, an unveiling. The entire process serves to suggest that the monuments conjure something, reveal something, and transport those present to a different time and place, in order that they may then work toward a particular future. The ceremonies ritualize a process whereby ordinary people are reminded, but for a moment, of a glorious past marked by Christian gentlemen and Christian warriors.[53] At the unveiling of the Robert E. Lee statue in Richmond on May 29, 1890, for instance, all these elements were present. Between 100,000 and 150,000 people gathered and performed the well-known motions. One observer said that he felt as though he were "assisting at a combined funeral and resurrection."[54] The proceedings were paradoxical: a kind of celebratory funeral that Southerners had been building toward through their remembrance of the war and their ritualistic resistance to Reconstruction.[55]

Of course, not *every* member of the South took part in these ceremonies. Indeed, the very existence of Southern black people problematized the Lost Cause narrative; the wordless question issued to black folks by these ceremonies was the one articulated by W. E. B. Du Bois: "How does it feel to be a problem?"[56] The monuments of this second wave and the Lost Cause generally served to keep black people in the past, frozen in time. Their place in the Confederate narrative was only as loyal antebellum slaves.[57] The apotheosis of this is the "faithful slave" monument that was proposed and very nearly placed on Massachusetts Avenue in Washington, D.C. in 1923, only a year after the unveiling of the Lincoln Memorial. It would have featured a "mammy" seated on an altar surrounded by three children.[58] Thankfully the monument was not approved, but some monuments commemorating "faithful slaves" were constructed.[59] This struggle between dominant myth and suppressed counter-memory was present at the Jackson unveiling in Richmond. Only days before the parade, Jubal Early and some of his fellow Confederate veterans threatened to boycott the event because there were rumors that the governor, James Kemper, was going to allow black militia companies and civilians in the procession. Their involvement, Early wrote, would be an "indignity to the memory of Jackson and an insult to the Confederates," and should be utterly excluded. Kemper decided to allow the small contingent of black marchers in the parade, at the back of the procession. Kemper said the inclusion of this group, who promised to "humbly" honor Jackson, would "vindicate our white people against Radical lies." The black contingent ended up not attending, and only a few former slaves of

Jackson were present, but this exchange exemplified something crucial: in the Lost Cause mythology, the choice was either to eliminate black people from Confederate memory altogether, or to declare them loyal and stick them at the back of the parade.[60] Monuments in the era of the Lost Cause, then, were meant to control history and promote white supremacy, and white Southerners were very successful in this effort. As Edward Pollard wrote in his sequel tract, *The Lost Cause Regained* (1868), "To the extent of securing the supremacy of the white man and the traditional liberties of the country—in short, to the extent of defeating the Radical party—[the South] really triumphs in the true cause of the war, with respect to all its fundamental and vital issues."[61]

This "true cause" speaks to the other markers of this era of Confederate monument building: lynching and Jim Crow. It is far from coincidental that this explosion of memorialization to Southern virtue and honor corresponds with the height of lynching in the United States. In the South, the combination of private nostalgia, public memory, and extreme antipathy toward Reconstruction politics produced a lethal environment for black persons and the experiment of black equality.[62] Southern Democrats at this time were pushing against political threats (or gains) that they despised, in particular the Fifteenth Amendment to the Constitution (1870), which was designed to protect the right of freed black men to vote. Subverting or getting around this law was the name of the game, and the first wave of voter suppression was conducted through grassroots militias, who tried to prevent black men from voting by way of intimidation, violence, and assassination of prominent political leaders. These paramilitary forces carried out an insurgency by which white Southern communities could resist unwelcome developments such as racial integration and black involvement in politics. Whereas initial waves of violence were carried out in the early years of Reconstruction, the peak years of lynching occurred in the 1880s and 1890s, which took highly ritualized forms by the 1890s.[63] This included gatherings, church services, songs sung, and sometimes even pieces of the victim taken as souvenirs.[64]

These murders deeply affected the black psyche, and their power far outstripped their statistical frequency. In terms of sheer numbers, lynching was an extraordinary occurrence, especially when compared to the more mundane and quotidian forms of intimidation that African Americans experienced under Jim Crow. But in part because of its relative rarity, lynching generated a level of fear and horror that overwhelmed these other forms of violence. The story of even a single lynching travelled through the region with speed and force.[65] Lynching was more than a killing: it was a cultural practice designed to control behavior and paralyze people into inactivity and shamed silence.[66] The practice of lynching continued steadily through the 1920s, which was the same era in which the bulk of Confederate monuments were constructed.[67] Thus, when a lynching was performed in the town square, the murder would often have been done under the watchful eyes of a marbleized Confederate soldier or general.[68]

Consider the case of North Carolina, in which this kind of vigilante violence reached unprecedented heights in 1898 with the only successful *coup d'etat* in U.S. history. Only three years after the state as a whole had placed a Confederate monument on the capitol grounds where the legislature met, some in Wilmington were distraught that a majority of Populist white and recently freed black representatives were elected to power. And so on November 10 a group of heavily armed white men stormed the government building, banished the elected officials, and then marched into the black neighborhoods of Wilmington, killing anywhere between nine and three hundred people.[69] This was a carefully orchestrated response to black enfranchisement, to the collaboration between black and poor white farmers, and to the horror at seeing this fusion government emerge in both the 1894 and 1896 elections. Powerful Democrats fought to break the fusion, and decided that appealing to race could drive a wedge between poor whites and blacks.[70] Democrats were wildly successful in this campaign, winning victories across the state in 1898, aided in part by the "Red Shirts," the militant arm of the Democratic party who intimidated and disrupted Republican meetings and black church services. These tactics did not affect Wilmington's fusionist government, however—their mayor was not up for reelection—and so, two days after the election, Alfred Waddell led two thousand men on their campaign, forcing the mayor, the police chief, and the board of aldermen to resign at gunpoint before rampaging through the city, looking to "kill every damn nigger in sight."[71] Waddell was then appointed mayor. There was no federal response, and a bevy of disenfranchisement laws followed, as Democrats were now emboldened to legalize their new social order.[72]

No adequate accounting of Confederate monuments erected in this time period can neglect either this violent background or the legitimation of this violence through the enactment of Jim Crow laws. It was during Jim Crow that most of the Confederate monuments were erected—including one in Wilmington, dedicated in 1924. Laws intentionally designed to disenfranchise black persons, as well as poor whites who could not afford something like a poll tax, were passed in rapid succession. The violence of lynching and vigilante intimidation was thus encoded into law, providing a veneer of objectivity to a system seeking to mask its original violence from itself.[73] In this context, placing a Confederate monument on a public street, at the courthouse, or on the grounds of the state capitol sent a message that any effort to challenge this legal arrangement would meet staunch resistance. Confederate monuments carried an unspoken message: "Don't forget who's in charge here." Or as one black man reportedly said when he observed the 1890 dedication ceremony of the Robert E. Lee monument in Richmond: "The Southern white folks is on top—the Southern white folks is on top!"[74] Against such a backdrop, it is what is *not* represented in Confederate monuments that is revealing.

In this sense the coup in Wilmington was actually the beginning of the battle, as in the following years those in power cemented their legacy through a war of memory, which was a central plank of the assault on African American equality during the age of Jim Crow.[75] A particular version of history was enshrined on university campuses and the statehouse lawn, in statues and markers exalting the very men who overthrew a legitimately elected government on explicitly racist grounds.[76] This pattern was repeated across the United States: white mobs would terrorize black communities, followed by monuments "objectively" memorializing dead Confederate soldiers. As such, Union Brigadier General

James S. Brisbin's letter to Republican Thaddeus Stevens, penned in December 1865, proved to be prophetic: "The moment [the South] lost their cause in the field they set about to gain by politics what they had failed to obtain by force of arms." Emerging laws governing black behavior, he argued, would "reduce the blacks to a slavery worse than that from which they have just escaped."[77] The hope that these monuments helped express was that, while the Confederacy itself was defeated, God Almighty might enable Confederate principles to succeed in a different form and for a later era.[78] It was as though the weed of white supremacy had been clipped, but its roots were left embedded in the soil, ready to disturb future generations.[79]

The Victory Won: Reconciliation without Justice

The country's move toward white supremacy as represented by Jim Crow and lynching was both completed and hidden from view as calls for "reunion" were issued by white people in the North and the South, and an explosion of monument making began in the United States.[80] As Confederate monuments continued to be constructed, a final aspect of this picture was the trend to bring "sectional animus" to an end, but without any sort of reckoning with the racialized violence or white supremacy that had happened and continued to happen. Monuments erected during this time became a top layer of memory placed over unhealed wounds—a kind of forgetting in service to the supposed aim of reconciliation.

The drive to reconciliation posed real dangers to black communities seeking peace, let alone justice, in a country marked by racialized violence. The move toward reunion between the North and the South was largely bought at the high price of barring further discussion of justice for black Americans, for it was "divisive" to discuss concrete steps to undo the reentrenchment of white supremacy in the decades after the war. The simplest way to describe what happened is that the majority of white Americans grew weary of fighting and wanted instead to enjoy "peace" with one another. This shift left the more ardent voices in the North seeking justice for the wrongs of slavery marginalized even within the Republican party—the party of Thaddeus Stevens was replaced with that of Rutherford B. Hayes. This cultural shift certainly marginalized Frederick Douglass, who by the 1880s seemed to be fighting a losing battle as to why remembering the past (well) was crucial, what he called "the mirror in which we may discern the dim outlines of the future."[81] The most unreconstructed voices in the South were similarly marginalized by this move—Jubal Early was replaced with voices of the "New South" that sought better business relations while retaining the gains of white supremacy. In a society that was fast industrializing, such tensions were bad for business.[82] Even some Northerners appreciated nostalgic remembrances of a "simpler time" in an age of rapid industrialization and the vices that came along with this new era, both real and exaggerated.[83] As the Republican Party became the party of big business in the Gilded Age, many powerful people stood to gain from a quick, painless reconciliation as industry migrated from the Northeast to the South amid increasing fear of immigrants. Northern capitalists wanted to expand into the South in order to exploit its cheaper, un-unionized labor, and messy arguments about racial justice only delayed such plans.[84] In the eyes of W. E. B. Du Bois, it was as though white America could not face what it had done and was doing—it was "ashamed"—and as such had kept certain wounds hidden and unhealed through a warping and reshaping of memory.[85] The question was which tradition was going to prevail going forward: the ideals represented by Lincoln's Second Inaugural or the counter-revolutionary vision of the Lost Cause.[86] Increasingly, it was the latter ideology that won favor among politicians and historians, as it more readily served their interests.[87]

One way to narrate this shift is as a move away from "vernacular" motivations for memorializing the past—local expressions of grief for lost friends and ancestors with little interest in national programs of reconciliation—to "official" calls to remember which deemphasize personal devastation and highlight the importance of national unity, especially since such unity is good for the business interests of those in power, both North and South.[88] As time passed, the narrative of the Lost Cause served the interests of the elites of the entire country, as it helped hide the shame of Southerners who would rather not remember a humiliating defeat, as well as a rising class of Southern industrialists who wished to resume business with the North—and assume the role once played by the Southern aristocracy. In order to absolve the South of guilt, it was necessary to deemphasize activities focused on grief for the dead or the defeat itself.[89]

Calls for unity had been slowly emerging, particularly with the growth of reunion days in which soldiers from North and South would come together, salute one another, and shake hands—unsurprisingly, a practice that was not immediately popular but grew as time went on, deemphasizing the "controversial" issues of slavery and highlighting the mutual "valor" that was present on all sides.[90] Many Southern politicians made the pragmatic decision that the South would be best served by refusing to dwell on the injustices of the past. Rather quickly, the fashionable position was to focus on the future and the present. The past was dead; what was done was done. There was nothing one could do about it now in any case. The only thing to do was to move forward.[91] Still, holdouts continued to resist this move. What finally brought "reconciliation" to completion was war: both the Spanish-American War and World War I. Fights over the causes of the Civil War—or "the war between the states," as Lost Cause advocates called it—were relativized in importance once men bled and died together on the battlefield. Nothing unified like a common enemy, and the bonds of reconciliation (again, with the necessary caveat of excluding black people, even black soldiers, from the proceedings) were forged through international conflict.[92] No surprise, then, that monuments erected in this time reflect this reunionist bent.

Monuments always reflect the interests of those who have the resources to commission, design, and commemorate history in the ways they desire. Monument making is not neutral, but reflects certain realities of power, aesthetic commitments, and collective memory. As such, it is not surprising that Confederate monuments' stress on valor and sacrifice, and their general silence on slavery or race, served to push discussion of these issues underground.[93] Even Northerners—who were in no way devoid of white supremacist views—liked the idea of reunion, and clung to these attitudes as a point of stability in an age of rapid change.[94] To change these symbols would be to change the meanings and purposes to which they were originally put, especially their messages of race and power—and since some elements of the past are always forgotten in any remembering, the better question to ask is which elements are being neglected in any commemoration. In the case of Confederate monuments, the memory of sacrifice for a "united" states required a sanitized version of history that left huge groups of "others" out of the narrative.[95] Those "other" stories did little to serve the goal of reunion, and as such black voices tended to look on this reunion with suspicion. Douglass saw as early as 1875 the danger in easy calls for sectional reunion: "So sure as the stars shine in the heavens, and the rivers run to the sea, so sure will the white people North and South abandon their quarrels and become friends. . . . If war among the whites brought peace and liberty to blacks, what will peace among the whites bring?"[96]

Whether or not Confederate monuments were erected to white supremacy is debatable, insofar as it may be too crass of a formulation about the causes and effects of monuments and how they connect to deeper cultural attitudes. But in their later forms, Confederate monuments undoubtedly served to perpetuate white supremacy, reflecting a mythos that was indicative of the entire white population. Fifty years after the end of the war, a Confederate monument stood in nearly every Southern town,[97] implicitly memorializing what Martin Luther King would later call "negative peace," which is peace without justice, or merely the absence of tension.[98] Calls for reunion and monuments put up during these ceremonies masked as much as they revealed, not out of any conspiracy from the top, but from a deep combination of white supremacist memory and a desire to end animosity.[99] Monuments erected to serve this end did their work, creating a feedback loop that shaped the perceptions of the Civil War and Reconstruction for years to come—creating the very past it sought to "objectively" commemorate.[100] The last trick of Confederate monuments was to hide from people the fact that this cover-up had occurred, and instead assumed the status of common sense history. In short, Confederate monuments reflected a peculiar fact about monuments in general: once they are erected they come to appear as natural facts, as if their arrival and presence was preordained. Monuments exercise a curious power to erase their own political

origins and thus take on an air of sacrosanctity, such that to relocate or remove them feels something like a desecration—like one
is altering an entire way of seeing the world.[101] In this context, it
is no wonder that some rise to defend Confederate monuments
almost by instinct.

The Task Ahead: Competing Theologies, Competing Visions

When the monument to Stonewall Jackson in Richmond was
unveiled in 1875, the dedication ceremony was religious in tone
and fervor. Jackson himself was held up as a picture of Christian
piety by preachers and speakers at the event, and attendees wept
with emotion. Chaplains prayed and hymns were sung, including a performance of Martin Luther's "A Castle of Strength Is
Our Lord." On this day, the use of theological imagery was made
particularly blatant by the presence of a massive, thirty-two-foot-
high "Grand Arch" to the dead general, featuring an angel of
peace ascending to heaven, a Bible, a cross, and the words "Warrior, Christian, Patriot."[102] Far from an aberration, Christian rhetoric was usually employed any time a Confederate monument
was dedicated in the South. Speakers would convert the growing
number of statues dotting the landscape into parables-made-stone,
using Confederate monuments to teach religious and moral lessons. What is more, the use of Christian imagery was not limited
to pious speakers at monument dedications. Theological phrases
and symbols were often inscribed on the monuments themselves,
including such phrases as "Our cause is with God" and "In hope
of a joyful resurrection."[103]

Even the most muted Confederate monument almost surely
contains the seal of the Confederate States of America, which
includes the official slogan of the CSA, *Deo Vindice*, meaning
"Under God, [our] vindicator" or "God will defend us." Of
course, the God assumed to be doing this defending was the
Christian God: written into the Confederate Constitution itself
was the explicit assertion that this nation was a Christian nation,
rather than the Deist and purportedly heterodox vision of the
North. The "us" this God is vindicating is almost surely not black

people, and what God is vindicating this "us" from took on new significance in the years after the Civil War. The way this theological language performed would change with each generation as circumstances changed and as Confederate monuments were received anew in each era. Put simply, Confederate monuments have a stance toward the past, but this stance is only ever made in the present. Critiquing the theological assertions inscribed on Confederate monuments involves unpacking them as authentic expressions of a particular theological vision of the world. Confederate monuments do not express a "pseudo-theology" or cynically misuse Christian imagery in order to manipulate and control the populace. Confederate monuments manifest a genuine theology that must be understood and undermined as such.

This is reflective of the era in which Confederate monuments were constructed, of course. The entire Civil War, including its lead-up and aftermath, was framed in theological terms and was itself seen as a kind of theological crisis. That is, the war in part came to be seen as a referendum on competing visions of providence and God's will for the country.[104] The postbellum trauma that white Southerners were working through was not just the carnage of the war, but also the realization—if only inchoate—that one's previous vision of the world, up to and including one's exegesis of scripture, had been proven wrong, or at least made illegitimate. No surprise, then, that monuments dedicated in the war's aftermath reflect this religiosity, which of course was deeply Christian in its expression. The response to this crisis was less often to face up to the reality of societal complicity in something like the sin of racism and slavery, and more often to assume that white Southerners were being punished by God for personal weaknesses like drunkenness, moral laxity, or worldliness.[105] Indeed, white Southerners generally came to manifest the psychological phenomenon displayed in the now-classic study *When Prophecy Fails*: namely, when a group of people have a basic conviction that is tied to a specific historical outcome, and that outcome does not come true, often the cognitive dissonance this creates is too much to bear, and people end up doubling down on their previous conviction, becoming more committed to the cause after the failure, even engaging in further proselytizing efforts.[106] The increased fervor of the Lost Cause after the defeat of the Confederacy, reflected in these monuments and their dedication ceremonies, bears a resemblance to this phenomenon. As such, investigating the theological contours of memory and self-deception manifested in Confederate monuments—the stance Confederate monuments take toward the past—is called for.

Even if Confederate monuments were not explicit in their invocation of Christian narratives and imagery, it would still be valid to assess their theological significance. All constructed objects communicate not only through explicit messages but also in their aesthetic form. No created thing—whether a building, bridge, or monument—is value neutral. Although there is a tradition in the West of limiting things of value to the explicitly verbal, paying less attention to the physical expression or form a message takes, this assumption is being decisively undermined from several angles in philosophy and theology. Scholars challenging this assumption seek to recognize that the shape or "vessel" a message comes in does as much to communicate as the message itself, subtly expressing things besides what is explicit or obvious.[107] In the case of Confederate monuments, the very shape and design of the structures assume values and aesthetic ideals that can fairly be called theological. A broad movement is forming that takes this shift seriously, grouped under the heading "theopoetics," which combines the Aristotelian emphasis on *poesis* (to do, to make) with the recognition that the things humans shape with their own hands end up shaping their view of God, often in ways that are deep and unnoticed.[108] Confederate monuments in form as well as content assume particular visions of what society should aim for, what is beautiful and powerful and good (as opposed to ugly and weak and bad). Their stance toward the past, which happens in the present, aims toward some future, a kind of eschatological end that should be venerated and respected.

Monuments are special cases regarding the way they shape human character and perception in their design. It is true that even seemingly innocuous buildings form human character in particular ways, though few think about this reality as it is happening. But monuments are unique in that they are explicit and self-conscious about their intended formative function. Everyone knows—designers, commissioners, and viewers in subsequent generations—that the purpose of a monument is to show someone what matters, to manifest some set of ideals behind and beyond the statue itself. This may even be a feature of how images work in general: the power of an image rests not simply on what it shows but on what it does not show, what is absent or hidden from presentation.

What monuments add to this feature of images is an explicit sense of time. Monuments stake claims on where a people have been, who is included in this "we" today, and where this "we" should be headed. As such, theological analyses of Confederate monuments should organize around these loci: past, present, and future. Confederate monuments involve questions about the nature of history and collective memory. Who gets to remember? What stories are not included in this telling? Do people ever remember "as is" or is interpretation always already included? Confederate monuments assume an aesthetic ideal toward which some people are said to be aiming—whiteness and the virtues associated with white heroes. And Confederate monuments do this work in the present, manifesting past realities and future hopes in the world of today. Each generation consents anew to how (or if) they will receive Confederate monuments, and as such contests over how to deal with monuments are always contests of power. To be sure, monuments' relationship toward past, present, and future are interwoven, and can be distinguished only for the purposes of analysis. And yet by distinguishing them one can untangle the theological convictions implied by each "direction" of Confederate monuments, having to do with memory, sacrifice, whiteness, reconciliation, community, and power. Identifying these theological convictions opens up possibilities for altering Confederate monuments in a way that enables people to proceed more faithfully into the future, despite a complicated and, at times, horrific past that cannot be erased.

2

Past

Memories Constructed

Ghosts live tortured lives. They haunt a world that would rather forget. They live lives mostly unseen, unnoticed; they conjure pasts that terrify. While the world grows ever more enamored of the promise of progress offered by technology's mastery of time, these old souls invoke sad, tired, and unwanted stories.

Jonathan Tran[1]

Jefferson Davis, the first and only president of the Confederacy, was not a universally beloved figure, even in the South. Unlike other prominent Confederate leaders such as Robert E. Lee, who enjoyed widespread acclaim before and after his death, Davis was treated with a degree of ambivalence, perhaps because of his perceived failures as a political leader, or perhaps because of his reputation for being aristocratic, aloof, and overly formal. After avoiding execution for treason and spending two years in federal prison, Davis threw himself into what would become his post-war passion project: defending the South's actions during the war. Davis was a true believer in the historical renarration that is the Lost Cause tradition, and he spent the last twelve years of his life

Fig. 2.1 Jefferson Davis
Statue,
Richmond, Va.

spreading its gospel. Davis vociferously defended the notion that
the South fought for a state's right to secede rather than slavery,
that the Confederacy had not "rebelled" but had been sovereign
over its land, and that white supremacy was natural and good.

Davis' apologetic efforts culminated in his voluminous book,
The Rise and Fall of the Confederate Government, which defends each
and every Lost Cause tenet. Going beyond the constitutional or
legal case, Davis argues that the Confederacy had a divine right
to do what it did, laying the blame for war solely at the feet of the
North. Davis also paints an Edenic portrait of slave-master relations prior to the war, which he argues represented an ideal balance between labor and capital that was only upset by Northern
aggression and the false promise of freedom. Slavery had brought
Africans out of "heathen" darkness by introducing them to Christianity, turning "a few unprofitable savages" into "millions of effi-
cient Christian laborers." Now, black folks were being tricked by
Northern politicians who "trained their humble but emotional

natures to deeds of violence and bloodshed, and sent them out to devastate their benefactors."[2]

Given his post-war efforts, it is no wonder that Davis' statue on Monument Avenue in Richmond, Virginia—dedicated in 1907—is basically a giant tribute to the Lost Cause and its false interpretation of the Civil War. The monument has Davis standing in a statesman's pose, one hand extended upwards as an appeal to the future while the other rests upon a literal "book of history." Inscribed behind him are several phrases, including *Deo Vindice*—appearing just beneath an allegorical, angelic figure named "Vindicatrix" pointing to heaven and representing "the spirit of the South"—and "Defender of the Rights of States." As a 67-foot-tall, 50-foot-wide spectacle, the monument stands less as a celebration of Davis himself and more as a sacred tribute to an entire way of facing the past.

When it comes to events that reflect poorly on one's people, the temptation to self-deception is strong. What a community remembers about its past reveals who they believe themselves to be and who they hope to become, and so it is neither easy nor pleasant to face the more troubling aspects of one's history. Of course, *what* one remembers is linked to *how* one remembers, as memories are not free-floating collectibles but are selected, narrated, and transmitted materially—and the material things that prompt memory color the memories themselves. People shape objects of remembrance that in turn shape their remembrances.[3] To investigate any object of memory is to get a sense of both a society's openness to alternate ways of narrating its past and to the stories which have been screened out of its collective remembrances. A monument is just one among a constellation of objects that shape a collective into a people through a particular narration of the past. Even so, monuments have a unique role to play in this process, and in the American South, Confederate monuments are an important means by which narratives about the Civil War are disseminated.

Part of the reason passions are excited when Confederate monuments are threatened is the ingrained sense that monuments are inherently venerable, and the (correct) assumption that to alter these statues might engender a wider shift in perception about

American history. Confederate monuments themselves encourage this feeling by way of the events they hold up as worthy of remembrance as well as the form of remembrance they encourage. On the one hand, Confederate monuments almost always contain references to the past and the importance of remembrance, focusing in particular on remembering the virtues of the deceased and their sacrifices. In order to analyze the way Confederate monuments employ these inherently theological themes with sufficient thickness and clarity, one must understand the concept of collective memory as it relates to material religion—in this case, the civil religion of the Lost Cause. On the other hand, Confederate monuments have a stance toward the past irrespective of what they actually remember. The design of Confederate monuments suggests that the way they remember is sufficient, universal, and closed to further narration. Thus, despite the ostensibly Christian themes that accompany these statues, upon deeper inspection most Confederate monuments betray a mundane vision of history and an idolatrous conception of sacrifice.

As such, one strategy for disrupting Confederate monuments is employing Christian theology to complicate the memories they conjure, remembering the narratives they tell (and leave untold) through the dangerous memory of Christ, whose unique sacrifice Christians confess is the key to viewing history aright. Through this lens Christians can see that people are called to face and confess wounds from the past, rather than attempting to hide from them, deny they exist, or transfigure them into a tale of past glory or moral innocence. Ironically, even certain attempts to redress the problematic history evoked by Confederate monuments—that rightly recognize their one-sided and supremacist nature—can reinforce a kind of historical denial ("This is not us!") that leaves wounds unfelt, unbound, and thus untamed as they continually return to the present.

Remembrance and the Forging of Collective Identity

It is rather unremarkable to note that memory plays a central role in forging individual identity. However, something analogous is true for collectives: groups of people share memories that are disseminated and passed through time, a phenomenon known as collective memory. While individual and collective memory are both important and reinforce one another, there is a strong case to be made that collective memory should take priority, and not merely as a corrective to the overemphasis on the individual in dominant strands of Anglo-European thought. Maurice Halbwachs, a seminal figure in collective memory studies, argues that group memory is logically prior to individual memory and is the fount from which individual memory springs. Memory binds collectives together, helps demarcate the boundaries of a community, and provides the framework for individual memory.[4] The basic insight regarding collective memory, which informs all subsequent uses of the term, is that some social framework precedes any individual act of remembering.[5] Specifically, "social framework" refers to the various relational networks—from family to friends to civic circles—as well as the linguistic-symbolic order through which people acquire the very capacity to remember.[6] Collective memory in this sense is not uniform; it is rather the recognition that individual memory is always dependent upon social "hinges" that enable the door to swing—hinges that are shared and that most of the time go unnoticed.[7] Thus, acknowledging the reality of collective memory need not lead to the overdrawn conclusion that individual memory is not real,[8] but it is to become attentive to the feedback-loop quality between individual memory, collective memory, and the cultural soil that underlays both.[9] Collective memory and individual memory exist in a complex relationship, whereby individuals remember within sociocultural contexts that are shaped by various symbols, monuments, and other media.[10]

Collective memory is a helpful frame through which to analyze Confederate monuments' relationship to the past, particularly in the way collective memory highlights the creation of group identity through corporate remembrance, and the way collective memory is reinforced through objects and physical locations. From their inception Confederate monuments have taken part in a process whereby particular memories are selected and highlighted in order to construct something called "Southern" identity. Things remembered (and not remembered) create a community's view of itself, providing the group with a kind of self-portrait that can evolve through time even as it gives the group a way of recognizing itself amidst divergent narratives and traditions.[11] The process by which group identity is created is complicated, of course, and connects with public contestations about who or what a given public should be. Something like collective memory can only emerge from such contestations, which typically divide between "official" expressions of memory and "vernacular cultural" expressions thereof. Official interpretations of the past chiefly serve to support those in power who have an interest in maintaining the status quo, easing conflict, and reducing the power of factions or narratives that would threaten the attainment of their goals.[12] That is, those in power desire to create a particular kind of social unity that does not easily admit of counter-narratives issuing from subaltern communities. By contrast, vernacular expressions of memory do not have the same level of interest in social cohesion, and are not as reliant on officially endorsed rituals, ceremonies, and media.[13]

In any case, group identity arises out of this interaction between vernacular and official memory, and over time becomes a part of the fabric of society. The collective memory that emerges goes deeper than any specific political or historical issue that might be recounted, but rather describes the fundamental matters of a society's entire existence, not least its present structure of power and the meaning of its history.[14] "Common sense" knowledge about the past emerges from this tension, creating the frame through which particular events are understood, which explains why challenges to standard interpretations of the past are heated: because they disrupt arrangements that have been accepted and potentially uncover fissures that have been ignored. All this is but to say that collective memory is variegated and complex. There truly are pockets of collectivities that remember different pasts and remember the past differently, as even the slightest attention to African American narratives about their experiences in the United States makes clear. Thus, it is important to keep in mind that no collective memory or collective identity is monolithic, and any suggestion otherwise can be nothing other than an expression of power.[15] Indeed, being open to stories that do not make it into an official self-image is a sign of healthy collective memory.

Most analyses of collective memory note that the process of constituting collective identity does not happen by magic but through various rituals, ceremonies, and objects. Collective memory does not exist just anywhere, but tends to gather around particular geographical locations, buildings, documents, and monuments—what Pierre Nora calls "sites" or *lieux de mémoire*.[16] It is through various material objects that memory is transmitted, that the past becomes present, and that traditions are reinforced. This insight is obviously relevant to monuments, which combine elements of materiality, functionality, and symbolism.[17] This is not to say that collective memory is limited to or contained "within" particular material artifacts, but rather that collective memory emerges from the continual, dynamic interaction between social practices, the mental dimension of individuals, and objects designed to participate in and stimulate this process.[18] As such, any robust conception of collective memory must include its material dimension, or it is woefully incomplete. Collective (and individual) memory is unthinkable without the mediation of narratives through various objects, oral communication, photographs, documents, and monuments; this includes the various rituals of remembrance that get associated with monuments.[19] Monuments conjure, manifest, and mediate collective memory, encoding information that prompts remembering and forgetting.[20]

Of course, objects of memory such as Confederate monuments do not simply report on the past, but shape and construct it. Monuments are not empty containers for collective memory; rather, they leave a "trace" on the events conjured. The medium of memory shapes the act of remembering, both in the object's explicit descriptions and its aesthetic form. And as various media coalesce—as more and more monuments are built with a similar aesthetic and message, for instance—entire worlds of memory are created, networks of memory which any singular monument implicitly manifests.[21] As such, while collective memory is diffused throughout a culture, it can be partly touched in and through monuments. It is through such objects that cultural memory can be accessed, including by members of the imagined community of memory itself.[22]

On its own, the concept of collective memory is helpful for understanding Confederate monuments' stance toward the past. Monuments do not respect neat divisions between past, present, and future; nor do they respect the boundaries sometimes set up between politics and theology, public and private—and neither does collective memory. Collective memory is an umbrella concept that integrates knowledge from a variety of fields, showing the connections—whether functional, analogical, metaphorical, or otherwise—between seemingly disparate phenomena, including monuments and historical consciousness.[23] But the usefulness of collective memory for understanding Confederate monuments truly opens up when it is connected to the field of semiotics—the study of the function and interpretation of symbols.[24] In particular, the force of Confederate monuments' stance toward the past becomes apparent when analyzed through speech-act theory.

Speech-act theory seeks to understand how language "works" as an ordinary, social, embodied reality. The seminal work in this field was written by J. L. Austin, who pioneered a multi-layered scheme for analyzing how words work by focusing on an utterance's *sense*, its *referent*, the *intention* of the speaker, and how this all *performs*. The basic idea is that language does not just refer to facts about the world (although it certainly works this way as well). Words work on many levels at once, and are active—are speech-*acts*—more than empty, neutral containers of information. Several facets of speech-act theory are directly relevant to analyzing monuments: the recognition that meaningful or "happy" communication requires a basic physical structure that is understandable by others—one's words cannot be garbled or in some kind of secret language; the recognition that any communication finds its place within some appropriate social context that enables it to "perform" in ways it would not or could not in another setting[25]; and the recognition that an utterance aims at affecting some state of affairs in the world such that its message must be understood, at least to a degree. If each level is satisfied, communication is achieved and a kind of "uptake" has occurred.[26]

Speech-act analysis can be applied to public, stable, material communications like monuments, and yields unique insights about any given monuments' performative power. For instance, the phenomena employed by a monument must be comprehensible to the average viewer. In the case of Confederate monuments, highly abstract art would not do. Part of the point was that these simple images could be immediately recognizable by most viewers (man, Anglo, soldier, horse).[27] Additionally, monuments are incomprehensible outside their social (and historic) context, and some social context is always implied by any speech-act.[28] Context says a lot about what a monument is intended to say, and to change that context is to change its meaning. The same monument performs differently when placed in a cemetery, in front of a courthouse, or in a museum, even if nothing else is changed.

Finally, one must attend to the intended affective force monuments have on viewers. Discussions on this front are necessarily complex, as any symbolic expression admits of multiple uptakes, multiple ways of being received—both in their immediate historical context and the unfolding contexts of later generations.[29] Debates about public expressions of memory arise in no small part at this level, with different viewers sensing different messages in monuments. This third moment is especially relevant to understanding Confederate monuments, as the majority of them explicitly tell viewers what the uptake should be—what should be valued about this past, why it matters to the present, and what ideals it projects into the future. Put differently, Confederate monuments intend—and in most cases happily evoke—a particular stance toward the world, born of implied narratives that give the monuments their deeper meaning.[30] It is precisely when these implied narratives begin to lose their cultural cachet that the monuments chafe where they were once celebrated or tolerated—at least by certain segments of the population. Confederate monuments are speech-acts made stone.

Speech-act theory is also helpful for understanding how monuments contain an excess of meaning, going beyond what is explicitly stated. To be sure, pure speech-act theorists have tended to focus on utterances themselves rather than their result, but any complete use of speech-act theory should consider what an utterance leads to, even if to do so takes one past the moment of speech (or monument-communication) itself.[31] As such, speech-act theory allows one to see that the way Confederate monuments perform in social context is a critical part of understanding their relationship to collective memory, and that it is possible to disrupt and problematize a Confederate monument's intended uptake.

Combining collective memory and speech-act theory, one can say that monuments are tangible spaces around which "essentially contested concepts" having to do with cultural memory are evoked.[32] While these contests can be heated and even violent, they can also uncover societal tensions that are then able to be investigated—including tensions lurking deep in the collective unconscious. Confederate monuments function this way: they reveal problematic convictions and fault lines in the United States, but in so doing they provide a unique opportunity to investigate and theologically critique American culture. Regarding Confederate monuments, then, the key questions are: What part of collective memory do these statues reveal? And what do Confederate monuments assume about the past in their design and location? With these questions in hand, one theme regarding Confederate monuments' stance toward the past becomes immediately clear: an overriding emphasis on remembering the virtues of those who fought, particularly their valor and sacrifice. Even if this theme is not explicit on or around the monuments, it is baked into their construction, lurking just beneath the surface. Implicit in this emphasis is an attempt to convert the trauma of the war and its aftermath into something triumphant, and a deadening silence about testimonies that would complicate this renarration, in particular testimonies about the brutality of slavery and the continued violence of white supremacy.

"For Our Altars and Hearths": Evoking the Power of Sacrifice

Consider the Confederate monument in Wilmington, North Carolina. Dedicated in 1924, the statue is atypical in many ways, and yet it distills themes found in other Confederate monuments into a particularly potent form. Designed by Henry Bacon, the man who also designed the Lincoln Memorial in Washington, D.C., the Wilmington monument departs from the standard "common soldier" aesthetic or a depiction of a famous general. Instead, the monument features a triumphant soldier, hatless and beardless, stepping overtop a dead comrade. He is resilient, steadfastly looking into the distance—due north, in fact. He is in stride, gun grasped tightly in his right hand as he moves forward with a cape flapping behind him. He has a book strapped to his belt on his right side—perhaps a Bible—and a canteen on his left. Finally, looking closer than the broad outline of the statue, his Anglo face bears a look of concerned determination. His brow is knit with a look of frustration, with a slight uptick in the inside of the eyebrows, suggesting a faint feeling of sadness. His lips are shut, jaw set, and lines mark a still-young face. The striding soldier represents the virtue of courage, while the dead soldier represents the virtue of sacrifice. It is hardly surprising that courage is highlighted in this statue, as it was the valor of soldiers on both sides of the war that was celebrated as the United States moved toward reconciliation in the post-Reconstruction era—although certain people always spoke against this false equivalence, not least people of color.[33]

Moving from the monument itself to the accompanying inscription, the viewer reads an injunction to remember these virtues of sacrifice and courage, and in so doing to preserve these idealized figures of the past: "Confederates blend your recollections; let memory weave its bright reflections. Let love revive life's ashen embers, for love is life since love remembers." To remember is obligatory, for to forget would be tantamount to a kind of second death for those who fought in the war. Conversely, to remember is to resurrect the very virtues enshrined by these men, making their sacrifices present once more. The intended object of this sacrifice is made clear by the last line of the poem: "Pro Aris et Focis." Colloquially this is translated "For God and Country," but the literal translation is "For Our Altars and Hearths." Its traditional use is to signal attachment to what is most dear, most worthy of sacrifice, but the origins of the phrase are not irrelevant here. In Roman antiquity, the "altars" signaled by the phrase referred to the altar upon which the guardian deities of one's home would rest, protecting and reinforcing the boundaries of one's abode, neighborhood, and city, providing spiritual security and good luck.[34] As such, a deep theology of sacrifice is evoked by the phrase, tied to the death and actions of Confederate soldiers, in order to suggest

FIG. 2.2 The Monument
to Confederate Sacrifice,
Wilmington, N.C.

that they fought to protect God and country, or (more literally) on behalf of the nation's domestic and religious-sacrificial life. Of course, by 1924 the Lost Cause civil religion had been well established, making it rather clear which God, which altar, which country, and which hearth is being called to mind.

While these themes are uniquely visible in the Wilmington monument, they are actually quite common in Confederate monuments, although they are usually evoked with more subtlety. For instance, the typical common soldier statue has a line dedicated to "our Confederate dead." Often, this is accompanied by words that connect the meaning of these deaths to the virtues of those who fought and died, transforming meaningless death into meaningful sacrifice. The monument in Graham, North Carolina (1914), for instance, just outside the courthouse, features a typical reference to "the bivouac of the dead," a line from a poem by Theodore O'Hare that describes those who died as being in an eternal camping ground. On the sides of the monument are references to "immortal glory" gained through death, and on the front: "To commemorate with grateful love the patriotism, valor, and devotion to duty, of the brave soldiers of Alamance County." Of course, these common virtues were ideally represented in the generals, who formed a kind of heavenly council for the Confederate civil religion. Any sacrificial virtues exemplified by ordinary soldiers are amplified and perfected in the generals, particularly Jackson and Lee. This emphasis became so pronounced in the South that it formed what came to be known as a cult of sacrifice.[35]

Thus, when it comes to Confederate monuments' stance toward the past, the first theme to emphasize is the inherently theological notion of sacrifice—a theme that continues to be influential in American civil life to this day. It is hardly surprising that theological themes would show up in monuments erected during this era, as the United States at this time displayed an unusual degree of religiosity.[36] But it is interesting to note which Christian themes were emphasized, and how they were used. Above all, the notion of sacrifice was consistently taken up by commentators and orators, and not just in the South. Horace Bushnell, for instance, narrated Northern victory in terms of the blood sacrifices of its soldiers, the price paid for freedom. Blood cemented a national unity that was "forever sanctified."[37] Many soldiers were explicitly counseled that their purpose *was* to die, to sacrifice for home and nation.[38] This point was so pronounced that the supposed neutrality, even transcendence, of sacrifice became a point of reconciliation between North and South. As Oliver Wendell Holmes put it in 1895, he believed in very little after the war, but of one thing he was certain: "That the faith is true and adorable which leads a soldier to throw away his life in obedience to a blindly accepted duty, in a cause which he little understands, in a plan of campaign of which he has no notion, under tactics of which he does not see the use." Holmes had faith in sacrifice itself, no matter what for or how meaningless it seemed.[39]

Striking this theme was tricky for Southerners given their defeat and their widespread belief in providence. With such a strong view of God's control over the world, mundane events were thought to be taking place against the larger backdrop of God's design. Robert E. Lee and Stonewall Jackson were famous for their strong providential beliefs, as was Lincoln.[40] As such, the Civil War and its aftermath were seen as a kind of theological referendum on whose vision of God and whose scriptural interpretation was correct. By itself, the fact that different people could claim to know God's will in diametrically opposed ways was theologically troubling (was God against himself?), let alone what it said of God that he could will such devastation.[41]

But for white Southerners the issue went deeper: once lost, the almost unbearable question was whether God was against them, and whether their loved ones had died in a futile and pointless quest.[42] Such questions touched on the very core of Southern identity and what the South was aspiring to be. What the Lost Cause and its monuments served to do, then, was convert these latent feelings of guilt and trauma into a victory, even if a victory of a different sort. The monuments increasingly served to highlight the principles of those who fought, which had been defeated but were not lost. To save these deaths from meaninglessness, they needed to be turned into sacrifices, vindicating the reasons these men fought and died—reasons which explicitly included resistance to "racial amalgamation."[43] In order to rescue these "timeless virtues" for future emulation, it was necessary to decouple them from the purpose to which these virtues were exercised in actual historical context, because otherwise they would not appear so pristine. Put bluntly, what is *not* mentioned in any Confederate statue is the underlying cause for which the Southern states seceded and fought, as well as the subsequent racial violence (both legal and extralegal) that accompanied the erection of these monuments to honor and sacrifice.

As such, the possibility of mourning was eclipsed by the duty to remember triumphantly, repetitively, and selectively. This is significant especially because of the very nature of trauma. Trauma is not inherent to a given experience. Rather, trauma is constructed, meaning that an event has to be received and interpreted as traumatic in order for it to function as such, individually or collectively.[44] So when Confederate monuments shift from lament to sacrificial imagery, they enable the kind of imaginative work necessary for a community to avoid the traumatic and redefine itself in more palatable terms. It was possible to receive the events of the Civil War in this way precisely because of the constructed, ongoing, interpretive nature of trauma. The collective identity that was emerging in the South was constructed by narrating the past in particular ways.[45] White Southerners were able to re-member a collective past in terms of sacrifice, and in so doing avoid a more complicated rendering of history.

While sacrifice constitutes the *what* of Confederate monuments in relationship to collective memory, these monuments also embody theological convictions about *how* remembrance functions. Namely, Confederate monuments tend to reinforce the notion that they are simply "reporting" the past rather than taking a stance on the events they memorialize. Confederate monuments embody a performative neutrality that assumes certain beliefs about the nature of the past and the role monuments play in the remembering process. Of course, the notion that Confederate monuments are at all neutral or innocent historical markers cannot hold up under honest scrutiny. It is abundantly clear that Confederate monuments narrate a specific version of the events they evoke, and during their construction everyone knew this was the case. The design of the monuments, the inscriptions featured, and even the origin of the stones used were hotly debated, in some cases delaying production.[46] The meaning of these monuments could not be left to chance nor open to interpretation, but needed to be spelled out as clearly as possible. This marks a difference between the aesthetic of earlier Confederate monuments, which typically employed a muted obelisk and were placed in cemeteries, and later monuments that were more explicit, ornate, and in places of public power. Confederate monuments increasingly narrated collective memory for the viewer through detailed imagery and verbose inscriptions, naming the parts of history that should be preserved and the parts that are unimportant or "secondary." Viewers are explicitly directed toward the virtues of those who died, and nowhere else. More representative of these later statues is the Baltimore monument to Robert E. Lee and Stonewall Jackson, dedicated in 1948: "They were great Generals and Christian soldiers and waged war like gentlemen."[47] No points are awarded for subtlety, and there is no room in the statue's design for any other way of understanding these men's actions.

The assumption is that monuments should do the entire work of remembering for people. Rather than prompting a conversation or narrative retelling about an inevitably complicated collective past, over-narrating in this way forecloses on any other way to describe history. *This* is what happened, and no other narrative or memory is relevant to the telling. All one needs to know is in the monument, rather than seeing the monument as prompting a living collective to remember anew. Monuments designed in this way allow people to abdicate the work of remembrance. Early Confederate rituals, Memorial Days, and dedications were practices, coupled with the erection of monuments themselves, that served to pass on a particular way of remembering the past. But as these rituals tailed off, the monuments themselves came to do more of the work of remembrance in the South.[48] Other memories and narratives were blocked from being considered, and the multidirectional nature of memory was flattened.[49] Moreover, the way the monuments functioned as speech-acts was designed to hide the necessity of interpretation from the viewer, as well as the constructed nature of the history they tell, and thus very little room is left for subaltern stories to find voice. Because of their performative neutrality, Confederate monuments could be seen as reporting objective facts about history, rather than being the result of an imaginative and power-laden process.[50] The problem is that relying on monuments to do the work of remembering for a people leaves little room for understanding the significance of the events recalled, other than the reasons that are already given by the monuments themselves. It heightens the possibility of remembering poorly, even if in great detail.

Remembering Rightly, Remembering Christologically

Confederate monuments take a stand on the events they memorialize, constructing a version of the past that is by no means self-evident. In itself this is not a problem, as monuments always function in this way. Every monument makes choices about how to frame and narrate the past; even more basically, they highlight what is worth remembering and what is not.[51] Neither collective memory nor history is a simple matter of chronicling "all" the facts as if they were isolated valueless collectibles, for no one truly thinks that *all* facts are necessary to a faithful account of the past—and to attempt to name them all would lead to an incomprehensible historical narrative. No history of the Civil War includes descriptions of the political situation in Russia at the time, or the length of Stonewall Jackson's beard, or the precise amount of milk consumed during the Battle of Gettysburg. Remembering the past always takes the form of a narration rather than a chronicling.[52] As such, the question with Confederate monuments in relation to the past needs to be properly named: it is not whether they are selective but the way in which they are selective, how they interpret what is selected, and whether these speech-acts induce the wrong reaction in people.[53] Christians should be ready to answer this question with their theological convictions coloring what a wrong and right reaction entails.

What is needed is a conception of remembering that is drawn from Christian resources, which directly contradicts the version of remembrance assumed by Confederate monuments, and which therefore enables Christians to name and undermine one aspect of Confederate monuments' deficiency in relation to collective memory. The quality of Christian responses to Confederate monuments is affected by how the act of remembrance is conceptualized, and whether Christians have recourse to a conception of the past other than an immanent, "just the facts" theory that assiduously avoids (or obscures) questions of power and perspective. Such a view of memory makes it hard to even see the semi-constructed nature of the past, let alone gather resources to disrupt narratives that assume an aura of inevitability.[54] For Christians, different theologies about the act of remembrance enable divergent imaginative horizons for undermining the power of Confederate monuments. Put simply, if one adheres to a picture of the past existing autonomously—and along with it, a view that memorialization simply reports the past and remembers for people—then certain responses to Confederate monuments will be harder to envision. Christians should not fall into a (tempting) support for remembrance as the neutral recalling of autonomous history, but should seek to view history Christologically—with all the nuances and subtleties required of this position—thereby opening other options for disrupting Confederate monuments than are typically considered.

Of course, Confederate monuments reveal the dangers of collective remembrance. While calls to remember tend to be treated as self-evidently good in a post-Holocaust world, Confederate monuments show that people can remember poorly, and that remembering can as easily hinder justice and reconciliation as aid in its arrival. Humans often transform the memory of injustice, real or perceived, into a warrant for further violence.[55] If memory is dangerous in this way—and Confederate monuments show that it is—then why endure the risk of remembrance? Christians risk remembering because it can serve to bring healing and justice to a broken world, prefiguring the transformation that will fully happen at the end of history. In any case, there is no choice but to remember.[56] Before the end of all things, it is simply a given that the past will haunt the present. The real question is *how* to remember, and in what ways might memory be made to enable collective flourishing. Especially in situations of conflict and past injustices, the goal of Christian memory is for people to remember in such a way that they may one day embrace—even enemies, even victim and victimizer. Christians care about memory insofar as it can bridge the divide between adversaries, remembering together in order to reconcile with one another.[57]

In this way, memory is central to the aims of justice and the healing of past wrongs, but memory cannot do this automatically or on its own. The mere act of remembering is not enough, for one can remember poorly, or self-deceptively. Memory is polyvalent, able to lead to healing but also despair, and many places in between. Worse, remembering grievous evils from the past is particularly hard because to revisit such moments can reopen old wounds, and thus enable the past to reinvade the present.[58] Memories can be used to wound others as well as heal; can perpetuate injustice as well as bring about justice; can create a person who is not liberated by but imprisoned within the past, doomed to repeat it.[59] What is needed is not just remembering per se, but remembering rightly—remembering in ways that bring justice and healing to the world.[60]

There are different ways that Christians can conceptualize how right remembering functions. One compelling vision is that remembrance is important insofar as it prepares for an eschatological amnesia whereby people are freed from injustice's lingering effects. Eventually, for atrocities and injustices to be made right in any meaningful sense, some element of forgetting must be operative—at the very least, forgetting the pain associated with such events. And since pain is not an extra element to an otherwise intact memory that can easily be brushed aside, to forget pain is in some ways to forget the essence of the event itself.[61] Thus, if it is really the case that all tears will be wiped away when God makes all things new, then forgetting evils suffered would seem necessary to that end. Of course, in the meantime, memories of wrongs suffered are ineradicable, and as such the best one can do until then is to ensure that one's memory is truthful and that painful memories are placed within the framework of one's life story and the life of one's community. In this way memories of evil might be directed toward protecting the vulnerable, forging solidarity with the oppressed, and preventing the repetition of similar atrocities in the future. Remembering is indispensable to achieving justice—but as one aspect of a process whose hope for completion lies outside of memory itself.[62]

And this is the crucial point. On this view, the memory of wrongs suffered serves an important but necessarily penultimate purpose. In the world to come (and only then)—after truth is told, after justice is done, after wrongs made right—final healing comes through forgetting wrongs done and wrongs suffered.[63] This is because wrongs suffered cannot be "made right" or "made meaningful," but remain forever *wrongs*, such that healing can only come by forgetting they ever occurred.[64] Theologian Miroslav Volf is the most prominent contemporary advocate of this position, which he summarizes with simplicity and starkness as "either heaven *or* the memory of horror. Either heaven will have no monuments to keep the memory of the horrors alive, or it will be closer to hell than we would like to think."[65] Monuments raised in this life that are painful or problematic will not remain standing in the world to come, either in reality or in memory. The choice presented by this view is eventual amnesia or continued torture by the past, which parallels a choice commonly presented concerning Confederate monuments: either remember the past even though it is a form of torture, or forget about it. Remembering rightly means remembering the past as is, and in anticipation of eventually forgetting the horrors contained therein.[66] As nuanced and helpful as this view remains, there are compelling reasons to question whether the vision of history that it is built upon is adequate—reasons that are relevant to understanding Confederate monuments' orientation to the past.[67]

Another vision of how right remembering works would push back against historical realism: the notion that the past exists "as is," and that there is such a thing as "what really happened" that is independent of any point of view.[68] It might seem as though historical realism follows from the Christian conviction that nothing in creation happens apart from God's presence, and therefore that there is a transcendental grounding for this view of the past, even if humans never have full access to such knowledge. For such theologians, Christians have a stake in affirming universality of this sort insofar as Christians affirm that God is not bound by the vicissitudes of time.[69] Further, this sort of historicism is often affirmed as a way for victims to combat victimizers' attempts to forget their misdeeds or lie about them.[70] Christians certainly do have a stake in affirming that God is present to all events in history. But this conviction does not necessarily lead to belief in "autonomous history" and the attendant theories of remembrance as bare recollection. Theologically, it can also lead to the conviction that the past is viewed aright when viewed in relation to Christ, the Alpha and Omega whose particularity is what saves all of creation, not his relationship to some wider, more universal vision.[71] And philosophically, there are reasons to doubt the notion of "history in itself," because history, memory, and facts are only intelligible as they find their place within a hermeneutical circle that is always already ongoing—a narrative by which they are made meaningful.[72] The question about monuments thus becomes not *if* they will assume some narrative about reality, but *which* narrative will be conjured—and if that narrative directs the memory of wrongs suffered toward justice and healing.[73]

This distinction has significant consequences for the ethics of memorialization. If history exists autonomously, then the memory of horrors suffered cannot be redescribed. The path to healing must lead to forgetting such horrors were ever inflicted; otherwise a remainder of that evil echoes into eternity. But if remembering rightly means remembering with and through the memory of Christ, then facing a traumatic past will mean coming to terms with painful memories by way of Christ's own suffering, who remakes the past without erasing it.[74] In other words, on this view the eschaton will be marked not by the total erasure of horrific memory but by the kind of forgetting inherent to the process of renarration—the renarration of the world through Jesus' particular story of forgiveness, which engenders worship of the eternally scarred Lamb. This process transforms the memory of suffering as it is set within a wider context of development, but if people are to know why they are worshipping, it is important that memories remain, however transformed, so that they at least continue to know themselves as the same people who previously suffered and thus know what they have to be celebrating.

While on the surface this may seem like a relatively minor theological disagreement, it actually affects one's stance toward the role and deconstruction of monuments. If history exists "as is," then the only way to address evil now and evil remembered is by way of a forgiveness that is a one-time event of giving and receiving, necessarily followed by forgetting the wrong committed—even if this begs the question of what reconciliation is.[75] Publicly remembering troubling events will mean adding information to what is already present. The problem with this is philosophical as much as theological: if facts are always already valued, given that they are selected and given the silences inherent to that process, then right remembering can never be the simple expansion of more facts.[76] Indeed, the very picture of collecting facts about a history that exists as is—the "storage model" of memory (as in Plato's cabinet or Augustine's hall)—does not adequately account for the reality that the "contents" of memory are neither fixed nor always accessible, but are affected (even if just in a minimalist sense) by the present.[77] Rather than modes of address that assume historical representation as mere vehicles for the transmission of knowledge (Lessing-like "husks"), any addition or historical fixing (which Confederate monuments surely require) must establish a right relation to that knowledge.[78] Thus, remembering with an eye toward forgiveness focuses not on a singular exchange or a single moment of "fixing" a problematic past, but on a process of forgiveness and renarration that is never exhausted.[79] Theologian Jonathan Tran summarizes this position by inverting Volf's aphorism: not "heaven *or* the memory of horror," but "heaven *as* the rememory of horror."[80]

If the fullness of Christian redemption is not dependent on historical realism, however modified, nor on forgetting as a way to go on, then it will instead be tied to renarration, in the same way that healthy communities process trauma by telling stories.[81] The past is often horrifying, but it is remembering well rather than forgetting that allows life to go on.[82] Integral to this claim is the recognition that the past is not dead or passive "stuff" to be analyzed, with memory being the simple retrieval of facts. Rather, the past is active and agential, haunting the present in ways both obvious and hidden. "Right remembering" is thus less a passive mental exercise and more a form of hospitality toward the past; it recognizes that the past always holds a degree of power over the future, and works to inherit this past in such a way that it does not solely do harm in the present.[83] More specifically, right remembering will move toward forms of memorialization that encourage the ongoing addition of stories and renarrations over time, recognizing that no monument can do the full work of remembering for a people.[84] The goal will not be to forget—now, or ever—but to remember without hate, to remember in hope.[85]

As such, a good starting point for disrupting Confederate monuments and the conversation surrounding them would be to reframe the notion of the past often assumed by supporters and detractors alike as autonomous, neutral, or a bare accounting of "just the facts." This is challenging because the monuments themselves typically reinforce this performative neutrality. Such rhetoric allows supporters of the monuments to hide (from themselves) the very real bent contained within the monuments, and opponents to imagine that simply taking the monuments down would free society from the racist ideologies that they conjure. Ironically, assuming that monuments do the work of remembrance for a people leads to a dialectic between those who argue one must never alter a monument, because to alter a monument is to alter the objective past and thus cannot help but be a matter of "propaganda," and those whose only imaginative response to Confederate monuments begins and ends with removal—out of sight, out of mind. At the very least, this analysis prevents people from saying that to change, play, or "screw" with monuments can only be the result of bias, or a desire to inject politics or ideology into a historical debate.[86] Monuments always already contain such commitments; the question is if they are truthful or not. All someone is saying when they claim that to alter a monument is to introduce bias into collective memory is that they prefer the narrative of the past as it is, and do not wish to have it disturbed in any way.

There is no question that Confederate monuments are terribly misleading when it comes to the past, which is why removal is one appealing option for responding to them. But if right remembering means finding ways to recontextualize and renarrate horrific events from the past, then other responses begin to come into view—not as a matter of moderate compromise, but as a means of getting at the soil from which such monuments spring. It suggests a different route altogether: a search for ways to reorient and disrupt the "uptake" of Confederate monuments by situating them around the crucified Christ, who enables people to face even such a past as this. With certain monuments removal is not a simple option to exercise on a logistical level; the path to disruption will be through some form of renarration. To take just one obvious example, the giant engravings of Confederate generals on the side of Stone Mountain, Georgia cannot be pulled down by protesters. Resituating or renarrating is likely the only option at Stone Mountain. And Stone Mountain may provide an example of the imaginative frame required going forward, since those generals are at least as indelibly engraved within Southern culture and Southern (white) minds as they are on that mountain.

A deeper point about responding to Confederate monuments may reveal itself through this theological argument about remembrance: if one cannot simply opt out of the past—no matter how much one may wish to do so—and if the past is a matter of narration rather than mere reporting, then *simply* tearing down Confederate monuments may only serve to drive this troubled history further underground but leave it otherwise unaffected. It is at least possible that many Americans—especially white Americans—wish to take down Confederate monuments in the belief or hope that this legacy is in the past and should be forgotten. This inclination is understandable, and in many ways laudable, but the question remains whether it is a path to justice. The legacies of the post-war South can be adequately addressed through the removal of monuments only if Confederate monuments do all or most of the work of remembering for the American South and if the past exists as an autonomous collection of facts such that forgetting is possible in this manner. If either point does not hold, then other paths for disruption will need to be sought—as they should—coupled with the removal and alteration of these statues. In no way should Confederate monuments remain undisturbed in their narration of the past, untruthful and unfaithful as they remain. But as Christians go about working to engender the disruption of Confederate monuments, it is important to remember that no response exempts one from this history.[87]

Theological Disruption: Lynching and the Crucified Christ

What would a deeper disruption of Confederate monuments entail? When Confederate monuments remember the past, they consistently evoke the theological concept of sacrifice. Thus, the beginnings of a Christian response to Confederate monuments could involve shifting the sense of the collective past embedded in these monuments such that they evoke not a pagan conception of sacrifice, but Christ's sacrifice. Disrupting the appeal to sacrifice is no trivial matter, for it is a central conviction of the civil religion of the Lost Cause; as such, one must recognize that to alter convictions about sacrifice is to scratch an ideology—a theology—and should expect the kind of instinctually defensive reactions that always come when ideologies are disturbed. And make no mistake: reorienting memory around the one sacrifice of Christ has the potential of radically unsettling Confederate monuments.

Connecting remembrance and sacrifice is far from arbitrary. Even at a surface level, there are etymological connections between memory and monuments in a variety of languages.[88] But more deeply, the concept of remembrance is frequently connected with sacrifice in the New Testament and Hebrew Bible: remembering well, remembering God's faithfulness in the past, remembering Christ's saving work. The two events most prominently associated with the call to remember in the Bible are the Exodus, with all the blood-sacrifice imagery contained therein, and Christ's death. The central ritual of remembrance in the Christian life is the collective memory invoked each time Christians take the Lord's Supper. Christ is remembered, his death proclaimed and made present in the remembering—and a particular form of remembering at that. The word *anamnesis*, which is used to describe the Lord's Supper, does not denote the simple recollection of bare information, what historians would call "chronicling." Rather, *anamnesis* is a type of recollection that leavens and liberates the present; it is not limited to individual recollection but is evoked in the ritual and verbal activity of communities. In the same way that recalling the Exodus event during the Passover meal makes these events mysteriously present, and that this recollection is not "neutral," so with the Lord's Supper.[89] This process of remembrance, spurred by material phenomena, forms Christian identity. In this way memory sits at the heart of Christianity—the memory of Christ, whose memory is dangerous insofar as Christ's suffering challenges the interests of the powers that be.[90]

Because of this connection, Christians have a stake in remembering well, with the particular memory of a particular life serving as the fulcrum-point for Christians' sense of what right remembering looks like. Christian remembrance of the past "remembers" Christ's body, whose own life and death provide a potential counter-discipline to the disciplines of the state.[91] This also includes the state-related disciplines of the Confederacy and the Lost Cause. Christians' use of sacrificial language should enable resistance to the calls for further sacrifice issued by other entities. Sacrifice of this kind—pagan in nature—is zero-sum. It calls people to empty themselves in order to fulfill something for another. But Christian *anamnesis* is not simple recollection, but performative and participative—and to participate in the sacrifice of Christ does not subtract but adds to a person's true end.[92] Christian sacrifice creates martyrs rather than victims, people who witness to the end of victimization and sacrifice itself by way of Christ's death (Heb 10:1–18).[93] As such, to participate in Christ's death undermines the concept of sacrifice that is found in Confederate monuments and that is used to bind American society together, in favor of living into an eschatological future in which all things are made new and blood sacrifice is no more.[94]

This is but a way of saying that Christ's salvation is sufficient for the world, and further sacrifice is not required. God has given all of Godself in Jesus Christ and has no need of further bloodshed.[95] Christians should resist calls to sacrifice for other principles and recognize that such calls are idolatrous. This temptation clearly manifests itself in and with Confederate monuments. The Lost Cause rhetoric always flirted with such idolatry, invoking sacrifices that are very different from Christ's own self-giving. For instance, one anecdote tells of the aged Robert E. Lee on Washington College's campus happening upon some Confederate veterans arguing. One veteran insisted that any good Confederate soldier had automatic entry into heaven. "Just then General Lee came along, and the veteran asked him to confirm this interpretation. 'No, my good friend,' Lee replied. 'I'm afraid not. That may be good Confederacy, but it's poor theology!'"[96] At times the idolatrous use of sacrifice language was put on monuments and memorials themselves, as in one marble drinking fountain to the Confederacy in El Dorado, Arkansas, which in its publicity statement said that "the water in it symbolized 'the loving stream of blood' shed by the Southern soldiers. Drinkers from the fount were thus symbolically baptized in Confederate blood."[97] Indeed, the use of sacrificial imagery in the postbellum South expanded from a concern to reclaim Southern honor to a quasi-cultic attempt to redress a cosmic imbalance, which connected in complex ways to black bodies.[98]

What does it look like to orient Southern memories around the remembrance of Christ in a way that resists the idolatrous exultation of sacrifice in general and the sacrificial rhetoric of the Lost Cause? What cannot be meant is simply "adding" Christian imagery to Confederate monuments, as if placing a cross in front of the common soldier statue in Wilmington would undermine its message. Not only would this strategy be laughably superficial, it would ignore the fact that Christian imagery is already present in and around many Confederate monuments. Something deeper is needed that shifts the way these monuments function. The use and function of sacrifice-rhetoric itself must be changed. This does not necessarily look like abandoning any use of sacrificial rhetoric, although there are good reasons some wish to do so, particularly given the ways sacrifice-talk is now fused with nationalism.[99] Nor does it look like a bland addition to monuments that does nothing to engender the sort of reckoning with the past that the United States has continuously put off. In other words, putting up a statue of Arthur Ashe—helpful as that can be in some respects—does little to disrupt the narratives and power behind Monument Avenue and the history of Richmond generally.[100] Nor still would *simple* removal be likely to do that trick, as the roots of these idolatrous moves have gone too deep.

Rather, the most interesting suggestion comes by way of theologian James Cone, who worked to remind (white) theologians that the Christ with whom they dealt was not a decontextualized or apathetic figure, but stood on behalf of the oppressed in every human society throughout history. Christ identified with the poor, the outcast, and the marginalized in his own time, and as such was deemed a threat to the religio-political establishment and was treated as such threats usually are: silenced by a quasi-legal process. In the United States, this identification is not rightly described in abstract terms, which ends up saying very little; because the historically marginalized in this country have been people of color, and chiefly identified (negatively) as black, Cone argues that God is black—obviously not in terms of skin color (as though race were merely a matter of melanin), but in terms of God's identification with those on the underside of history. This is a Christological point. While Jesus Christ stands over all statements about truth and is the very criterion for truth and beauty, it is also true that Christ is not separate from or independent from the oppressed of the earth, such that to truly know Christ is to know him as he is revealed among the poor.[101]

In this perspective, it follows that contemporary Americans cannot understand the power and scandal of the cross of Christ without understanding the lynching tree. The reason that this is so goes beyond parallels between the mob violence that led to Jesus' death on a tree (Acts 10:39) and the mob violence suffered by countless black persons under Jim Crow. Because God identifies fully and actually with the marginalized, to really understand Jesus' sacrifice one must understand that his crucifixion was the result of forces far closer to American lynch mobs than many white people would care to admit. Seeing this connection is necessary if the credibility and hope of the Christian gospel are to survive and if the Christian message about Jesus' cross is to have any chance of healing the wounds of racialized violence that have marked the American past, and continue to divide American church and society alike.[102] Even more profoundly, if God was present at every lynching and claimed their suffering as God's own, then the lynching tree is the cross in the United States. American Christians discover the real scandal of the cross when they realize that Jesus is met in and among the crucified bodies that are obscured and ignored every day.[103] "The real scandal of the gospel is this: humanity's salvation is revealed in the cross of the condemned criminal Jesus, and humanity's salvation is available *only* through our solidarity with the crucified people in our midst."[104]

Following this insight, perhaps adding stories of lynchings that happened around the same time monuments were constructed celebrating past "Confederate glory" is the clearest way to receive the judgment of Jesus' cross for today, in a way that would avoid tepid calls for "reconciliation" that circumvent the necessarily prior trip through judgment. Such a judgment would come not through forgetting but counter-memory—the hard, often painful work of facing suppressed, denied, or ignored memory, and in doing that work giving voice to an eschatological hope that Christians, at least, will be willing to live out their convictions.[105] By adding lynching markers around Confederate monuments, statues that were designed to intimidate and limit imagination might be transformed into sites of resistance and healing the deep, invisible wound that is race and whiteness.[106] If there is anything to the connection between the cross of Christ and lynching, placing memorials to victims of lynching would be a way of reorienting public memory around Christ in a more substantive and subtle way—even if most people would not describe this move in Christological terms. At the very least, it would remind Americans that lynching is not nearly as distant an occurrence as some might think.[107]

Constructing monuments about lynching is a risky endeavor, as it highlights ghosts from the past that endanger and subvert stories this nation tells itself about itself. To memorialize the events surrounding lynching well requires crafting forms of memorialization that do not purport to "set" the narrative once and for all, but remain open to counter voices and alternative narrations than the ones normally told. A major risk is that, in speaking about lynching at all, some people might come to celebrate these horrific events, while others will have an already-latent hopelessness reinforced.[108] Guarding against this possibility will include recognizing that those on the receiving end of suffering are also a resisting, resilient people, at once suffering and empowered.[109] That is, adding markers to lynching is not a sufficient response to Confederate monuments or a comprehensive approach to counter-memory. But such warnings do not negate the possibilities contained in this response, as it is important that Americans, and especially the white American South, become much more willing to be disturbed by the past. What remembering Confederate monuments through the lens of lynching avoids is both forgetfulness and nostalgic, triumphalist readings of the past that ignore or minimize suffering. In particular, it aims to puncture the "respectable" indifference that many white people have to Confederate monuments and the histories they tell and conceal—the same indifference that infects America today and which allowed the practice of lynching to go on for so long, out of sight and out of mind.[110]

As such, the suggestion to publicly remember lynching as a counter to Confederate monuments' false memory will be fiercely resisted. People tend to like their arrangement with the past, and do not wish to do this kind of memory work. Dangerous memories indict facile resolutions to past oppressions; they disturb complacency, timelessness, forgetfulness, and distortion, and few people enjoy being disturbed in this way. This is as true of Christians as anyone, despite the fact that at the heart of the Christian story is the dangerous memory of Jesus Christ that does not leave any aspect of creation undisturbed. Others will be concerned that remembrance of this sort instrumentalizes the past for the sake of white enlightenment, and to be sure, one must avoid accidentally glorifying such horrors or using them for the sake of one's own glory. And still others will simply resist facing something they do not wish to face. When the first lynching memorial was opened in Montgomery, Alabama in the summer of 2018, many celebrated its arrival, but others vocalized concern, arguing that sleeping dogs should be left alone. "It's going to cause an uproar and open old wounds," one fifty-eight-year-old said, continuing, "it's bringing up bullshit." Another: "I think they just need to leave it alone." (The "they" in the sentence is left unspecified, but in context it seems pretty clear who is meant.)[111]

Facing the connection between the sacrifice of Christ and the death of black bodies in the United States is dangerous. It directly counters the connection made between Confederate soldiers' deaths and Christ's sacrifice. The point, of course, is not morbidity. To face wounds of this sort is a kind of passageway; it allows people to recognize their own locatedness in history as well as invites them into the hard work of carrying memories differently. Christians, at least, should lead the way in facing painful and dangerous collective memories, refusing to shy away from wounds either individual or collective. In facing ourselves in this way, people may discover in their wounds not a death but a passageway to healing, to God, and to one another—discovering ways of remembering that neither retraumatize nor erase the past.[112] If Confederate monuments tell a particular story about the past, then adding markers to lynchings would be a powerful means of interrupting that story. The goal must be to find ways of facing this past that are flexible yet focused, and that attend to the implied vision of "the good" within most Confederate monuments, over which the crucified Christ stands in judgment.

But at this juncture, the question is simple: Is America willing to be freed from its demons?[113] Do people really want to face the ways the past has been constructed? Many do not. In the United States discussion of things like lynching, if it happens at all, is relegated to private and hushed conversations rather than the public arena, although this has recently begun to change.[114] Americans want to think of themselves as exemplary democratic citizens, participating in a grand experiment that is the envy of the world; few want to acknowledge that people could be so ruthless.[115] Or in the case of white folks, to acknowledge that one's own people have done such things. Even so, whatever justice and reconciliation is possible in this lifetime will only come by passing through the waters of truthfulness and remembrance—somehow viewing a complicated past through the eyes of the crucified.

3

Future

Whiteness Concretized

Hence are we called atheists. And we confess that we are atheists, so far as gods of this sort are concerned, but not with respect to the most true God . . .

Justin Martyr[1]

The monument to the Battle of Liberty Place was hard to find, and it was this way by design. In 1993 the monument had been moved from Canal Street in New Orleans to a location off the beaten path, tucked away just beside a parking garage. The goal had been to mitigate or at least hide the statue's offensiveness, but in January of 2017—only three months before it would be removed completely—it was clear that this strategy had failed. Fake blood was splattered on the ground next to the monument, and someone had taken a hammer to the inscription at its base, leaving it half-destroyed. The Liberty Place monument had attracted this kind of attention throughout its history, vandalized and graffitied by each generation.

This attention was well-deserved. The monument celebrated and memorialized members of the "White League" who violently removed the Republican governor from power in 1874. Many white Southerners disputed the legitimacy of the governor's narrow victory and resented the idea of being under the dominion of Southern "traitors" about as much as they resisted the idea of African Americans in power. Indeed, one local historian described the battle as "The Overthrow of Carpet-Bag Rule in New Orleans."[2] And so these aggrieved southerners staged a coup, which was opposed by city police and the former Confederate general (and Lost Cause scapegoat) James Longstreet. Within three days the federal government had reasserted Republican rule—marking a key difference between this incident and the coup in Wilmington, North Carolina two decades later—but it pointed to the profound disdain most southerners had for Reconstruction, which was soon abandoned with the Compromise of 1877. When the White League came to power a few years later, they decided to create a monument celebrating this "battle." Erected in 1891, the monument listed the names of those who died fighting to reinstate white rule; one might say it commemorated those who fought for the Lost Cause rather than the Confederacy as such. This subtext was made text in 1934 when two inscriptions were added, which read: "United States troops took over the state government and reinstated the usurpers but the national election in November 1876 recognized white supremacy and gave us our state." And, "McEnery and Penn, having been elected governor and lieutenant governor by the white people, were duly installed by the overthrow of the carpetbag government, ousting the usurpers Gov. Kellogg (white) and Lt. Gov. Antoine (colored)."[3]

Because of its overt racism, the monument was altered over the intervening years. In 1974, Mayor Moon Landrieu agreed to place a plaque next to the monument that described the events of Liberty Place as an insurrection rather than a battle, and noted that the inscriptions to white supremacy were later additions. In 1981 the plaques that mentioned white supremacy were covered up. In 1993 a new inscription was put at the base of the monument, adding the names of those who died defending the government, and (in a rhetorical flourish reminiscent of Donald Trump's response to the Charlottesville riots) stated that it honored those "on both sides" of the fight. It ended with an appeal to look ahead rather

FIG. 3.1 The Battle of Liberty
Place Monument,
New Orleans, La.

than behind: "A conflict of the past that should teach us lessons for the future." Finally, on April 24, 2017—a day that three different states celebrate Confederate Memorial Day—Moon Landrieu's son oversaw the removal of the monument, which began at 1:30 a.m. by workers wearing bullet-proof vests, masks, and helmets. The workers were also provided sniper cover. Importantly, Mayor Mitch Landrieu justified this move not only because the monument distorted the past, but also because it was "an affront to our present" and "a bad prescription for our future."[4]

To be sure, the monument to the Battle of Liberty Place was unique in how clearly it pointed onlookers to the future, both in its early forms in which the hoped-for future was one of white rule, as well as later when people attempted to divert its performative power to other "lessons for" the future, even if those lessons were left unstated. But an orientation to the future is present in all Confederate monuments, which is unsurprising given that a monument is an object that stimulates memory in order that a people may coalesce around shared aspirations—a means by which people can communicate their values and desires to future generations.[5] Put differently, monuments are never just about the past, but ask people to remember in order to shape present collective identity and manifest some particular future. Monuments signal the conscious and subconscious ideals of a people, often through the representation of exemplary figures, and contribute to a community's sense of direction.[6]

Generally speaking, Confederate monuments seek to orient society toward an ideal that was explicitly named in the Liberty Place monument but is implicitly signaled by most Confederate monuments: the goal of white supremacy. In Confederate monuments whiteness takes on the character, not just of an aesthetic ideal, but also a kind of eschatological horizon, which is seen most clearly once one realizes that monuments communicate in ways beyond what they explicitly "say." Monuments always contain a surplus of meaning. In Confederate monuments, this surplus is signaled by pointing the viewer toward the future and whiteness at one and the same time. And if one recognizes that this racialized ideal was a theological development, then these monuments that reinforce white supremacy come to be seen not just as wrong but idolatrous—as signs of a rival eschatology. It stands to reason that if theology created and bolsters whiteness as an ideal, then theology can also be used to disrupt Confederate monuments in their aesthetic orientation to the future, which is their most subtle and most pernicious aspect. By seeking alternative forms of memorialization that aim toward a more faithful, equitable future, Americans might begin to hope for an apocalyptic disruption of whiteness that comes from outside of their own resources and imagination.

Monumental Aesthetics: Implicit Meaning and Visions of the Beautiful

Every monument carries meaning beyond what is immediately evident. Indeed, part of the power of communication is the way messages can be coded within the primary communicative act. Sarcasm provides a case in point: it is a device through which a speaker is able to be nasty to another person while retaining plausible deniability if one read a transcript of the conversation: "What? *All* I said was that I *love* your outfit!" In some cases, the intended meaning of an utterance can even contradict what is explicitly stated. In order to catch sarcasm, one cannot simply read the words themselves. One must understand the communication in its wider context, including the history of relations between the two people in question. This is no less true of Confederate monuments. There are subtleties of visual communication baked into a monument's history, its physical placement, the time period in which it was erected, and the way it represents its subject matter.

There are many avenues leading to the insight that the meaning of monuments is deeply contextual and multilayered; one such avenue is speech-act theory. One of the insights to be gleaned from speech-act theory is that in order for an utterance to be "happy," one must attend to multiple levels of communication at once: not just the bare utterance, but also the social context within which any utterance takes place, and the way an utterance is understood by an interlocutor. This analysis helps one better understand how speech works, of course, but it also destabilizes what words mean insofar as social contexts themselves shift and change. As time passes, new interpretations of words are possible as new contexts "house" these communications. Put differently, the meaning of language is not exhausted by the signs themselves or even what they immediately intend to represent; meaning is also found in the way words are taken up by later hearers, who can use and interpret the same words very differently. Additionally, speech-act theory allows one to see that there is an excess of meaning with any utterance, to the point that understanding what is going on with any statement is more complicated than a technical analysis of "just the words." The surface level of meaning is important, of course, but there are also meanings that are wordlessly implied or contextually illuminated once utterances are considered in their full context. Analyzing a speech-act, then, means recognizing that while there is not an unlimited number of ways an utterance can "mean," there is an inexhaustibility of meaning in every communicative act that is never fully settled.[7] Even descriptions of mundane and communally accessible phenomena are not *fully* captured by language; words can be adequate without exhausting all that there is to say about something as ordinary as the smell of coffee.[8]

Much philosophical and theological work has been done on how words specifically function in this multifaceted way, and for good reason; but these insights apply to images as well. In the same way that the meaning of a speech-act is not exhausted simply by paying attention to what is said, so does an image have its own surplus of meaning. An image can be approached from a virtually inexhaustible number of angles, and in order to approach any image well, one must note and respect this surplus rather than attempt to resolve or dissolve it.[9] Also similar to utterances, no image exists in a pure state, but finds its place in an already-ongoing cycle of interpretation and background information that is assumed by the viewer. Ludwig Wittgenstein called this phenomenon the "hurly-burly" of life: the mixed-up series of actions, judgments, and concepts that make any single action (or any single monument) intelligible.[10] As such, competent analysis of a given monument will utilize many different disciplines, as no symbolic image exists in a vacuum but is always already connected to other spheres of influence (political, theological, psychological, and so on).[11] The realm of aesthetics is never totally isolated from the sociopolitical or the theological, because the imaginative storeroom from which the symbolic background is "filled in" is stocked by one's cultural context, which itself is constituted by various intertwined social, political, and theological convictions.[12]

It follows that there is always more to a monument than what meets the eye. Monuments contain hidden and contextually specific meanings that go beyond what they say they represent. This surplus of meaning makes monuments important but also dangerous, for it suggests that a monument's precise significance can never be settled once and for all; their meaning can change over time and for future generations, and as such they always have the potential of disrupting a people's sense of what is going on in the world.[13] Because this excess of meaning cannot be explicitly signaled by the monument itself, it will often be revealed in a monument's design and aesthetic form, which subtly prepares people to consider certain possibilities in the world as imaginable, and others as unimaginable. By putting material together in this or that way, arranging and rearranging symbolic forms over time, people set for themselves the limits of what can be seen and thought, enabling certain ways of inhabiting the world.[14] The question regarding Confederate monuments thus becomes: What are these statues "saying" in their very form and aesthetic presentation? Not if, but how do Confederate monuments manifest meanings and convictions beyond what is immediately evident, but may be seen if one delves into their historical context? Because people have an aesthetic before they have an ethic, Christians wishing to investigate Confederate monuments' significance must do so not only in terms of what the monuments assume to be good or what they assume to be true, but what they assume to be beautiful.[15]

And make no mistake, Confederate monuments assume a particular vision of what is beautiful, and even what is ultimate. The people who constructed Confederate monuments understood the importance of their design, intuitively grasping that the way these figures were portrayed would shape future generations as much as any of a monument's overtly didactic qualities. The designers of Confederate monuments and those who sat on memorial committees were greatly concerned with the aesthetic dimension of monuments, for they knew that before any words were read on a plaque or inscription, the images themselves would impact viewers and stick with them long after they left. The goal was to create a fusion of horizons between the monument and the imaginations of future viewers.[16] In the case of Confederate monuments, the primary means by which this imaginative fusion was achieved was through the notion of "the ideal human form," which was something of an obsession in the nineteenth century and assumed the idealizations associated with "classic," Western art. The concept of an ideal human form was drawn from the belief in a God-given or natural racial hierarchy—a belief that was bolstered by pseudoscience, phrenology, ways of reading scripture, philosophy, and carefully crafted histories, among other things—and which created a genuine aversion bordering on anxiety in representing people of African descent.[17] If "the Negro" was sculpted or portrayed at all, it was vital to signal his or her inferiority. Thus, the notion of the ideal human form—which is unequivocally behind the design of most Confederate monuments—was mapped onto theological and political values that were common at the time, and was explicitly reinforced by Christian habits of thought. While it is true that some monuments were explicit in their commitment to white supremacy—the monument to the Battle of Liberty Place being a prime example—the commitment to whiteness is usually found at the level of the aesthetic surplus of meaning. However nuanced one wishes to be about Confederate monuments' history and placement, it remains true that the majority of Confederate monuments manifest a commitment to whiteness-as-beautiful and a white future that is embedded in their very design. This commitment is rarely explicit, but this does not make it any less real, present, or pernicious. In fact, one could argue that the message of white superiority becomes more powerful for this aesthetic subtlety and non-verbal presence, as it enables a (semi)plausible deniability in the monuments' defenders. Confederate monuments in this regard are less monuments *to* white supremacy (as is sometimes claimed) and more monuments *of* and *for* white supremacy, a subtle nuance but one that is important in both understanding their danger as well as paths that lead to their genuine dismantling, and dismantling the ideologies they conjure.

The problem and allure of whiteness is only deepened once one recognizes that white supremacy has always been a theological, even Christian idea. The notion of whiteness was born of particular uses of Christian resources, and as such its articulation and representation is deeply theological—or better, theopoetic, a category that stresses the notion that the things people make (and not just "think") end up making them and creating certain realities in the world.[18] White supremacy is not a set of rational truth claims held by individuals; it is much more a spiritual conviction that is felt and experienced as one goes about shaping the social world in particular ways. The concept of whiteness takes *form*—verbal, visual, sensual—and that form affects one's way of imagining the world, as much as or more than the "idea" itself.[19] As such, one could say that Confederate monuments both manifest and encourage a semi-theological devotion to white superiority. The constellation of symbols and statues devoted to the Lost Cause are powerful instances of whiteness being concretized.[20]

The White Ideal: Common Soldiers, Heroes, and Racial Hierarchy

Despite the fact that many of the high-profile controversies surrounding Confederate monuments have been generated by statues of Confederate generals, those monuments are not what one is likely to find in a typical Southern hamlet or city square. Instead, what one will probably find is a statue dedicated to the everyday Confederate soldier, a nameless "type" representing the ubiquity of Southern virtue, valor, and sacrifice—what came to be known as the "common soldier" statue. Confederate generals (particularly Robert E. Lee and Stonewall Jackson) represented the apex of these virtues, the idealized and aristocratic exemplars against whom all Southerners should measure their actions. Common soldier statues, on the other hand, represented the ordinary Southern hero who faithfully embodied the same narrative but in more humble, quotidian ways.[21] Statues to generals and common soldier statues are thus linked not simply by the time period they were typically constructed within, nor by the fact that they were usually placed in public settings, but more deeply by the ideals they manifest. This contrasts with monuments placed in contexts of memorialization and death. Put bluntly, in their very design common soldier statues manifest convictions about the ideal human form which are drawn from a purported hierarchy of the races as well as assumptions about what constitutes true masculinity. The monuments that proliferated throughout the South after 1875 served as marble embodiments of a set of beliefs that were fast taking on the character of a civil religion.[22]

To be sure, some Confederate monuments were dedicated immediately following the Civil War, and these statues tended to be placed in cemeteries or at the site of some significant event, though this was not universally the case; these early monuments also tended to display signs of mourning and remembrance of the dead. However, most Confederate monuments were commissioned and dedicated a generation later—between 1885 and 1915—with a major uptick occurring after the turn of the twentieth century.[23] The later monuments were erected in service to the Lost Cause and were specifically meant to commemorate a Southern golden age that those in power hoped would return someday. Speakers at dedication ceremonies would frequently exhort audiences to remember the greatness of the Southern past, and to emulate this greatness in the present for the sake of the future. For example, at an 1887 monument dedication in Smithfield, North Carolina, Alfred Waddell (of Wilmington coup infamy) argued that Southerners should refrain from speaking of a "New South," because it "is tantamount to an insinuation that there is something about the antebellum South to be ashamed of"—as if the slaveholding South was not an ideal society to aim for once more.[24] Even though these later monuments always spoke of honoring the dead, their physical placement (increasingly in the town square, beside the courthouse, or at the state capitol), as well as the sharp increase in their construction across the South, suggests that other factors were at play.[25] In particular, the speed with which monuments were being put up and the popularity of the common soldier design suggests that something about this time period itself was driving construction—a time period that is centrally marked

Fig. 3.2 "Common Soldier" Statue and Monument, Raleigh, N.C.

by the reassertion of white rule through lynching and the birth of Jim Crow.[26]

The design of common soldier statues is consistent, even bordering on formulaic, which is no surprise given that their production was something of a cottage industry in the postbellum period.[27] A common soldier statue usually features an unidentified male soldier with Anglo features and of average size. He will be standing at ease or at parade rest, either leaning on his gun or resting it on his shoulder. It is rare that a common soldier will appear as a combatant or show any signs of having fought in a war at all, whether through torn clothing or physical markings.[28] Quite the opposite, the figure exudes control over his body combined with a vigilant ease. The man will be standing rather than sitting, prepared but not anxious: a person who is not transcendent (as Lee or Jackson would seem), but worthy of emulation.[29] Finally, the common soldier is usually elevated some distance from the ground, at the lowest with his shoes at eye level, but sometimes reaching sixty or seventy feet in the air—an honor normally reserved for a local hero or general rather than the common foot soldier.[30] Coupled with the requisite dedication to those who died, such monuments are meant to be unobjectionably praiseworthy; one could theoretically be offended by those who were in power for this or that decision, but only the most callous, traitorous, or obtuse could object to an ordinary soldier being ordered into battle.

Or so the monuments would have you believe. If one knows the cultural milieu out of which these monuments emerged, things become vastly more complicated. Paying attention to this context reveals that common soldier monuments are far from innocuous, but in the aggregate represent an aesthetic North Star that is meant to lead society into the future. This is particularly evident if one analyzes Confederate monuments within the framework of the predominant aesthetic assumptions and constraints of Western artistic expression, particularly regarding depictions of the human body. The goal of the common soldier monument was by definition to be universal in its reference points, representing the generic man who fought in the war. As such, designers and sculptors had to choose what would represent the prototypical soldier-citizen.

The generic facial features needed to condense all those who fought for the South into a standard "American" type, which was not easy to define. But whiteness was obviously a prerequisite.[31] The reason this was obvious has to do with the belief, fully developed by the nineteenth century, that the Anglo body represented the epitome of strength, beauty, and rationality. The further a body deviated from this aesthetic ideal, the further removed it was from the universal values embodied therein. Needless to say, the "Negro" was seen as the mirror opposite of this white ideal, but the arbitrary nature of this designation—of what is considered truly "white"—is revealed by the fact that categories of people who would be considered white today were not considered white at this time; the most famous example of this is the Irish.[32] Thus, because the phenomenon of the common soldier statue was at its base a depiction of the male body, its design was never neutral or simple, but a politically and racially fraught affair. Earlier soldier monuments were simple obelisks, sometimes inscribed with individual names, and thus tended to erase the difference between soldiers in death. Death united all those who fought and died. But when the common soldier statue exploded in popularity, Confederate monuments entered inherently racialized terrain.[33]

In response to these dangers, most white sculptors avoided depicting black people in any form, which served to erase (or eclipse) black experiences from public memory. When sculptors did not take the path of avoidance, their work almost inevitably manifested a belief in white superiority, in ways both subtle and overt. If people of African descent were represented at all, they were depicted in a position of passivity and bondage. This unwritten rule was followed even in abolitionist art that attempted to support the cause of emancipation. A good example is the famous nineteenth-century picture of the pleading male slave in chains and on bended knee, which always carried the inscription: "Am I not a man and a brother?"[34] These beliefs were manifest in certain sculptural formulas for depicting the human form, which included placing black bodies in a sitting or kneeling position (similar to the female body), and white bodies standing or active.[35] Many abolitionists assumed the picture of the black body was associated with infantilism, danger, disorder, and a lack of control; they simply argued in favor of educating and "elevating" black people from this mean estate. Thus, defenders of and apologists for slavery often employed a very similar logic, the only difference being that one thought it was the institution of slavery that elevated Africans from "barbarism," while the other thought that this was achieved through the goodwill of educated white people.[36] The common strand between the two, which is deeply ingrained in most Confederate monuments, is a paternalism that assumes white folks in power know what is best for those who are beneath them, even better than they know themselves. In the postbellum South, there was general agreement on the superiority of the white race, with several positions existing within that framework ranging from full-on revanchist racism to the more common, "respectable" acceptance of white dominance built on conservative paternalism, which tended to welcome the end of slavery but remained nostalgic for the supposedly harmonious race relations of the prewar South.[37]

Fɪɢ. 3.3 The Emancipation Monument, Washington, D.C.

While white paternalism is ubiquitous in common soldier statues, it is also on full display in the "Emancipation Monument" in Washington, D.C., demonstrating that the problem of white superiority in the United States is far from confined to the American South. Dedicated in 1876, the monument features a standing Abraham Lincoln with his left arm outstretched, hand hovering over a crouching, nearly naked black man. The idea behind constructing "The Freedmen's Memorial" was to represent in public space the newly integrated nation, but in the process it reinforced white paternalism in a profound way. The black body depicted in the statue is not so much an exemplar for other black folks to admire as a means by which white mastery and benevolence is revealed. This "freed" man retains the archetypical markings of a slave: naked, showing no sign of personal agency or enculturation, directly in contrast to the fully dressed and standing Lincoln.[38] Unsurprisingly, Frederick Douglass disliked the monument, arguing that it was more a monument to Abraham Lincoln than to

Fig. 3.4 The Robert E. Lee Monument, Richmond, Va.

black people or black liberation. For Douglass, the monument reinforced the argument that freed slaves should be grateful to their masters for freeing them, rather than subverting the master-slave logic altogether in favor of a story of human beings escaping bondage.[39]

The Southern versions of the white-hero monument, of course, are the monuments to Confederate generals, which are similarly marked by paternalism and an idealization of self-mastery. Among these monuments, the pinnacle is reserved for Robert E. Lee. This is not simply because Lee was and remains the central hero of the Lost Cause mythos, the decorated general who only reluctantly fought for his "country," Virginia, and who was only defeated by the Union's superior numbers. It is also because Lee was seen by sculptors of all stripes as representing the ideal human subject, a strikingly handsome man of means and dignity, the very embodiment of repose, manly beauty, and strength—a ready-made subject.[40] In both his prominence, stature, and beauty, Lee was perfectly suited to signal the climax of the white aesthetic ideal, toward whom all should aim and against whom all should be measured. Even the decision to have Lee on his horse, Traveller, is meaningful. To be sat on a horse in this way signaled "power in repose," representing his mastery over an inferior (yet powerful) creature, and was alluring to white Southerners who wished to show they were still in control, or else remember that kind of control in the hopes of achieving it once more. The unspoken message (which was sometimes made explicit during dedication ceremonies) was that granting limited privileges to black people should not and need not undermine the natural and good truth that was white rule.[41] Lee, and to lesser degrees all the other statues of generals, represented ideals that should continue to be pursued in the future, and was seen at the time as part of a national campaign to legitimate white supremacy in the national consciousness.[42] The Civil War had settled slavery, as Edward Pollard wrote in the original Lost Cause tract; it "did not decide Negro equality."[43] Monuments to Lee and common soldiers alike aimed to decide that question for the future of the South and the country. Indeed, the Lee Monument in Richmond, Virginia was placed in a part of the city that had yet to be built;

it literally sat in Richmond's future and beckoned the city toward him.[44] The politics of aesthetics worked in the Lee monument to disguise white power through the veneer of "civilization," with whiteness serving as the sign and prerequisite of what counted as civil, of course.[45]

The point in describing the monumental representation of the white hero is to highlight the aesthetic backdrop against which all Confederate monuments were designed, particularly those erected during the height of construction around the turn of the century. The power of the common soldier monument was its ability to tap into this aesthetic ideal, with the key difference being that its effect was cumulative. That is, the function of the common soldier statue is felt as part of a collective, in which towns have a figure of this sort in the public square. Monuments of a general are particularly potent versions of this narrative—a higher distillation of the same beverage—but the common soldier monument provides day-to-day reinforcement through its aesthetic form, reasserting and reestablishing a social identity that was lost during the Civil War: the normative white soldier and citizen.[46] The white male is placed at the doors of power, a quiet if unassuming reminder of the racial status quo. In fact, the common soldier is dangerous precisely because of its ubiquity and seeming banality. Nobody needs to study it with any depth in order for it to do its work. Common soldier statues are simple, even simplistic, monuments, able to be understood almost immediately, and as such they distilled massive "civilizational" issues concerning what a nation should aim for into an uncontroversial and boring form.[47] Whatever their differences, common soldier statues are united in one major, implicit uptake: that whiteness is beautiful, powerful, and ultimate.[48]

It should be clear that "whiteness" does not simply mean the amount of melanin in one's skin or having Anglo-European facial features. Whiteness is not the mere difference in skin tone but the social gradations and distributions of power that get linked to these differences—purported ontological differences associated with physical variance that are in fact socially constructed. Of course, to say that race is socially constructed is not to say that race is unreal, fake, or infinitely malleable. Race is constructed, but it has a social reality, meaning that after it is created it is real in its effects, particularly on the people in society who are racialized as "black," "white," and so on.[49] Even at its earliest modern usage the category of race imposed social meaning on physical variations, and as such had to do with ways of structuring society rather than any genetic differences between people.[50] While based on physical differences, race was and remains a sociopolitical category which took its modern form in the eighteenth century after centuries of development. Particularly in the American colonies, race was useful in creating a sense of otherness between certain groups, a move that helped reinforce the defenselessness of labor, broke up solidarity between workers, and encouraged the belief that some groups of people were naturally more fit for certain types of jobs than others.[51] It did not take long for whiteness to become a full-on ideology, in which whiteness was equivalent to "truth" and "virtue" even as it was taken as neutral, universal, and "un-raced."[52] If whiteness became the norm, then the black body was its opposite: not self-sufficient, ugly, morally bankrupt (a belief that was often justified by a particular interpretation of "the curse of Ham"), excessive, even monstrous.[53]

And so whiteness is not simply a matter of physical difference, but is an inherently "valued" social category, a way of seeing the world that is deep in the marrow of the United States and largely unquestioned even by those who argue for "racial tolerance." It produces "the white gaze" which can be internalized by white people *and* people of color: the condition by which one sees oneself primarily through the dominant class and its categories.[54] Put simply, people are trained to prefer whiteness as natural and normal, including those who do not benefit from it.[55] Over time, whiteness as an outlook was baked into a social structure that awarded systematic privileges to those of European descent.[56] The inheritance of whiteness is a pattern of social relations that outstrips any single actor's good or bad intentions, although individual prejudices can, of course, mirror these structural realities. An entire racial ideology has emerged that explains and justifies the status quo, which is reinforced through common frames of reference. These frames of reference are based on common experiences, narratives, and symbols—symbols designed by those in power to explain how the world either is or ought to be, and that can then be taken as "common sense."[57]

Even the most seemingly innocuous Confederate monuments work at this symbolic level: they are material objects that reinforce a racialized story about how the world ought to be. Confederate monuments are far from alone in doing this work, of course, as the imaginative hierarchy that is white supremacy employs a variety of symbols to reinforce itself, as well as the forces W. E. B. Du Bois names (and capitalizes) at the end of *Black Reconstruction*: "Religion, Science, Education, Law, and brute force."[58] But monuments remain important players in this process, especially in the South, encouraging deference to the power of whiteness as natural and ideal. Confederate monuments help reproduce an aesthetic that tells anyone who is not white that they are in danger—unless, as AME Bishop Daniel Alexander Payne put it in 1869 with regards to lynching, "he or she exhibits both in word, and deed, the spirit of a slave."[59] Given that this is the case, it is incredibly important to understand how Confederate monuments reinforce these messages of race and power.[60] Not if, but how.

Transcendent Whiteness as Eschatological Goal

Confederate monuments reinforce whiteness in their aesthetic form, and thus are worthy of theological investigation, as the construction of whiteness as aesthetic ideal has always been a theological, and specifically Christian, project. That is, the category of whiteness is not fully understood within an immanent frame of reference. Rather, the white aesthetic signals a commitment that is metaphysical in nature, and which includes something like an eschatological vision—that is, a view of the end toward which all things should aim.

One does not have to be a theologian to recognize this truth. One of the central insights made by philosopher George Yancy is that whiteness assumes the trappings of the sacred. As a way of seeing and imagining the world, whiteness is more than "just" a social construction; it has become a transcendental norm, meaning that it is tied up with what is fundamentally right and wrong, good and bad, beautiful and ugly.[61] "White" is a way to name, stabilize, and substantiate one's ontological superiority over others, even if one is poor or disenfranchised. It is this aspect of whiteness that has historically offset solidarity among poor people, keeping poor white people complacent even in the face of their own political or economic demise. During the main construction of Confederate monuments, this racialized division was certainly taking place.[62] The strategy of reinforcing white supremacy worked precisely because whiteness was not just a cynical tool of social control from the top but a theological norm that assumed the status of unquestionability and could even be internalized by black people—as it can be today.[63]

Whiteness as transcendental norm does not take root by accident, but is reinforced through various practices, symbols, and narratives. It operates at the level of stories, subtly fixing black bodies as inadequate and desiring of whiteness.[64] As outcomes are predictably produced by these myriad forces, racialized views are taken as basic facts about the world, and (following Toni Morrison) are "confirmed" through the construction of semiotic spaces designed to reproduce this system.[65] Whiteness as transcendental norm is reinforced every day through the variety of practices, ways of relating (or not relating), and semiotic spaces that pass underneath consciousness for being banal and barely worth considering.[66] Many Confederate monuments, particularly the (relatively) inoffensive common soldier statues, function in precisely this way, reinforcing a sacred backdrop of whiteness before which politics, entertainment, relationships, economics, and religion take place. Certainly any monument found outside of a cemetery or battlefield was intended to function in this way to some degree, though monuments in so-called death spaces can function at this level as well.

For theologians working in this area, the transcendent residue of whiteness can be traced to theological developments that are distortions of Christian convictions; that is, whiteness as it is manifest in Confederate monuments and elsewhere is not simply transcendent but Christian in nature, an aesthetic and an eschatological goal with Christian roots.[67] For instance, the modern conception of race was hierarchical, with "whiteness" placed at the top—the concept of the *Herrenvolk*. Blackness, by contrast, was seen as always and forever at the bottom of this hierarchy, with black bodies serving mainly to illumine the majesty at the top.[68] In this way the figure of the black body was taken to be, by nature, the *Untermenschen*.[69] But theologian Willie Jennings shows that the creation of this hierarchy was enabled by several theological developments, not least European colonialists divorcing Christian identity from Israel. That is, Israel was increasingly excluded from European articulations of Christian identity, and thus the process of becoming Christian had to take on new ontic markers. Before Israel was marginalized in the European Christian imagination, the Christian affirmation was that the story of every people group cracked open before the reality that was revealed by Israel's God.[70] Insofar as this theological narrative held, it was both inappropriate and unnecessary for Christians to force the people of one culture to assimilate to another or to assume a false sense of uniformity; instead, Christians were to submit to one another's language and customs in a kind of Pentecostal harmony.[71] But as Israel's election was displaced as a central point around which Christian identity found its trajectory, an idealized European identity and aesthetic took its place.[72] Basically, European Christians forgot that they were included in the covenant of Israel as gentiles, and that all ethnicities are grafted onto the people of God in a way that expands but does not negate Israel's election. Theologians would point out that God entered freely into covenantal relationship with Israel, but then would use this point to argue that God was now free *from* Israel, and thus attachable to other people.[73]

Unmoored from Israel, the picture of Christian perfection could be remapped onto a racial hierarchy in which the European Christian was at the top, the new people of God,[74] and "converts" at the bottom. The darkness of one's skin came to be associated with the likelihood of, or "natural" proximity to, salvation.[75] What is at stake with this racial development is not "just" a particular ideology or political reconfiguring of ethnicity, but a distortion of the Christian vision of creation. Aesthetic judgments concerning "burnt" or "damaged" black skin became signs of a particular way of seeing and imagining creation, with some bodies by nature closer to God and some further away. Anyone could still, of course, be graced by God, but with black folks this would happen despite their race.[76] The conception of peoplehood that is born of this theological shift uncouples humans from any connection to the earth, with Western Christians afterward having an inability to see themselves as intimately tied to the land. Rather, "race" becomes a free-floating aesthetic category that can be applied to people across the globe, uniting people who have little in common other than melanin levels.[77] A racially segregated imagination is henceforth cemented within Western Christianity, leaving many people unable to see how they are imagining the world as well as how the world is shaping their imagination.[78]

Whiteness mapped onto a theological hubris whereby becoming a disciple of Jesus Christ looked like being assimilated into European aesthetic (and economic) practices, rather than being rooted in the resurrected Jesus who gives the Christian a new identity that is harmonious with his or her cultural background and yet is shaped by a new reality of love and belonging.[79] Put simply, to be saved was to become white, and to be white was to be closer to God.[80] One practical result of these theological shifts is the perception that white people are in a natural position to save others and the world. Black people and others "lower" on the racial hierarchy are seen to be fundamentally in the position of learners, the natural and perpetual recipients of instruction. In Immanuel Kant's racial typology the Negro is described in precisely these terms: "They can be educated, but only to be a servant; that is to say, they can be trained."[81] By contrast, the white body was perceived to be not just aesthetically beautiful but a fundamentally acting and instructing agent who can fashion the world in his own image—a move that can be traced to Europe's earliest colonial ventures.[82] From the Iberians to the British, those considered white tended to see themselves as agents of God and the good, ordained to bend creation to their will. Whiteness signaled a category of people who conditioned the world rather than were conditioned by it—who rose above being conditioned by others and creation—and who thus put themselves in the position of God insofar as they assumed activities reserved for God alone.[83]

By the time Confederate monuments were constructed these theological shifts had long been sunk into the American DNA, and are implicitly recalled in and by them. Thus, the theological notion that whites are aesthetically beautiful, closest to God, and in an intrinsically better position to instruct the world is evoked by both common soldier and Confederate general statues. In their form more than anything they say, they are reminders of a theological argument that justifies white paternalism as not just natural but desired by God himself. White paternalism is reinforced both in each statue's individual design as well as their proliferation across the United States, which serves to place a white man in spaces of power throughout the country.[84] Put differently, they presume a vision of God and creation that is deeply alluring, at least to those who benefit from it.

Of course, whiteness as a theological development is not static. Especially as conceived by European colonialists, racial being always implied movement toward a kind of "endless becoming" that organized around the white body.[85] That is, whiteness is both a present and future ideal; like the kingdom of God, it is both now and not yet, moving toward and awaiting its perfection. Whiteness is the end toward which political, economic, and aesthetic matters should and do move, and this ideal is now imperfectly present in white people and culture, awaiting its final consummation.[86] So understood, whiteness is best seen as an ever-expanding way of structuring the world, for if whiteness is the perfection of what humans were meant to be (as Kant explicitly argued), then it is almost a duty for this vision to be spread across the globe. In a sense whiteness awaits its own perfection until this spread is complete.[87] Whiteness comes to be conceived as playing its part in an unfolding drama whereby it brings solution to divisions in the world in no small part by bringing autonomous, universal reason to those unfortunate groups who have purportedly failed to attain it.[88] Thus, while it is rarely put this way, whiteness can be viewed as a kind of eschatology—as the final "end" toward which all things, and certainly all people, should be oriented.

At its most extreme, this eschatology is so encompassing that all other racial groups should be eliminated, while in its "softer" forms other groups can continue to exist as long as they remain clearly subordinate and deferential. The most subtle (and thus perhaps most pernicious) expression of this logic is the rhetoric of being color-blind, which purports to judge people in neutral terms irrespective of ethnic difference (think of misuses of

Martin Luther King's mention of judging "by the content of their character")—but uses categories to make these judgments drawn from the same logic that produced whiteness in the first place. But whatever form it takes, however "nice" or vicious, whiteness expresses itself as an organizing principle that is totalizing: one must either conform oneself to it if possible (as did the Irish), or try to live in such a way as to avoid its wrath.[89]

Perhaps this eschatological dimension of Confederate monuments is most clearly represented by the bas-relief of Lee, Jackson, and Jefferson Davis on the rocky side of Stone Mountain, Georgia. At this site of the so-called second founding of the Ku Klux Klan in 1915, the gigantic engraving was begun in 1924. However, progress was slow, and the work was not complete until 1970. Clearly, the motivation behind these depictions was not any kind of lament for the dead or processing of trauma, as it was completed over a century after the war's end. It is darkly fitting that the bas-relief was begun during Jim Crow and completed during resistance to the civil rights movement. Stone Mountain is about something else: depicting the permanence and inevitability of these heroes for the Georgia of today and the Georgia of the future—heroes who by this time had long been baptized as not just perfect generals and perfect gentlemen, but perfect Christians.[90] These images project a demigod status whereby they, and white men following after them, are competent to charge forward in time. Adjust to their march, the relief seems to say, or get out of the way.

With all this said, it is hardly surprising that monuments erected during the height of Jim Crow exclusively and repetitively represented the ideals of humanity in the form of the white male body. To represent the black body in any way other than subordinate would have been tantamount to a kind of heresy, cutting against the grain of a particular vision of the ultimate—a particular theologic. Analyzing Confederate monuments in their racialized and future-oriented aspects reveals that they are not concerned with the past, history, or accurate remembrance so much as with projecting an ideal onto the future—an ideal that did not need to have a good connection to any historical reality. The common soldier in particular represented an idealized

FIG. 3.5 Confederate Memorial Carving, Stone Mountain, Ga.

myth rather than an actual figure. In this way, the common soldier monument parallels the cultural notion of "the mammy," which was an equally racialized, idealized, and fictional figure that *almost* had its own monument. The fact that the United Daughters of the Confederacy proposed a mammy monument in 1923 in the same historical moment that common soldier statues were being constructed gives the lie to their (perhaps subconscious) intentions in constructing Confederate monuments: to project a vision into the future.[91]

Theological Disruption: Subversive Icons and Idols Overthrown

The problem with Confederate monuments is not that they have a future orientation; the problem is the nature of this end, which is the theological aesthetic of whiteness and white ultimacy. This aesthetic can be detected in individual monuments and their inscriptions, but it reveals itself more clearly as one zooms out, at which point one can begin to see what they are doing at the macro level beyond what they are saying. Cumulatively, Confederate monuments help reinforce a white aesthetic as "common sense" in the United States, which has deep theological dimensions. If all this is true, then critical treatments of Confederate monuments are incomplete if they neglect the theological dimensions of this racialized way of imagining the world.[92] Confederate monuments mark out a particular theological vision, and people who find them appealing are attracted to them at this level, whether they realize it or not; it is a theological, aesthetic appeal as much as a rational one. To truly disrupt Confederate monuments requires attending to them in their theological dimension, for it is at this level that their appeal to the future finally rests. Not simply on a notion of what is good, or what is true, but what is beautiful.

What is needed in order to disrupt Confederate monuments, then, is not an abandonment of theology but a counter-theology—a counter-gaze, a counter-vision of the future—that can open up space to disrupt these monuments' eschatological commitment (a commitment, of course, with an appeal that is much wider and deeper than any statue). This requires nothing short of a different articulation of God than the one assumed by most Confederate monuments, one which will sound like heresy to partisans of the statues. And of course, that is exactly what it is: a disbelief in one deity, born of faith in the most true God. Without this focus, simply removing monuments will leave the underlying vision they represent untouched and unaltered. Monuments may be removed without disrupting the idol that is whiteness.

If it is true that what people consider beautiful comes before what they consider right or good—if aesthetics precedes ethics—then a theological disruption of Confederate monuments must emerge from an alternative vision of what is beautiful. To put it as bluntly as possible, Christians are not supposed to think of whiteness as supremely beautiful.[93] Rather, Christians are supposed to confess that Jesus Christ reveals the fullness of God's beauty to the world, the image of the invisible God as well as the truly Human One. Whiteness is not ultimate; Christ is ultimate. Christians are supposed to confess that Christ shapes what is considered beautiful and gives Christians a direction to follow. This kind of affirmation can sound simplistic, and can even function as an excuse to not trouble oneself with such "contentious" matters as race or white supremacy—an inherently privileged move. But it need not function in this way. It depends on who is making this affirmation as to whether or not it liberates from or reinforces the status quo.[94] This affirmation sounds different when it assumes the vision of Christ articulated by liberation theologians: the God who is and has always been on the side of the oppressed and marginalized, rather than those who are perched atop the ideological hierarchies of their own creation.[95] When Christ is affirmed by liberation theologians, he is rightly seen as a disruptor of such hierarchies, whose crucified body gives witness to the upside-down nature of God's power, wisdom, and beauty—upside-down at least when viewed from the perspective of whiteness. Of course, it can be hard to imagine what it would look like to truly restructure the unjust hierarchies that mark society, especially given the extent to which whiteness has entrenched itself in every facet of the United States, including the church. To question whiteness is to question an entire way of organizing the world. But some theologians do, and in so doing show that monuments assuming or celebrating this ideology are not just "historically inaccurate" or "politically incorrect," but idolatrous. To disrupt Confederate monuments at this level, theologians must tap into this vision of Christ from below, making it clear that these statues stand as idols to the god of whiteness. Confederate monuments should be disrupted such that they change from idols to icons pointing to the God of Jesus Christ—or be destroyed.[96]

From this starting point, at least two paths of disruption are available, which share as a goal the dismantling of white supremacy. These paths should be thought of as complementary rather than mutually exclusive, in that it depends on the context of each monument whether one or the other should be taken. The first is the path of "iconography," which attempts to change the uptake of Confederate monuments away from whiteness. Given the primary markers of whiteness as a way of structuring the world—paternalism, aesthetic superiority, associating "white" (modern Anglo-European) values with the sacred—a truly disruptive "iconography" must subvert these commitments, even if the monument itself is left intact. Any such strategy must at least serve to remind white people that every group comes to God as learners, and that self-styled white people are in no way superior to any other group. It could involve moving monuments to settings in which a fuller story can be told about their construction and the history they attempt to recount: a cemetery, a battlefield, or a museum. Or it could involve leaving a monument where it is, but introducing other statues around it that alter the story it tells. For instance, part of the power of the common soldier statue is the fact that it is often the only physical image in a given space, which helps reinforce the notion that it represents "the universal man." Adding other statues around (certain) Confederate monuments could undermine this presumption without making a single alteration to the common soldier statue itself.

An example of attempting to disrupt Confederate monuments by adding other monuments nearby has been tried with the inclusion of the Arthur Ashe statue on Monument Avenue in Richmond—a compromise that still offended partisans of the Confederate monuments because it was seen as an intrusion into a semisacred (white) space. The strategy of the Ashe monument has promise, but the problem is that the designers tread so lightly that it had the effect of promoting black inclusion in an otherwise white space; the logic of Monument Avenue itself was left untouched. Paths of "iconography" that are truly disruptive will need to be more creative and purposeful about the figures chosen, their placement, and their intended uptake. For instance, it would be much different if someone like Frederick Douglass, W. E. B. Du Bois, or John Brown were put in the place of Ashe, or a visual homage to the abolitionist movement in Richmond. One could also imagine monuments to Virginia's Reconstruction government, to "scalawags" of the day, or anything that would undermine the paternalism inherent to statues as they stand. Statues could be erected that show that white folks were not the perpetual heroes of the South but stood in profound need of learning and tutelage themselves—which they refused—and thus undermine the very logic of the master-slave framework that continued even after the abolition of slavery. The Virginia Civil Rights Memorial, opened in 2008 on the grounds of the state capitol, is an excellent example of a memorial attempting this kind of work. Possibilities are endless, but the point is that it is possible to disrupt the underlying theology of whiteness through Confederate monuments without advocating their (necessary, universal, and immediate) removal.

Of course, if such additions are successful in forging icons out of idols, it is likely that they will move certain (white) people to despair as they begin to recognize the depths of their sins and the sins of their forefathers, as they realize that the wrongs of the past cannot be undone, and as they see that the same logic operates today in altered form. If the triumphant eschatological vision of whiteness falls away, it may be replaced with mourning and lament. But this may not be a bad thing. One of the functions of these "icons" should be to present a counter-vision of the end that is not the triumphalism and paternalism of whiteness, but an end that is multiracial and in which whiteness no longer has the sacred overlay that it currently enjoys—as difficult as that is to imagine. If people note the gap between that vision and the contemporary world, and if that leads people to despair, that is good insofar as it forces people to sit with the pain caused by whiteness. Before any healing or justice related to these monuments can occur, Americans must come to recognize that the end Confederate monuments have pointed toward is monstrous—even anti-Christ. And if, in the process of confronting this eschatological vision, some people are robbed of a shallow sense of optimism and trust in perpetual historical progress that is mislabeled "hope," all the better, for such hope is little more than a balm that reinforces the way things have been.

Instead, an alternative would be to make space for voices on the underside that have been silenced or muffled; their being heard would weaken the intellectual defenses and "must be" status of white supremacy because they disorient the status quo.[97] Whereas progressive white people seek an eschatological hope that does not come to terms with the past, and revanchist voices seek simply to glorify that same past, what is needed is a hope that directs white people to the good, to God, by moving through the cleansing waters of despair. White people need to hope for a despair that wipes out false gods and focuses attention on the one true God.[98] Such iconographic tutelage might force a painful yet crucial renunciation of the hubris that would lead someone to say, upon learning of white supremacy, that society should fix these ills or simply manufacture the United States out of the problem. The desire to quickly fix whiteness comes from a well-meaning place, but it does not grasp the depths of the challenge. Instead, such additive-destructive work should foster a longing for a community that does not exist, an eschatological reality the shape of which can only become clear as one loses faith in the way things are.[99] In the meantime, when it comes to the racialized system surviving "as is" but simply with more people included within it, the goal should be to smash that system altogether, and thus to be "post-hope" with regards to the status quo.[100] This kind of disruptive judgment will only sound like bad news to those who have an interest in the continuation of the world as it is—which is built on "progress" at the cost of others' well-being—but it will be good news to those who are not invested in this world, who have hungered and thirsted for justice with and among the oppressed.[101] The point is not to serve as a "middle way" between destruction and leaving Confederate monuments alone. The point is that there may be ways to add monuments that are more disruptive of white supremacy than simple removal, and those ways should be tried.

With all this said, there are circumstances in which another path of disruption should be taken: namely, the destruction of these idols to white supremacy. Recognizing that Confederate monuments point to a future (and not just the past) is the strongest reason to remove them, as this reveals that their work is ongoing. Having recognized the future-oriented nature of Confederate monuments, most will just need to go, especially if that is the will of the community within which they sit.[102] There is a place for simply tearing down monuments marked by white supremacy, in defiance of decorum or law, as happened on August 14, 2017, when a group marched to the common soldier statue in Durham, North Carolina and yanked it down two days after the Charlottesville riots. But a word of warning is called for here: while it may seem like destroying Confederate monuments would almost automatically help destroy white supremacy, it is possible to remove a monument without affecting (or perhaps even reinforcing) the underlying ideology it represents. The destruction of white supremacy will not occur with the destruction of Confederate statues. In order for removal to do this kind of work, it must be done in such a way that it at least has the chance of forcing people to reckon with the legacy and ongoing power of white supremacy. It must open onto a wider disruption. A major temptation when it comes to taking down Confederate monuments, despite their real and pernicious effects in society, is that it might tempt people—in particular, white liberals—to think that they are somehow free from this ideology. Whiteness is not so easily escapable, but is Hydra-like, able to take on more "respectable" forms even after its more egregious representations are removed. In any case, whiteness as a theological aesthetic and eschatology has already been baked into the structure of American society. To remove Confederate statues without addressing this reality would be like entering a house with profound structural damage, replacing the furniture, and calling it a day. Again, this is not to say that removal should not be done. But it is to say that the *how* of removal is important, not because removing Confederate monuments is "too fast" or "not nice," but because quick removal may be too nice—if it avoids the painful process of forcing people to face who they really are. In order to aid in the destruction of whiteness, something more will be required.

This is easy to say, of course; naming what this "something more" actually entails is altogether more difficult. It must surely include frank discussion of why removal needs to be done, even hosting something like public rituals of truth telling and corporate repentance. It might also include the erection of new monuments to replace those that have been removed, which hopefully tell the painful story of antiblack violence in this country and the struggles against it. Something like this has been suggested as a replacement for what was formerly known as Lee Circle in New Orleans, which is a good idea: any vacated public space should be filled with intentionality rather than left open. Whatever is done, the goal of all such efforts should be to subvert the narrative that whiteness is ultimate, even as these efforts will not manufacture a quick or easy solution to a centuries-long evil. But they might at least unmask whiteness as a principality and power (Col 2:15), and thus prepare the way for a future destruction that comes from outside the realm of cultural representation.

It is hard to say much more in advance about what good, subversive strategies for removing Confederate monuments will entail. This is partly because any recommendation that would bring about the reckoning that is needed will also seem unworkable in the current political climate, such that thinking through disruption through addition *or* destruction is to grasp at a world that is hard to imagine. Most people do not want to recognize the "white face" these monuments helped give the nation—some wish to ignore it while others wish to relegate this problem to Confederate monuments alone. But it is a likeness that the United States has yet to challenge with any real vigor or determination, because to do so would require a much deeper examination of the structures of power in this country.[103]

If something like this reckoning is to occur in ordinary time, white people will need to begin a process of regularly dying to themselves and what they had previously thought was ultimate, confessing that their aesthetic vision has been corrupted and stands in need of profound correction.[104] Everyone will need to be open to the judgment of a past that cannot be "fixed," and an eschatological future that cannot be controlled, but which one can await with a hope beyond hope. It is profoundly true that the United States stands in need of a grace that it cannot give itself. Such grace can only come from a God who suffered, who was and is uniquely present to all those who are oppressed and marginalized—and whose grace cannot be received without disrupting one's commitment to an oppressive status quo.[105] Altering or destroying Confederate monuments is a means of liberation when it prepares for this divine disruption, and thus engenders change in the present.

4

Present

Wounds Obscured

There is never time in the future in which we will work out our salvation. The challenge is in the moment, the time is always now.

James Baldwin[1]

In the years following the coup of 1898, Jim Crow took root in
Wilmington, North Carolina as it did throughout the South, and
it was during this time that the city set aside public space for a
Confederate monument. This particular monument was dedicated in 1924 to "the soldiers of the Confederacy," some of whom
would have been involved in the coup itself. This monument is not
a sign of mourning in the aftermath of a war, nor even a marker
of the Lost Cause—that fight had by this point been fought and
won—but rather a sign of ideological reification. The statue was
placed on a well-traveled street in downtown Wilmington, pre-
sumably so "everyone" could enjoy it as they walked the street,
but this prominent placement also proved to be a danger to its
very existence. Because it sits in the median of South 3rd Street,
the monument has been hit by a car three separate times over the
last sixty years, including in 1999, when the collision caused such

significant damage that the monument was removed for several months. But the removal was brief. The foundations were reset, the statue made to look even better than it had before the crash, and in no time the monument was restored and ready to welcome the new millennium.

This event serves as something of a parable about the ongoing power of Confederate monuments and why it is important to think about the way to remove them, at least if their removal is to be lasting. Despite the fact that this monument was all but destroyed by a reckless driver, its return was inevitable precisely because it was knocked down without intentionality, without an organized effort to keep it down. More importantly, the cultural narratives that gave rise to the monument and continued to supply it with meaning were untouched by this means of removal. The sign was disrupted, but the narratives that sit within and behind it were left undisturbed, and as such the monument returned rather quickly and with little discussion. Without doing any work in the cultural soil in which the monument sat, its removal was akin to plucking a dandelion and thinking one had destroyed the weed. It looked nice for a moment, but the roots were left in place, and so the flower returned.

All this is but a way of saying that while monuments are oriented to the past and the future, they are also always maintained in the present, reinforced by narratives that have contemporary traction. Even at the most basic level, someone has to cut the grass around the monument, clean the grime off the base, ensure it is not sinking into the earth, and so on: all tasks that must be performed and funded in the present. Monuments do not maintain themselves. The Wilmington incident illustrates that Confederate monuments must be analyzed in their orientation to the present no less than the past or future, and that the soil holding them up in the present is richer than some imagine. Thinking of Confederate monuments only as past relics or something for future generations to debate allows people today to evade their own responsibility for perpetuating the monuments as they sit—or perpetuating cultural attitudes and narratives that give the monuments their power. It is easier to rage against signs of the past or bemoan an allegedly inevitable future than to lament in the present and work to undermine manifestations of white supremacy in one's own world.[2]

Confederate monuments are caught in a kind of feedback loop, shaping as well as being shaped by contemporary cultural narratives. Monuments are unique material objects in which descriptions of the past and visions of the future collapse onto the present—visions whose contemporary force is often revealed precisely when they are challenged, as when someone calls for a monument's removal.[3] But the way Confederate monuments manifest this reality has profound theological resonances that need to be unpacked if one wishes to get at the root of this particular weed—in society and in oneself. If monuments are understood as revealing something about a society's present as much as its past and future, then there is no mere act of commemoration, nor a simple way to signal a hope for the future; every monument makes demands of the current generation even as it helps shape that generation in its own image.[4] Monuments are public things that are fluid and evolving, despite their appearance of fixity. Put differently, monuments create and are sustained by a community that places itself in the same story as previous generations, and thus create a particular space that takes on the air of the numinous. To analyze Confederate monuments as objects through which theological narratives are conjured is to imagine ways in which these monuments might be altered such that they serve as passages to a more just society in the present.

Recent theological treatments of trauma provide a helpful framework for analyzing the way Confederate monuments might be used to bring about a modicum of justice and collective healing in American society. As they currently stand, Confederate monuments bring past wounds into the present, and as such they beg the question as to how society should face, heal, celebrate, deny, mourn, or welcome such wounds. Rather than forgetting or suppressing these wounds, certain Confederate monuments could be altered to serve as a passage through wounds, allowing a diverse society to face and even begin to transfigure wounds that are not as distant as some might wish. Nonetheless, analyzing Confederate monuments in terms of their present performative power pushes one to the limits of monuments' transformative potential—for good or ill—and toward the necessity of active responses to what lies beneath such monuments by real people participating in ongoing rituals of recognition, mourning, and repentance. To truly address the wounds that Confederate monuments both conjure and suppress, space needs to be created where the practice of mourning can occur—where varying yet interrelated wounds and stories of woundedness can be shared in a way that does not rewound in the process.

Even so, counter-memorials and additions to current monuments can aid the process of collective mourning. In certain cases (though certainly not all or most), reconfiguring or problematizing still-standing Confederate monuments can be an effective way to encourage Americans to face their collective wounds, thus upsetting the soil from which these monuments arise. There is a peculiar power in redirecting the meaning of a monument toward ends that it did not intend—or even better, ends that are the opposite of what it intended; it performs a kind of aikido on these cultural talismans, transforming objects meant to intimidate and diminish into objects that can instruct and spark more fruitful collective self-narration. In any case, if Confederate monuments are removed without any corporate reckoning—or removed in a way that lures people into thinking that white supremacy is ancient history—then these ghosts of the past will continue to haunt the present, and the work of justice will be put off for yet another generation.

"They Left Us a Story, A Story to Live!": The Fiction of Monumental Stability

Monuments are in a constant state of flux. Despite the fact that a monument is often taken to be a permanent and unchanging fixture of a town or city, its meaning necessarily shifts as each generation receives it anew, reinterpreted in light of new experiences, subsequent events, and the inclusion of previously marginalized voices. Recognizing that monuments change undercuts the argument that to alter, relocate, or remove Confederate monuments is to intervene into an otherwise static situation. If one assumes that monuments are stable speech-acts in their own right, then to change Confederate monuments in any way would be akin to butting into a conversation that one has no right to interrupt. Confederate monuments should be left alone, the sentiment goes, and any decision otherwise could only be driven by an ideological desire to "rewrite history," or anachronistically judge the past by the standards of the present. This response fails to recognize that monuments constantly change as they manifest the ideals of the past in and among present social networks, and if no such adaptation were to occur, then both monument and memory would fade.[5] Confederate monuments are re-inherited by each generation, so the question is not if one will make a choice in relation to these monuments, but what that choice will be—even if that choice is to uphold them in their current state.[6] A vote to "do nothing" is a vote for the status quo. This does not settle the question of Confederate monuments, of course, but it does mean one can dispense with arguments that proceed as though keeping monuments up is any less of a choice than to alter or remove them.

The majority of Confederate monuments were constructed during a memorialization boom at the turn of the century, during which time American cultural leaders sought to create a nation of dutiful, orderly, and united citizens.[7] The people who commissioned Confederate monuments did so with the express desire of constructing an imagined community that was bound by common narratives about the past (selected memories, ideals drawn from these memories, ways of framing these memories, and so on), and vigorous debates ensued regarding their design and placement.[8] Of course, every monument is the result of power struggles and debates that are now mostly forgotten.[9] Monuments are birthed from some contingent past that was at that time present, and is only past from the vantage point of the present.[10] At their very inception monuments inspire arguments about historical memory, how to narrate the past, what values are important for future generations to hold, where the monument should be placed, and the question of funding—all arguments that are political in nature. The variety of social processes that give rise to a monument are hidden from view once the monument is complete.[11] Even aspects of monuments that one may think avoid the political or are pre-political fall under this umbrella. For instance, the simple act of selecting something as worthy of remembrance is not just a matter of memory, but the result of political negotiations and struggles having to do with who gets to participate in such conversations, what equal participation in such a process looks like, and so on.[12] And once some event is selected, how it is described is far from ideologically neutral. There is a massive difference between naming the events of October 12, 1492, "the Castilian invasion of the Bahamas" as opposed to "the discovery of America," even though both phrases could be used to describe what happened on that day. To name a fact is to impose a reading upon it, and all description puts an event into predetermined lexical fields that forecloses on other definitions of the event in question.[13] Thus, a monument's appearance of stability covers over a process of negotiation and interpretation that begins the moment the idea for a monument is proposed, and that does not stop once it is erected; it only changes form as each subsequent generation receives the monument anew.[14]

Thus, while monuments have intended messages baked into them by their original designers, that meaning has to be granted to them by people in the ever-changing present.[15] No narrative or representation of the past is "automatically" renewed in the present, but relies on people's (at least implicit) consent to receive it, renew it, and continue on in the way it describes what is going on.[16] For this reason, the processes that give rise to monuments are as important as the monuments themselves, and a real danger with monuments is that they will tempt people into thinking that once they are constructed, the work of memory is complete.[17] Ideally, monuments push against this inclination, self-consciously generating continued debate about their own origins and leaving space for additions to the narrative they tell. Monuments should display the contingency of their viewpoint and design, or else have that feature added to them through additions, subtractions, or recontextualizations. At their best, memorials are designed in a way that points to their own changing nature, to the diversity of viewpoints that will come to any such space, and to the arguments that preceded their emergence. Polemics, which will inevitably continue after its completion, should be a central, animating feature of a memorial, rather than seen as a weird by-product of monument creation.[18]

In any case, a monument is meaningless without people who imbue it with meaning, including through the actions people take around the monument itself: pilgrimage to the monument, rituals one participates in once there, how one is directed to move within and around the monument, and so on. Activities of this sort constitute a monument's meaning for a people and can change its meaning over time.[19] One prominent example of this phenomenon is the way the Lincoln Memorial in Washington, D.C. gets its power not just from the design of the monument itself, but the way in which visitors sojourn to the city, walk the National Mall in order to climb its steps, and recall subsequent events that happened at the same location. Most notably, these events include Martin Luther King Jr.'s speech on the steps of the memorial in 1963, which significantly altered the meaning of the Lincoln Memorial for visitors. Indeed, a plaque now marks where King once stood.[20]

Recognizing that monuments receive much of their meaning in the present reframes the conversation about Confederate monuments, as it shifts the focus from the past or the future to one's own context. The conversation becomes more intimate, and perhaps uncomfortable, for it means that one has to pay attention to how the events portrayed in a monument map onto contemporary situations and struggles. What makes a monument faithful to the past is not merely a matter of factuality but also an honesty with regard to how it re-presents the past given present circumstances. For example, to represent slavery well does not mean *simply* getting the facts in order or *simply* denouncing slavery as an institution of the past without recognizing its lingering effects today. Faithfulness to the past with regard to slavery includes denouncing the racist present within which representations of slavery are produced.[21] People should not leave a monument to slavery patting themselves on the back, as though white supremacy is gone or as though American society is not still shaped by the attitudes that justified slavery in the first place. Or as though people today are different kinds of humans, somehow immune from committing grievous evils. It is possible to focus on the past in a way that diverts attention from contemporary injustices that are continuations of previous ills, and thus protects oneself from having to deal with the present. Monuments at their best aid people in facing the present through the past, such that one leaves something like a Holocaust memorial with the understanding that no amount of historical research, additional facts, or World War II movies is a substitute for organizing against the rise of white supremacy and anti-Semitism today.[22] At its best, a monument will also make it clear that it represents a particular perspective that is colored by its time and place.[23]

Attempts have been made to bring these elements together in monuments; a good example is the Monument against Fascism in Hamburg, Germany, also known as the "disappearing memorial."[24] In 1986 the monument was put up in response to a rising neo-Nazi movement in the city, and stood at forty feet tall. The monument was relatively sparse: a hollow, square aluminum column in the center of the commercial part of the city. Uniquely, the monument was slowly lowered into the ground over a period of seven years, mirroring a fading of memory into the collective subconscious that never totally disappears. As the monument was lowered, people were encouraged to carve messages into the monument; it invited vandalization of itself in a way that was at once interactive and risky (as one cannot control what messages will show up). The hope was that people would consider not just the fascism of ages past but also the current forms that they were facing, as it is much easier to condemn something that is now gone than a practice that one currently faces and perhaps even benefits from.[25] The intent of the overall design of the monument was to put the burden of memory back on the people. While a monument could remind people of the dangers of fascism, it could not resist fascism itself. That responsibility falls on the people and the way they tell their story. Thus, the monuments' instability encouraged people to do the work that the monument intentionally refused to do.

All this to say, Confederate monuments cannot be assessed separately from contemporary debates about race, the resurgence of white nationalism, and the activities of the alt-right. People are not complaisant prisoners of the past; nor is the past escapable.[26] The work is to trace the narrative thread connecting Confederate monuments' vision of the past and the future, to honestly consider how that narrative needs to be reframed, supplemented, or contradicted, and to name how that narrative is perpetuated by contemporary policies and practices in the United States. Confederate monuments themselves often encourage making connections of this sort, directly imploring the viewer to carry on its message in the present—a point that was always made during their dedication ceremonies. As was written on the common soldier statue in Winston-Salem, North Carolina—which was erected in 1905 and sat next to the old Forsyth County courthouse until 2019—"They gave us great glory; what more could they give? They left us a story, a story to live!"[27] Of course, as people pushed back on this story over time it appeared less and less innocuous. For instance, on February 8, 1960, the first sit-in demonstration in Winston-Salem began directly across the street from the monument. Carl Wesley Matthews and others would have sat at a counter in direct view of the monument, and the crowd of white people dumping food on their heads would have been backgrounded by a vigilant Confederate soldier. At the time, surely, many in the white mob would have looked to the statue and gained encouragement in "living the story" of their grandmothers and grandfathers. But

Fig. 4.1 "Common Soldier" Statue, Winston-Salem, N.C.

after the success of the sit-in, and with the placement of a plaque commemorating the acts of civil disobedience now in direct view of the monument, that story appears in a less flattering light—a light that begins to expose the implications of this story being lived out in the present.[28] All Confederate monuments ask contemporary society to value the story they tell, and because of this they remain open to contemporary response, which can include reimagining or even rejecting its narrative. If Confederate monuments invite people to live into a story, then people also have a right to refuse the invitation.

Storied Stones: Narrative Theology, Transitional Objects, and Unacknowledged Wounds

In practice, people recognize that there are times when monuments should be destroyed and times when they should be maintained. While a typical reactionary response to changing monuments based on subsequent events is that it is ideologically "totalitarian," "illiberal," or even "Stalinist," this view is hard to hold with consistency. In a previous era, the same voices that decried any change to Confederate monuments also cheered when statues to Stalin and Lenin were toppled after the collapse of the Soviet Union.[29] The question is how to determine when alteration or removal has become the appropriate response to a monument, and there is no avoiding the fact that it will be present circumstances that make it seem necessary to remove a monument. People living *now* are the ones who decide on a monument's power in light of subsequent history and current events; the people of today are permitted to alter monuments as they see fit.

In the debate about Confederate monuments, the way they function as objects of value and significance in the present tends to be eclipsed by (equally important) considerations about the way they narrate the past or point to the future.[30] But the way people "hook in" to the story Confederate monuments tell is no less important or theologically weighted. Indeed, Confederate monuments utilize a species of typological reasoning, standing as they do as objects that seek to create an imagined community across time. The communal narratives conjured by Confederate monuments—even narratives that are present only in their implied negation—accidentally reveal a number of interrelated, collective, barely hidden wounds that mark the present: the trauma of the Civil War itself, white supremacy, and the stories of antiblack violence that lurk just beneath the collective consciousness of this country. In making these wounds visible, there may be a hidden opportunity to transition through them by way of acknowledgment and lament, and in that process to begin to change the cultural soil that gave rise to Confederate monuments in the first place.

Viewed through the lens of speech-act theory, it is obvious that Confederate monuments communicate at many levels at once, not only (or simply) referring to things in the past or implying things about the future but also symbolically making certain narratives and values present. Further, it is intuitively clear that much of a monument's meaning is filled in by the audience and that people today participate in the communicative, remembering, envisioning project of any Confederate monument. This happens in ways that are both simple and profound. At the simplest level, viewers must identify a thick book in a common soldier's waistband as a Bible. At the most complex level, when a monument makes reference to "a story to live," the audience has to know, or fill in, what this story is and entails. But either way, the communicative act happens in the present, through a complex back-and-forth process between object and viewer. Once this phenomenon is recognized, it is clear that the primary point of Confederate monuments is to make the past, or a certain vision of the past, typologically present. This does not happen by magic or accident, but by directing people to view reality in a particular way, and inspiring people to tell a particular story about the United States, whiteness, the glory of military sacrifice, slavery, and Southern manliness.

In this way, Confederate monuments utilize a deeply biblical form of reasoning and remembrance in which people are encouraged to tell, retell, and place themselves within a narrative about God and the world. Throughout the scriptures, people are encouraged to place themselves within the story that is being told, asking questions of it, pushing back on it, but identifying themselves with those in the narrative. To take just one example, in Deuteronomy 6 there is a question (or challenge?) issued by a hypothetical Hebrew child: "Why should we keep these laws?" The answer parents are instructed to give is, "We were Pharaoh's slaves in Egypt, but the LORD brought us out" (Deut 6:21). Of course, strictly speaking, this is incorrect. On any dating of Deuteronomy, neither inquiring child nor parent would have been in Egypt, and yet the parent is told to respond, "*We* were slaves."[31] It is assumed that making a typological link in this way is both possible and good; the reader is beckoned to inherit these narratives by placing oneself within the sacred stories of scripture, in the same way that Confederate monuments beckon viewers to place themselves in the narratives that they conjure and, indeed, in the "space" they create.[32]

Even more to the point, throughout the Bible memorials are usually important insofar as they inspire people to tell a story about why a memorial was built in a particular place. In their bare materiality, biblical monuments do not describe an event in full detail. Instead, biblical memorials are simple, often consisting of little more than a collection of stones: public prompts of memory that are obviously in flux and require ongoing maintenance. A good illustration of the typical role and function of biblical memorials is found in the book of Joshua. In one version of events, as the people of God are crossing the Jordan River and entering the promised land, Joshua instructs twelve men to set up twelve stones to commemorate the occasion—to serve as a sign among them (Josh 4:6). Again, the meaning of these stones is related to the task of narrating the events to one's children: "When your children ask in time to come, 'What do those stones mean to you?' then you shall tell them . . ." (Josh 4:6-7). With the inclusion of the phrase "to you," this story implicitly affirms the subjective and multilayered nature of any such telling. "What do those stones mean *to you*?" Not, "What do those stones mean universally, forever and for all time, from every point of view—*sub specie aeternitatis*?" And yet the stones are not inconsequential to this process: they center and organize any such retelling, spurring and subtly guiding the conversation as it continues through time.[33]

All this to say, noting the ways a Confederate monument functions in the present is theologically weighted. One can think of it as a species of narrative theology, wherein stories about the Lost Cause that have deep theological resonance are brought into the present. As these narratives are heard and affirmed, a particular community comes into being, strengthened by the bonds, not of physical proximity, but the imagination.[34] Of course, the way each subsequent generation is faithful to this narrative necessarily changes as circumstances change, but a people is created that is bound by this common story. It is true that one can only say what one should do if one can answer the question, "Of what story or stories do I find myself a part?"[35] Confederate monuments provide a powerful set of stories that enable a particular moral sensibility. No wonder altering Confederate monuments is seen as threatening: to attack the monument is to attack someone's self-identity.[36] It is a violation of sacred space.[37]

The weightiness of Confederate monuments is only deepened when they are understood as public objects: things that are commonly owned and operated rather than privately held for the primary purpose of turning a profit. Humans require such "things" in order to be oriented to the world and each other—material objects and physical spaces that provide a framework for anything like a life together, objects which people can gather around, debate, argue with, even destroy. Public things are vital to the functioning of a healthy democracy; they are the *res* of the *res publica*.[38] Political philosopher Bonnie Honig argues that democracy depends upon fostering a common love for and maintenance of public things, and that without them the signs and symbols that constitute democratic life are debilitated. Public things are powerful, and a people's sense of the common good is connected to the way they treat things like monuments, bridges, roads, and parks. The power of these objects goes beyond their utility; it is found in the ways they enchant the world, mediating relations between people. As such, to exclude *objects* from the sphere of politics is to reduce social life to matters of procedure, polling, and policing. Public things are what people argue about, gather around, and even agonistically contest.[39]

Uniquely, Honig analyzes the power of public things by extending D. W. Winnicott's object-relations theory of child development to the societal level. Winnicott, of course, argued that objects play a key role in a child's capacity to develop and relate to the world. Infants need transitional objects (teddy bears, blankets, and so on) in order to learn how to relate to an external, objective world. As a child discovers the permanence of a chosen object, even after it is neglected or willfully destroyed, he or she develops a sense of their own subjectivity in relation to that which is not-them—and something analogous could be said for the healthy development of democratic societies. Democratic forms of life seem to depend partly upon objects that gather diverse citizens into a self-governing collective, having given up notions of individual omnipotence and instead found a sense of integrated subjectivity, responsibility, and agency.[40] Collectivities are formed and re-formed in relation to symbolically weighted objects whose meanings shift and evolve; these objects can fall into disrepair over time, to be sure, but the presence of public things seems to accompany the creation of a people, which in turn shapes behavior in obvious and subtle ways. As such, the question to ask of a Confederate monument is, "What sense of communal self is created by and through this object?" Or better, "What passage is created by this object, and where does that passage lead?"

As Confederate monuments make abundantly clear, reclaiming public things does not automatically foster communal flourishing or heal social divisions. At their best, things like monuments can bring people together to act in concert for the good, but monuments can also be divisive. A monument's power is ambivalent; it furnishes the world through which people encounter others in both agonistic and healthy ways.[41] Indeed, in the United States public things have often been used to signal racial superiority and limit the scope of who is included within the realm of "public"— the material means by which the exclusion of black and brown people is reinforced.[42] In a society marked by white supremacy, public things have served to communicate and reinforce the terms of a tiered system of citizenship. Even when divisive, though, public things can still serve as transitional objects in that they can focus organizing efforts, stand as objects to contest (or defend), and spur alternative visions of how society could or should be organized.[43] These considerations are important to arguments about how to respond to Confederate monuments: public things that obviously privilege certain stories (and people) above others. People are born into a world of things that they did not create—things that require a response, whether that response is marked by appreciation, rejection, or ambivalence.[44]

Through the lens of public object-relations theory, Confederate monuments no longer appear as untouchable monoliths that dwarf agency, but rightly come to be seen as objects that do something in the world. Confederate monuments conjure narratives that parallel and intersect with contemporary cultural scripts, and serve as passages to particular forms of life in the present. A monument's power rests in the narrations and renarrations that it enables or squelches. Further, object-relations theory opens up the conceptual space to think of a collective—like a growing child—as in development rather than static, and thus it is not required to hold every object forever, in the same way, or for the same reasons. If monuments are important because of their capacity to transition a people from one state to another, then it is easier to think of them as things that can be "let go" if and when their purpose has been served, exhausted, or no longer desired. Truly, there is a time to throw away stones, and a time to gather stones together (Eccl 3:5).

Like transitional objects, monuments gain their "enchanted" nature because people decide to instill them with that power. Whether an infant invests a teddy bear with value versus a blanket is up to her, not qualities inherent to the bear; and whether a society invests one monument with value versus another is similarly up to the society itself, not qualities inherent to the statue. Finally, this analysis does not confuse arbitrariness with unimportance. Once an object is invested with value, its capacity to shape the world is real. In this way are monuments objects of both facticity and fantasy in that they support the collective capacity to imagine, build, and tend to a particular world, naming the vision to be pursued and the malefactors to be defeated.[45]

Obviously, Confederate monuments have functioned as transitional objects in many ways throughout their history, though always with the desire to usher the United States into new eras while retaining the "virtues" of the Old South. But as layered as these meanings are, Confederate monuments invariably contain an element of woundedness that can either be acknowledged or suppressed by viewers today. The earliest Confederate monuments were explicitly born of the collective wounds brought on by the war itself. As complicated as the motives were for designing funerary memorials and placing them in settings of mourning, in large part they intended to help people mourn the loss of loved ones and the loss of a particular vision of the future. But other wounds were left unacknowledged even in these early monuments, breeding a silence that only intensified in later generations. In particular, Confederate monuments universally screen out the motivations behind the war, with no mention whatsoever of slavery. A retroactive silence was wrought by the monuments such that slavery was either "not as bad" as some made out, or totally denied as a motive for the war. Confederate monuments offered a renarration that allowed white Southerners, in their mourning, to avoid the full force of their trauma.[46] An additional layer of silence was added as Confederate monuments were erected in and around the context of widespread antiblack violence, coterminous with the greatest construction of Confederate monuments and their placement in places of public power. Needless to say, these monuments make no mention of such violence.[47] One would have no idea of its existence if one viewed any of these monuments, even as they subtly reinforced the logic of white supremacy that gave rise to such violence in the first place. Confederate monuments signal the beginnings of post-racial rhetoric wherein a cheap reconciliation between warring white people was achieved in part by eliding the cause of true racial justice and abolition, even while white supremacy continued to be official state policy. There is a profound irony in a monument that reinforces white supremacy simultaneously maintaining a performative neutrality. In this way, Confederate monuments are forerunners of a type of memorialization that trades in color blindness and cheap forgiveness—that discusses the past without context and without attention to ongoing liberation struggles in the present.[48]

Taking these elements together, the subtle, layered, performative silence of Confederate monuments encourages a habit of avoidance in people—and not just white people. Confederate monuments help create a contemporary society that largely refuses to acknowledge its history of antiblack violence, the continued presence of myths surrounding Anglo-Saxon superiority and its connection to property rights, and the way these myths haunt the present.[49] Confederate monuments serve as signs of intimidation to people of color and are inappropriate at best, re-traumatizing at worst. Confederate monuments reinforce a reluctance among white people to acknowledge the sins of their mothers and fathers, while also maintaining the chimera of color blindness. As one letter to the editor put it after Confederate markers were vandalized in Raleigh: "There is a day when the dead will be raised and all people will be judged before a just and holy God. Men will be tried by the state of their hearts, not by the color of their skin. Until then, we must not take vengeance for the sins or perceived sins of the past."[50] And Confederate monuments block white people from recognizing the spiritual wound that is created as the myths associated with whiteness and the systems of power born of these myths are maintained.[51] In these ways and others, Confederate monuments paradoxically reveal wounds hiding just beneath the surface of the body politic that their own removal, while helpful and appropriate in most cases, will not erase. Counter-memorialization and removal is important, but it will not mean much if the violence of the past is not reconciled with present conditions in the United States—if difficult conversations about the past and the present are avoided.[52] As they stand, Confederate monuments serve as transitional objects that have created a society that is marred by unacknowledged wounds—wounds that are hiding in plain sight.

Facing and Transfiguring Wounds

If Confederate monuments help breed a society marked by carefully maintained avoidances, and one grants that this avoidance has been negative for society as a whole, then the obvious question is what might force Americans to face themselves, difficult though that may be. From the perspective of trauma studies, refusing to acknowledge wounds is not a path to wholeness and healing. Ignoring wounds does not make them go away, but simply allows them to continue doing passive, silent work. As such, people who study trauma tend to note the importance of coming to recognize and "own" unacknowledged pain; insofar as trauma is the "impossibility of narration," finding one's way to renarration is critical.[53] That is, if trauma is retained unwillingly and is spontaneously prompted by stimuli, then a step toward healing is finding the capacity to name the scripts and memories that are already doing implicit work, reappropriating symbols such that one's pain is no longer passively experienced. Altering public symbols associated with collective trauma (by renarrating the past in a way that is faithful to what came before) is not a matter of political correctness or secondary to the "real" work of material change. It is a way to create possibilities in the present that would not otherwise exist.[54]

However, for certain theologies it will not be immediately clear that facing wounds is good or important. There are different ways to approach wounds theologically, many of which are not helpful. One approach would speak of woundedness—if it is spoken of at all—as something to be overcome, often through sheer force of will. Another approach would deny that collective or individual wounds do this kind of work in the present and would think it unnecessary to focus on them in this way. If an individual is affected by traumatic stories and memories, that is their problem to fix. And still another theological approach would argue that wounds are real but should be forgotten rather than dwelt upon, a notion that can come in a variety of forms—conservative and liberal, mainline and evangelical. One might even suggest that whatever wounds people receive in this life will be woven into a glorious eschatological future, and as such one should not dwell on them in the present. Wounds are things set for erasure, and thus Christians should be people who keep their eyes on and prepare for this woundless world to come. One's theology affects whether or not one sees the value of facing wounds of the sort manifested by Confederate monuments, and as such what is needed is a clear articulation of the warrants Christians have for acknowledging collective wounds. Against calls to forgive and forget, undo, or deny collective wounds, some paths paved by Christian theology encourage people to face and (perhaps) pass through collective wounds into a world of justice, but in such a way that the wounds remain rather than disappear—healed but not erased.[55]

In her extended reflection on trauma, resurrection, and the Gospel of John, Shelly Rambo notes that major Christian traditions have been uncomfortable talking about wounds, and that this discomfort is revealed in the way theologians have treated the wounds of Jesus. On any plain reading of John, the wounds of Jesus figure prominently in his encounters with the disciples, especially Thomas—and yet Jesus' wounds are sometimes erased from Christian interpretations of this passage. In particular, John Calvin sought to distance the disciples, hearers today, and even Jesus himself from the marks on his hands and his side. For Calvin, one should believe in spite of one's senses rather than because of them, and thus Calvin shifts attention away from Jesus' wounds. Calvin instead focuses on the interactions between Jesus and the disciples as pedagogical in nature, and argues that the wounds were important in order to prompt the disciples' belief, nothing more. Calvin goes so far as to say that because the wounds' purpose was purely utilitarian, they only appeared to be on the body of Jesus, but were not actually there. The wounds are signs, types, that disappear from relevance once they serve the purpose of bringing the disciples to faith. Once they have been used to teach this truth to the disciples, the wounds disappear from Calvin's account of this passage.[56]

The theological implication, which recurs in traditions that emerge from this analysis, is that faith, healing, and resurrection come by recognizing—but then erasing—wounds, a process that happens quickly and in one smooth direction: doubt to faith, woundedness to wholeness. Wounds can certainly have a pedagogical usefulness for those who need such things, but they will not remain with people after healing is wrought, after faith is declared. The resurrected body moves forward unmarked, with wounds overcome or forgotten in faith. Once the marks serve the end of teaching or prompting a confession of faith, there is simply no reason for them to remain, even with Christ. Even more fundamentally, on this theological rendering the resurrected body *cannot* carry wounds forward because it assumes an eschatological vision that is unmarked by human limitation.[57] Thus, when it comes to collective trauma, this theology gives birth to a response that says that wounds stay in this world, and that the Christian hope is for their erasure. No triumph over death is imaginable that retains the marks of death.[58] In the meantime, this tradition would look askance at attempts to face and welcome one's wounds as too worldly, as backward looking, as too focused on "former things," and as antithetical to authentic faith. Applied to markers of collective wounds like Confederate monuments, it would likely lead to an instinct either to ignore them ("If these statues bother you, that shows you are still too invested in things of this world") or erase them ("We have learned those lessons and should move on").

But there is another, better way to read this scene in John that assumes a different relationship between woundedness and resurrection; if taken seriously, it could open up other imaginative possibilities for disrupting Confederate monuments born of the Christian tradition. Drawing on her work in trauma studies, Rambo argues that certain psychological wounds are not erasable from the "core" of one's identity. Some wounds remain with people, lurking under the surface even when ignored, and have a tendency to reinvade the present in odd, violent ways if they are not faced. People *live* traumatic memories much more than they *recall* them. As such, trauma is best thought of as what remains unintegrated and thus continues to return, preventing a person from engaging the world in the same way that they did before. Both individually and collectively, trauma does not name a problem that happened in the past but a problem of living in the present; it names a phenomenon by which the past is present, but in an invasive way.[59] Trauma becomes body, both the individual and corporate body. As such, the task is not to pretend trauma does not function in this way, as if certain wounds have not become a part of a collective story, but rather to find a way to come to terms with this reality. It is to reconceive, renarrate, reintegrate these wounds in a way that allows people to "go on." Healing from trauma means becoming a witness to one's own story and learning to take responsibility for the past as it continues to manifest in the present. Such responsibility is achieved through a continual process of covering and uncovering, appearing and disappearing, surfacing and receiving wounds. It means finding an afterlife—a way of afterliving—in the wake of trauma that is more than mere survival.[60] And because wounds will affect the present whether one acknowledges them or not, the question for Christians is not if but how to regard them theologically.[61]

This approach to trauma problematizes any simplistic division between healing and woundedness, seeing the two as on a spectrum and in continual relationship with one another. Life and death—endings and beginnings—cannot be clearly delineated but exist on a coterminous range, and resurrection is the promise that the seeds for new life are being planted amidst death. There are resources in the Christian tradition to think of resurrection in this way, rather than as the erasure or minimization of wounds. Indeed, Jesus' own resurrection appearances in John do not admit of any simple division between wound and resurrected body. Unless one is predisposed to argue that Jesus does not retain his wounds post-resurrection, a plain reading of the text reveals that wounds remain on Jesus' body, real and touchable at least in principle (whether Thomas actually touches the marks on Jesus' hands is unclear). As such, this scene in John describes an intimate social context in which unincorporated wounds from the immediate past return to the present, and in which the Spirit facilitates a communal wrestling with trauma, collective guilt, and fear. The entire scene provides a way of conceiving life after trauma that is marked by wounds but is also renewed by and through them.[62] Resurrection becomes a miraculous event that enables people to confront rather than erase wounds, to bring forward histories of death and suffering to be dealt with—or to be awakened by the witness of others to a past one only half remembers or remembers poorly.[63] Put differently, resurrection is no longer the hope for an unmarked or pristine body, but the weaving of a new body, healed and marked at one and the same time.[64]

Bringing trauma to the surface creates opportunities to break cycles of perception and traumatization by transfiguring a wound without erasing it, but this does not happen automatically; people can just as easily fall back into patterns of behavior that preceded a trauma's recognition. At its best, a surfaced wound serves as a passage into a new world; it enables a new awareness that changes the way people act in the present. But at its worst trauma is ignored or even glorified, and when it comes to the ongoing collective trauma of white supremacy in the United States, that is largely what has happened. White supremacy is a wound that requires acknowledgment if one is to be healed of it, even as it seems to uniquely avoid such acknowledgment. Racism itself is a wound, a logic that (mis)shapes the conscience, and as such simply removing its wallpaper will not undermine its power. Racism produces a tension that, left unattended, will ossify into an impregnable ideology that one internalizes, apologizes for, or even celebrates.[65] The pain this brings to people of color is clear, but it is damaging to white people as well. It begets a silence. As Wendell Berry described so well, there is an anguish implicit in white people's racism. Stories passed from generation to generation about race and white supremacy are told like something of a confession, "in the unspoken, even the unthought, hope that we will finally tell it to someone who can forgive us. But its pain has never been openly admitted to."[66]

Given the anguished, avoidant silence inherent to white supremacy, what is needed is a theology that enables reckoning with this reality and the way it affects social policy right now: in American social practices, policing, housing, mass incarceration, and so on. The problem in white America is that the wounds of whiteness are rarely acknowledged or integrated into the collective identity of the country, and so they continue to return in altered form. Confederate monuments stand as reminders of a wound that is largely ignored, and as such they perpetuate a form of not-seeing that is woven into group dynamics and individual imaginations.[67] Countering this willed blindness requires spaces wherein this wound could be recognized: where people begin to name and work through these wounds in a way that does not erase, ignore, deny, or minimize their reality. Because Confederate monuments stand as particularly obvious, public reminders of the need for this process to occur, they may provide something of an ironic opportunity to facilitate discussions and encounters about issues that might otherwise remain unacknowledged. This process may end with the monument's removal, contextualization, or destruction, but the encounter itself is what is desperately needed. America needs to acknowledge its wounds.

With all this said, acknowledgment does not come without its dangers. In creating paths to acknowledge wounds, one will simultaneously create opportunities to reopen wounds, and as such this process must be approached with care. In a provocative turn, Rambo reads Thomas' words to Jesus as a demand— "Unless I see and put my finger in the marks, I will not believe"—that symbolizes a desire to impose control over the situation and that may exacerbate Jesus' suffering.[68] Whether or not this holds up as an interpretation of this passage, it is absolutely correct as a warning about trauma and acknowledgment. Acknowledging surfacing wounds comes with the danger that such acknowledgment may inflict pain on another—or that one will be indifferent to that possibility. Thus, acknowledging the wounds of white supremacy and collective antiblack violence is risky, especially if one uses Confederate monuments to do so; it has the real potential to cause more harm to people of color today. As bad as ignoring wounds remains, a greater sin would be to glorify horrors of the past, using other people's suffering as a means to one's own enlightenment or even turning that suffering into something noble. But beyond the drive either to refuse to acknowledge suffering or to reinscribe it, there is a third way. Disciples are not called to glory in suffering but are invited to find in wounds a crossing. Wounds can alter perception such that one is reoriented to one's own suffering (rather than escaping or denying it); and as wounded people draw near to one another, they may discover more comprehensive, faithful ways of remembering that do justice to their wounds.[69] Taken seriously, this theological conviction would lead Christians (if no one else) to expand the search for ways to dismantle Confederate monuments and the wounds they simultaneously reveal and ignore. At the very least, it would create a community that is relentless in its desire to confess its wounds and to create spaces where such acknowledgment can occur. This group would know that it is only through acknowledgment that anything approaching justice and healing will be found in this life—anything like an afterliving in the face of layered, collective trauma.

Theological Disruption: Learning to Grieve
Injustices, Past and Present

If one affirms the importance of acknowledging and passing through wounds on Christian grounds, then what does that commitment look like when applied to Confederate monuments? Given that contextualizing or altering symbols can be helpful in renarrating a traumatic event or enabling people to receive a truth about themselves in a new way, changing Confederate monuments has the potential to enable forms of acknowledgment that Americans have largely avoided. At the least, Christians who recognize the importance of acknowledging wounds should affirm this point. As transitional objects that give passage to particular narratives into the present, the question is how might these symbols be made to encourage acknowledgment in a largely unwilling, indifferent (and indeed, white) population? A central challenge in a purportedly post-racial United States—where "racist" is a bad word and present manifestations of white supremacy are denied or downplayed—is to get people to see something that they have a vested interest in ignoring. At present, Confederate monuments block this recognition from happening, but given the fact that they touch on these topics at all and thus bring something to the fore that is usually unconscious, they may have the potential to be turned to other ends than they intended. That is, if Confederate monuments can be used to bring people to acknowledge their collective wounds, then they can serve as transitional objects to a different future that is not marked by white supremacy, forgetting the past, or a false neutrality—even if this (over time) leads to their own erasure. Strategies for using Confederate monuments for these purposes will vary, but they will be united in their attempt to get people to face their wounds, to narrate the world differently, and through this process to encounter one another—and in encountering others, perhaps also encountering Jesus himself. Any attempt at altering Confederate monuments involves imagining and working toward realities that do not presently exist; it involves a willingness to not take present reality with final seriousness, but to act in the hope that the future need not be like the present, and that the present need not repeat the past.[70]

One set of responses will attend to the monuments themselves. Monuments cannot do all or even most of the work that is needed to transition society toward justice, but they do prepare people to see the world in particular ways in their capacity to reify narratives about the past and future. As such, altering Confederate monuments rather than erasing them has the potential to prepare people to see the world differently—to jar people from complacency or place images in people's minds that are not easily forgotten.[71] Monuments cannot bring about anything like a full recognition of the violence wrought by Lost Cause theology, but they might help prepare someone to begin that process of recognition, undermining ideologies held largely without question. This is similar to an insight about the importance of public art made by none other than Karl Barth. Exploring the relationship between art and theology, Barth argued that art alone could never bring someone to a full affirmation of faith in Christ. Barth even questioned whether or not public art could midwife someone into that affirmation. But he did argue that aesthetic representation could serve as a hammer that smashed the narratives one told about oneself, quickly altering one's sense of the world in the way that few things can. Art can be apocalyptic: it can reveal what is going on beneath the surface as well as destroy old things in preparation for the new.[72] Because of this Barth argues that living into God's future—and acknowledging wounds—can include fashioning images with and for the world one finds oneself within. There is always a place for iconoclasm and the destruction of images that correlate with one's negative response to a particular state of affairs. But there is also an important place for messing with Confederate monuments through aesthetic creation that changes the performativity of these monuments, even though this cannot fully bring about the conversations and changes that need to happen.[73]

To this end, one way to bring about the kind of acknowledgment that is desperately needed is to focus on the act of aesthetic creation itself, altering statues or recontexualizing them through further creation in ways that force people to face themselves squarely. This advice does not come from any kind of love for Confederate monuments.[74] It comes from a belief that there is no avoiding the world of things into which all people are born.

Rather than attempting to avoid or erase all Confederate monuments, adding images around certain monuments has the potential of undermining the narratives that give the statues their power as well as reminding people that this remains a part of the story of this country. Rearranging and recontextualizing symbols that are already present can radically alter perception in a way that removal does not, for the act of aesthetic creation in this context puts things together differently such that the familiar becomes unfamiliar, the comfortable becomes uncomfortable. Further, aesthetic addition has the potential to open up conversations about what a positive vision for society should be going forward.

While there are many ways a community could follow this strategy, the Equal Justice Initiative (EJI) serves as something of a model for what it would look like to bring this national wound to the surface through aesthetic creation and addition. The creation of the first museum about lynching in Montgomery, Alabama functions as an open educational space that remembers victims of ritualized extrajudicial killings in the United States and traces this history of antiblack violence to policies and practices of today. What is truly unique about this museum is that it is designed to shift and change over time so that its message can be claimed by communities across the United States. The museum features a series of hanging concrete markers that list the name (if known), date, and location of a documented lynching. These stones are able and ready to be moved, relocated to the community in question if and when they decide to display it in their town. When this happens, a space remains where a marker previously hung in the museum—a kind of erasure of memory—while the still-unclaimed markers will stand out. Ideally, this space of the museum would one day be empty, signaling a wider willingness to face this collective trauma, but it is also ready to continue on even if such a reckoning never comes. As such it is a space that is at once hopeful and realistic, steady and ready to be taken apart. In any case, EJI provides a model for finding creative ways to bring about acknowledgment of collective wounds. Many of the towns that have claimed their lynching marker have done so with the explicit aim of countering the Lost Cause narrative conjured by their Confederate statues, awoken by the racialized violence of the past five years. For instance, citizens of Charlottesville, Virginia explicitly claimed their marker remembering John Henry James, a man lynched on July 12, 1898, in order to confront the Stonewall Jackson monument in town. Adding this marker to a lynching cannot heal the wounds of this event, of course, or automatically bring about justice in present-day Charlottesville. But it at least encourages people to face this history by bringing these wounds to the surface, which is a first (though not last) step in the process of healing.[75]

Altering, moving, or creating other statues around Confederate monuments has potential not only to foster a creativity and willingness to work with what is already present, but also to bring about a deeper reckoning about the United States' past and present than would simple and immediate erasure. As a strategy it is but one of several options for disrupting Confederate monuments. But it is an option that has promise precisely because it can force people to face their contradictions. It heightens the tensions in society in such a way that they are no longer possible to ignore—which is not a problem if one locates the power of resurrection in confronting rather than erasing life's complexity.[76]

Nevertheless, there are real limits to what can be achieved through aesthetic addition, however creative or disruptive such additions may be. No matter how many monuments are added or removed, facing collective trauma is ultimately something that has to be done by a community. That is, the organizational and memory work that enables people to begin to face themselves requires communal spaces that no monument can replace. People are separated from one another by fear; undermining this fear requires coming together in intentional meeting such that the narratives that keep people divided are undermined. In other words, the work of acknowledgment is ultimately done by and through a living community (as the story in Joshua 4 makes clear) with markers of memory being helpful insofar as they aid this work.

This insight seems to have been intuitive to the people who commissioned and erected Confederate monuments. When monuments were dedicated, there was usually a ceremony that marked the proceedings and that served to reinforce the narratives being conjured by the monument, rededicating people to the values evoked by the statue. Indeed, it was often during these ceremonies that the mask would slip and the coded language of Lost Cause ideology became explicit. To take just one infamous example, at the 1913 dedication of Silent Sam—the common soldier statue that previously sat on the north part of campus of the University of North Carolina—Julian Carr described how he "horse-whipped a negro wench until her skirts hung in shreds, because upon the streets of this quiet village she had publicly insulted and maligned a Southern lady." And yet the heart of the ideology is displayed when Carr states that the Confederate soldier stands for "the welfare of the Anglo Saxon race." According to Carr, "the facts" are clear: these soldiers' "courage and steadfastness" is to be praised because those virtues "saved the very life of the Anglo Saxon race in the South," and "as a consequence the purest strain of the Anglo Saxon is to be found in the 13 Southern States—Praise God."[77] These dedication ceremonies were as important as the monuments themselves. Confederate Memorial Days functioned in this way even more obviously, providing an annual opportunity for people to come together, to mourn, and (increasingly) to reinforce the theological tenets of the Lost Cause. The people gathered around a grave or monument, but the power was in the people who themselves carried the story forward in their day-to-day lives. The monuments were limited in their ability to do this work; their function was to focus the energy of people, to "catch" certain feelings and organize them into a coherent whole.

The danger of focusing on objects of memory, important though this remains, is that it can obscure the reality that people ultimately carry on these narratives and have agency (though limited) in this process. It can tempt one to either overvalue the power of monuments or undervalue them, but in either case focusing on objects of memory can make one think that people have little say in how to carry on or push back on the narratives that they inherit. But receipt of and repetition of these narratives is central to a monument's continued power.[78] As such, acknowledging the wounds conjured by Confederate monuments must include counter-organizational work that creates communities of people capable of coming together to recognize and confess the narratives that sit behind these monuments—something that is much easier said than done. This parallels what is seen at the end of the Gospel of John: the creation of a living community that has found the ability to recognize the returning wounds of Jesus. In the space in which the wounded Jesus breathes the Spirit upon them, the disciples encounter both Christ and each other in such a way that their fear is assuaged.[79] Thus, countering the peculiar sacred space created by Confederate monuments involves similar communal rituals that enable people to undo or retell the narratives the statues weave, and at the least undermine the patina of unquestionability they give to the Lost Cause and white supremacy.[80]

Focusing on a community's response is also important because when wounds surface, they can be responded to in a variety of ways, including ways that reify the same logics that gave rise to these wounds in the first place. Suffering comes to be viewed under the aspect of competition, wherein attention to one group's suffering takes away from acknowledgment of another group's wounds. What is required to counter this logic of competition is the creation of spaces that enable memories of suffering to be told and retold in ways that resonate one to the other.[81] In this way an ongoing process of retelling stories can go on that has no precise end point—certainly not in this life.[82] One should be wary of calls to "address" wounds as almost inevitably forestalling the kind of wound work that brings about true healing. Communities in actual space are capable, at least in principle, of doing this kind of work; monuments alone are not.[83] Given the fraught and complicated wounds conjured by Confederate monuments, it is vital to have communities that can intercept the ways these wounds can be responded to poorly. This is all the more true once one recognizes that the way the narratives behind Confederate monuments connect to current events is constantly shifting, such that one needs an ongoing capacity to discern how these narratives are being made manifest in the present.[84] Further, it is more than possible that one could connect current circumstances or practices to the narratives behind Confederate monuments (say, mass incarceration) but do so in such a wooden way that the next manifestation (say, the revival of "race science") goes unnoticed.

Making such connections is vital, but it is also vital that they are made with care.

Basically, there are limits to memorialization. Important though monuments remain, dismantling white supremacy requires ongoing practices of acknowledgment. Not tomorrow, not by the next generation, not by some other community over there, but here and now.[85] Some will seek to avoid this recognition, for facing collective wounds together does not promise to be a pleasant experience, but it is nonetheless vital despite (or because of) its difficulty. It is this combination of painful and necessary that makes the closest analogy to the process of acknowledgment the practice of mourning or lament. Lament counters apathy without becoming overconfident in one's ability to address moral evil or falling into an easy reconciliation. Mourning is a response that allows people to lament what happened in the past without purporting to fix it or offering a forgiveness that one is not in a position to give (or accept); it enables people to name and grieve the way these narratives haunt the present; and it moves away from the kind of verbose didacticism that marks the worst forms of memorialization.[86]

The practice of mourning refuses to accept that the way things are is the way things must be. It laments the power these narratives about sacrifice, whiteness, and the Lost Cause have had in this country; it laments the subtle and explicit violence these myths help fund in the present day; and it laments the fact that no matter what is done in the future to rectify these ills, it will not erase or "make right" horrors already suffered. Indeed, mourning is a unique practice that can only be done in the present, but always has its eye on the past and future. Confederate monuments, altered monuments, and new aesthetic creations can aid this process by "focusing" the practice of mourning. That is, monuments can steady one's gaze and sustain a conversation over a period of time that might otherwise lose steam. The best uses of monuments will be ones that are explicitly open to ongoing narration and that resist both nostalgia and ahistoricism. The practice of lament is best served by monuments that spur collective remembering while also recognizing their own limits, and that are able to be altered as time goes on. Monuments of this sort would point to rather than hide the arguments that preceded their construction, which would require seeing monuments as a part of a process that is never completed (on this side of the eschaton), animated rather than hindered by the forces of history that brought them into being.[87] Whereas monuments help create a people in the present, people in the present can also push back on monuments, reversing the feedback loop through practices like lament and turning objects of triumph into objects of shame and repentance.

Disrupting monuments in these ways will be resisted. White people in particular will be wary of this level of alteration and confession, likely concerned that to move in this way means losing something of one's identity. (The racist specter of "white genocide" lingers.) And the truth is, that might be so. White people might well lose their identity through a process like this. But if white folks lose this previously constructed identity, they might gain neighbors from whom they have been silently alienated; they might gain their humanity, which has been marred in the struggle to subtly maintain superiority; they might gain the beginnings of healing as they stop papering over the wounds of the past. And insofar as people become more truthful about themselves, white folks might gain a clearer picture of the God who remains on the side of the oppressed. After all, truth is not an abstract concept but a divine reality invading each contemporary situation, "revealing the meaning of the past for the present so that we are made new creatures for the future."[88] In any case, without acknowledgment the wounds of the past will continue to return to the present, unnoticed and unabated. Of all things to be avoided, chief among them should be removing Confederate monuments in a way that merely hides the evidence of a complicated history, enabling people to pat themselves on the back as they clear the way for future monuments erected to atrocities born of the same narrative logic.

5

Apocalypse

Disrupting Palliative Monuments

The most common lie is that with which one lies to oneself; lying to others is, relatively, the exception.

Friedrich Nietzsche[1]

It is a troubling and often overlooked reality that Confederate monuments continue to be built. The flow of construction has slowed, of course, but it has not stopped completely, even a century and a half after the Civil War.[2] This fact alone should give pause to those who would say Confederate monuments are about actively mourning the dead or learning lessons from history, for no one living bears the scars of this war, and a multitude of monuments already exist that can teach about the past (if one persists in the idea that this is the primary purpose of monuments). The creation of Confederate images in the contemporary world is a practice born of aggrievement and issuing from a minority of the population, which is a fact that the organizations spreading these images seem to intuitively understand given the creative ways they seek to avoid or mitigate public backlash.

Consider the infamous monument to Nathan Bedford Forrest that sits outside of Nashville, Tennessee, dedicated in 1998. Designed by white nationalist Jack Kershaw, the statue features the Confederate general and original Grand Wizard of the first Ku Klux Klan on horseback. Forrest is holding a revolver in his left hand, a sword in his right, and is yelling behind him. Aesthetically speaking, the monument is atrocious. Forrest's head is out of proportion from his body, and he has a crazed-yet-blank facial expression that puts the monument in the realm of the cartoonish. But its aesthetic offense is nothing compared to its obvious white supremacy, from which the monument's designer did not shy away. Kershaw once responded to criticism of the statue by saying, "Somebody needs to say a good word for slavery."[3] However, despite widespread criticism and derision, removing this monument or doing anything to disrupt its message has proven difficult due to the fact that it cleverly skirts the public-private divide. The statue sits on a local man's property and thus cannot be removed by public vote. And yet the monument was constructed in order that it would be unavoidably noticed from Interstate 65, and its construction was no mere private decision. The monument was approved and dedicated by the Sons of Confederate Veterans (SCV), and the state of Tennessee cleared trees from the side of the highway to ensure maximum visibility. Subsequent requests to replant trees in order to obscure the monument have been denied by the Department of Transportation. And yet, technically speaking, the monument is not public. Or better: it is public in its performance without being public in accountability.

In transcending the public-private binary in this way, the statue to Nathan Bedford Forrest exemplifies an emerging type of construction employed by groups seeking highly visible yet private land to display Confederate iconography. Another prominent example is the movement by the Sons of Confederate Veterans to place Confederate flags along I-40 and I-95 in North Carolina, one "for every monument taken down."[4] Flags are placed on private land but raised high above any highway barrier, as is already done in other states in the South. This strategy has even been employed on historic sites, as with the monument to Confederate general Joseph Johnston at Bentonville Battleground in

Fig. 5.1 Nathaniel Bedford Forrest Statue, Nashville, Tenn.

North Carolina, dedicated in 2010.[5] The statue sits on a piece of private land directly adjacent to the battlefield itself, but is clearly included within the public space. This arrangement enables these markers to avoid public backlash as well as allows defenders to shift the conversation to the sanctity of property rights when they are inevitably vandalized, as happened in December of 2017 when the Forrest monument was painted pink.

These trends should be worrying even to people who live far away from Confederate iconography or live in communities that are dismantling these monuments to the Lost Cause. The goal in dismantling Confederate monuments should not be a form of NIMBYism in which urbane sophisticates are happy so long as Confederate monuments are not in their own backyard and not directly in view—a temptation for communities entering into the complex question of what to do with these monuments once they are slated for disruption or removal. In some cases, a Confederate monument has been removed as an inveterate signal of white supremacy only to be sold to a community two counties away and put right back up, with no education or disruptive element.[6] But the goal should not be for Confederate monuments to exclusively sit in communities that glorify a particular vision of the past. The goal should be to change the soil from which these monuments spring (or are easily replanted within), which is a goal that cannot be achieved quickly or easily. That Confederate monuments continue to be built can breed a sense of frustration among those who want them gone, and a sense of fear that a neo-Confederate revival born of historical denial is forthcoming. At the very least, the defense and construction of Confederate monuments signals an ongoing cultural crisis.

This crisis has only been deepened by describing the theological convictions that give rise to and are reinforced by Confederate monuments, for it reveals that the beliefs that fund these statues are more intractable and widespread than is sometimes thought. Uncovering the theological forces that underlay Confederate monuments can be a discouraging exercise, but it is also important to understand just how deep the ideology goes that keeps these monuments in place, so that any practical recommendations for addressing the crisis they manifest has a chance to get at the root of the issue. At the very least, thick theological description of Confederate monuments forces people to be realistic about the scope of the challenge they represent. However, the seeds of a positive response are found in this theological approach as well. By identifying specific areas of Christian theology that are perverted by Confederate monuments, one also names the aspects of an effective counter-theology: a better conception of remembrance and sacrifice, a more faithful vision of the eschatological horizon beyond whiteness, and a willingness to face wounds as the path to salvation.

These areas of theological investigation lead to several interlocking strategies for disrupting Confederate monuments corresponding with their multifaceted orientation toward the past, present, and future. There are myriad strategies that one could employ to undermine Confederate monuments and the convictions that give them power. As such, exploring paths of disrupting these statues is meant to inflame people's imaginations and inspire other modes of response. Of course, given the shape of the political landscape as it currently sits in the United States, most recommendations regarding Confederate monuments are made in hope; but that does not mean thinking through responses is a useless exercise. If nothing else, imagining responses to Confederate monuments might at least shift the Overton window such that what may currently seem unrealistic comes to be seen as thinkable. In any case, Christians have a stake in the way theological concepts are utilized in public and whether these concepts are used in a way that aids or hinders the pursuit of the common good. Hopefully these recommendations will be of interest to people of other convictional communities as well, even as such people will have their own reasons for pursuing strategies that disrupt Confederate monuments. There is no need for Christians to hide their theological convictions in order to discuss matters of public import, lapsing into a false neutrality; such recommendations must only be offered in a way that recognizes their own limitations in scope and perspective.

From Palliative to Apocalyptic: The Ways Monuments Hide and Reveal

Because Confederate monuments vary in their performativity both in terms of their design and placement (cemetery versus courthouse, Confederate general versus bare obelisk, just after the Civil War versus the heart of Jim Crow), recommendations for disrupting them must be at least as multifaceted. To recognize this fact does not necessitate having any love for Confederate monuments, or to put certain monuments in a class of moral innocence they do not deserve. Noting the variance of Confederate monuments is a matter of intellectual honesty and robs defenders of a key way to hide their ideological commitments: namely, to rightly note that using blanket descriptions for all Confederate monuments leads to the condemnation of markers in cemeteries or battlefields that were put up just after the war's end. To be sure, this argument is probably not made in good faith. It is doubtful that vociferous defenders of Confederate monuments are any more comfortable destroying statues put up at the height of Jim Crow, or even the civil rights era, than those that were credibly constructed as signs of lament for the dead. But it does provide a fig leaf for such people to dismiss all criticisms of Confederate monuments as unreasonable or disrespectful. For this reason alone, it is important to nuance descriptions of Confederate monuments rather than seeking a once-and-for-all theory that can then be applied to them wholesale.

And yet there is an image that can organize the various responses to Confederate monuments, a theological lodestar that distills what is troubling about the vast majority of Confederate monuments and what is inadequate about most popular discussions on this topic: the image of the palliative monument. The most common use of the term "palliative" is in the field of medicine, referring to care that aims to relieve pain rather than address its underlying causes. Put simply, palliative medicine deals with symptoms, and in fact is often used to alleviate pain that is caused by medical treatments themselves, especially in the context of terminal illness. Such treatment plays an important role in providing medical care, but one should not confuse it with being cured. Palliative medicine provides "comfort care." Analogically, then, a palliative monument is a seductive type of monument that seeks to alleviate collective suffering without addressing the root cause of the pain, either by consequence or by design.

For the most part, Confederate monuments fall into this category, having served a palliative function in American society until quite recently, at least for a major segment of the population. With the possible exceptions of those constructed in the immediate aftermath of the Civil War and placed in cemeteries, Confederate monuments were designed to alleviate a sense of collective loss. Indeed, the very concept of the Lost Cause evokes a sense of palliative nostalgia. This nostalgic sensibility was often paired with implicit hopes for future glory ("The South will rise again!"), but these hopes were always built on palliated loss, converting collective psychological, spiritual wounds into a powerful and soothing sense of aggrievement. By focusing on the "virtues" of those who fought without mentioning the end to which these virtues were aimed, Confederate monuments diminish the capacity of Americans to face their collective, underlying wounds, constructing a myth of heroism and innocence in their stead.[7] What is more, certain recommendations for addressing the crisis occasioned by Confederate monuments are no less palliative. For those who recognize the deeply problematic nature of Confederate monuments, it is tempting to think that, if these monuments were simply removed (or perhaps just not talked about so much), then the United States could continue its march into a post-racial future. Confederate monuments problematize an otherwise inspiring story of American exceptionalism and unfolding racial justice, and thus to remove them would get American society "back on track." But the idea that this is the history and trajectory of the United States seems delusional and palliative in its own way. It is a comforting thought, but it doesn't square with the white supremacist, undemocratic, and imperialist machinations that have always been a major part of U.S. politics. Certainly the notion that the United States is anywhere near a post-racial society is hard to hold in light of the reemergence of explicit white nationalism and anti-immigrant sentiment on the national stage. The point, then, is to describe Confederate monuments as palliative in a negative sense insofar as they attempt merely to soothe the hidden wounds of the body politic without any plan for healing the underlying maladies of the American South and the United States as a whole.

But palliative has a more literal sense as well, one that is equally relevant to an analysis of Confederate monuments. The word "palliate" originates from a Latin term meaning to cloak, to mask, or to hide.[8] Palliative monuments, then, serve to cover over or hide the truth about reality, even if monuments typically purport to do exactly the opposite.[9] It is this obscurantist feature of Confederate monuments that is particularly dangerous. Confederate monuments hide, or at least minimize the importance of, major narratives about the South and the United States; they hide their orientation toward whiteness-as-ultimate even as they reinforce it; they hide the processes and arguments that precipitated their construction, giving the appearance of a unified and monolithic Southern culture. And in all this, they hide people from themselves.[10] Palliative monuments are problematic because they cover reality in such a way that they mask the power they nonetheless manifest in the world, thus delaying the sort of reckoning with the past that necessarily precedes healing and justice.

Theologically speaking, justice cannot come by hiding the past, but can only come by way of confession and repentance, called for by the Christ who remains wounded even after his resurrection and who taught that the truth will set his followers free.

In contrast, the contours of an alternative type of monument would not hide or numb, but rather reveal and disrupt—the apocalyptic monument. The literal meaning of the term *apocalypsis* is to uncover or reveal. If the palliative monument serves to cloak, the apocalyptic serves to uncloak, pulling the curtain back to reveal what was always going on behind the scenes. It may seem grandiose to describe any monument as revelatory, but it is appropriate insofar as monuments have the potential to reveal what a people hold most dear as well as more complicated realities that a society skirts or ignores. It is not hyperbole to say that the lynching memorial at the National Memorial for Peace and Justice in Montgomery, Alabama is revelatory: it reveals a truer, deeper story about the United States' past and present that can change one's entire way of seeing the world. If altered or moved to a different context, Confederate monuments could be revelatory in a similar way, revealing the United States to itself even if they are a part of the American story that one wishes was different. Other possibilities of public artistic expression can be imagined that are apocalyptic in this sense; this is a good thing, for a variety of strategies will be needed to awaken Americans from their palliative slumber, especially in a society that is marked by a deep level of self-deception when it comes to white supremacy and American exceptionalism.

But apocalyptic has another, more common sense that is equally applicable to monuments: not just revelatory but disruptive. Apocalyptic monuments are statues, markers, and memorials that, through symbolism and typological visions, witness to and even help bring about the end of a world. Of course, the end of any way of life is always two-sided: it will come as good news to those who find the present and past order of things unsatisfactory and oppressive, and it will come as terrible news to those who are comfortable with or benefit from the world as it is. As such, monuments that are disruptive of the current order of things will always be divisive and will likely emerge from the concerns and agitation of those on the underside of history, with the aesthetic

Fɪɢ. 5.2 Memorial Corridor, National Memorial for Peace and Justice, Montgomery, Ala.

goal of jarring people out of certain patterns of talking about and imagining the world. Monuments alone cannot bring about the kind of reckoning required for true and lasting societal change, but they might at least give voice to a group's desire for this sort of disruption, thus creating possibilities for that disruption to come about by other means.

Altogether, palliative and apocalyptic monuments can be thought of as types that sit at opposite ends of a spectrum. No monument is "purely" or even permanently on one side or the other. Monuments can move along this spectrum depending on what is changed about the monument itself and shifting historical circumstances. These categories, then, are meant to give one language to describe the performativity of particular monuments: whether they hide or reveal, whether they soothe or disrupt. Thinking in terms of a spectrum enables one to see that hiding and revealing are always in dynamic tension with one another; monuments always at once reveal *and* hide. The question is how open the monument in question is to its own limits of representation and remembrance. Christians have strong theological warrants to prefer monuments that lean toward the apocalyptic rather than the palliative. Monuments are good insofar as they witness to the ultimate apocalypse that is Christ himself, and bad insofar as they resist this apocalyptic event. Moreover, responses to monuments can be assessed as good or bad to the degree to which they inspire an honest reckoning with the past, and the degree to which they forestall such a reckoning for reasons of politeness, progress, or outright denial. Christians have a stake in disrupting monuments that perform a predominantly palliative function in society, preventing people from working and hoping for anything more—halting desire such that people are satisfied with injustice, or even just half-truth. Alternatively, in doing this disruptive work people might not only come to face themselves more honestly, but also inspire people to work for and desire a justice that must come from outside themselves, and thus to work for the common good under the sign of a judgment and a hope wrought by such images.[11]

To Move and Remove: When the Idols Need to Go

Assuming the preferability of apocalyptic monuments, what are some responses that would disrupt Confederate monuments out of their palliative state, altering their performativity such that the United States is opened to and prepared for the disruption of its own sacred narratives? Once one recognizes the historical context, racial animus, and form of remembrance manifested in Confederate monuments, one response is intuitive, even visceral: removal. Destroying or moving Confederate monuments is a key strategy in disrupting the theological narratives that these monuments assume and conjure in the world. In responding to these statues, it is probably the central play in the playbook. The question for Christians is *why* to utilize this option, and whether certain methods of removal may end up being counterproductive.

Before saying anything more about removal, it is important to reiterate that some Confederate monuments should probably be left alone.[12] These instances will be rare, and there is no hard and fast rule here, but certain monuments do fall into this category.

For instance, monuments constructed very near the Civil War's end have a more legitimate claim to being about lament for the dead—much more than one constructed in 1999 or 1899. But consideration of timing is not enough, as early monuments can be as problematic as later ones. It also matters where a statue is placed. Specifically, then, monuments that were constructed early on and placed in a cemetery or a battlefield ought to be thought about in a different light.[13] This is not to say that they are innocuous or innocent, for it is entirely possible for a people to mourn poorly or for the wrong reasons. But it is to suggest that early Confederate monuments in so-called "death spaces" should be approached as special cases, and their disruption should come by means other than destruction—regular communal gatherings of confession and lament, for instance. With this said, partisans of Confederate monuments should not be surprised if the intransigence of political leaders, racial tensions, and the continued presence of Confederate iconography in public spaces lead people to direct their frustration toward monuments in cemeteries. This happened with the obelisk to the Confederate dead that sits in Oakwood Cemetery in Raleigh, North Carolina, constructed in 1870. In January of 2016 vandals poured fake blood on the markers of nine high-ranking officers in the Confederate Army, including a towering statue to General George B. Anderson, which was spray-painted with the words, "The CSA fought for the right to enslave." Some graves were also painted. Actions of this sort in cemeteries may be misdirected and counterproductive, but it is not surprising that they occur. What seems clear is that monuments of this sort would perform differently if all other Confederate monuments were removed from public space or significantly altered, such that Confederate monuments were confined to cemeteries and battlefields—moved from the center of public space to the periphery.[14] If these were the only, rare Confederate statues that existed in the country, then this conversation would be different. But at present these monuments undeniably participate in a broader speech-act performed by a chorus of hundreds of monuments. Perhaps these monuments should not receive the same ire as others, but one should not be surprised that they do, at least until a wider reckoning with the past happens in this country.

Fig. 5.3 Oakwood Cemetery Monument to the Confederate Dead, Raleigh, N.C.

Regardless, monuments that could possibly be left alone are exceptions—especially since they do not constitute the majority of Confederate monuments. For monuments in public places of power—state capitol grounds, university entrances, courthouses—as well as monuments that are clearly celebratory in tone, removal is the easiest and most intuitive option. Removal is warranted especially by the fact that these monuments tend toward the mythic, going beyond "merely" remembering the past or teaching about civic pride. The majority of Confederate monuments represent a particular goal and aesthetic ideal in public, an implicit conviction about where society should be headed, a future that continues to venerate and defer to the white male. These monuments are about power: namely, the power of whiteness that forms an eschatological horizon for those caught up in its vision. Once one recognizes that Confederate monuments are not ideologically neutral, then removal becomes much more obvious as a live option, since there is no non-ideological place to go. If the construction and preservation of the monuments are laden with power, then advocating for their removal no longer sounds like an "ideological" option among otherwise neutral responses. For Christians, the option of removing a monument should be guided by the following convictions: that the crucified Christ is alone Lord of all; that Jesus has revealed the self-emptying, upside-down beauty and power of God; and that all human commitments and political ideals should be judged according to this standard, the true end of all things. Removing monuments—dismantling idols—does not in itself provide a constructive vision of what the cosmos aims toward. But acts of removal may witness to this end insofar as they clear away barriers that prevent people from seeing this end, and thus prepare people to see Christ by deconstructing narratives that keep them from recognizing the truth. Humans cannot make this end come about by clever activism or social engineering—not even by removing monuments that celebrate the antithesis of the way of Jesus—and people certainly cannot fix atrocities from history through these means. But destruction can signal a rejection of the idolatrous narratives that have been handed down, and a hope for something new to come to the world, even if one cannot quite see the form that will take.

Certainly, Christians of all people should know that the future need not be a dull repetition of the past and that the future reality of God even now breaking into the present radically changes one's perception of ordinary history. Those who hope for a future marked by God's justice and reconciliation will know that, while one should not forget the past completely, the temptation of nostalgia is also to be avoided whereby one is oriented to the past in such a way that one longs for it, even as one whitewashes what it was really like.[15] Not only does nostalgia create an idealized projection of the past that is a fantasy, but it can also prevent people from perceiving the new things God is doing here and now (Isa 43:18-19). As such, monuments that breed a nostalgic orientation to the past are in deep need of disruption, particularly if one does not want future generations to continue in the nostalgia of the past. Confederate monuments have become talismans of an era that never was, and insofar as it did exist was nightmarish to black folks, at the very least. To be sure, removing monuments comes with its dangers, not least the temptation to think that one has completely and adequately disrupted the narratives of white supremacy or neo-Confederate practice by removing a monument. But this only means that *how* a monument is removed is actually important (it is not merely a procedural point). One can remove without achieving structural change, and thus it is important to think through how removal can be done in such a way that the maximum amount of structural change is achieved through this action—or that the further work needed to make these changes is not foreclosed by the act of removal. Put differently, what happens in the months and years after a Confederate monument comes down is as consequential to the work of justice as the removal itself.

All this to say, and with all caveats and warnings heeded, most Confederate monuments should be moved, and many destroyed; they signal a narrative about the past that should be disposed.[16] The particulars of how to go about removing these statues is a separate issue, but in an ideal world most Confederate monuments would be removed immediately. For monuments such as the one to Nathan Bedford Forrest in Nashville, the ideal action would be to destroy it as quickly as possible. Other monuments could be moved to a museum in which viewers could be given a proper and full consideration of the history Confederate monuments allegedly attempt to portray. Another option would be to move certain Confederate monuments to a "death space," such that they are less likely to be taken as triumphalist celebrations of the Confederacy per se—a realistic compromise that has been proposed and enacted in some cases. For example, in 2018 the Confederate monument in Lexington, Kentucky was moved from the courthouse grounds to the Lexington Cemetery, thus changing the way the monument functioned in the cityscape without destroying it altogether. One has to go to the monument now in order to see it, rather than it being an unavoidable marker as one enters the purportedly neutral halls of justice. In any case, what should be avoided in removing Confederate monuments is moving them to a similarly public place, at least if the goal is truly to disrupt the narratives that gave rise to them in the first place. The irony is that by focusing attention on a monument, even if to attempt to destroy it, one may bestow upon it a mythic power that it previously lacked or had lost. That is, one may take the monument more seriously than its defenders. In fact, the potential for a monument to be defaced or destroyed is among the most meaningful aspects of its existence. To destroy, alter, or threaten to remove a monument may bestow a meaningfulness to a monument that previously did not exist, or exist in the same way.[17]

What to do with removed Confederate monuments themselves is one question; another is what to do with the vacated space. Ideally, cities would construct other monuments in the place that is left behind—other aesthetic representations and markers—in order to fill the space that was previously haunted by the ghosts of the Confederacy. To expel the spirit of white supremacy without filling the house with an alternative vision invites those same spirits to return sevenfold stronger (Luke 11:24-26). But a creative option upon removing a Confederate monument could be to leave the space intentionally and conspicuously blank, thus signaling the contingency of this response to a problematic history and an openness about what to do next. It would signal that a statue to the Lost Cause did stand here, and in this way serve as a kind of temporary confession as well as an expressed desire to move forward, even if one does not yet know what that looks like. In North Carolina, Duke Chapel modeled this option after a statue of Robert E. Lee that stood in the entrance of the chapel itself was defaced in 2017. The Lee statue was put there in 1932, but subsequently removed once the vandalization took place. After deliberation, Duke decided to leave the space open for the time being, as a sign of what had come before and an openness to what may yet come to be.

Regardless of the particulars, one thing is clear: the power to remove Confederate monuments (as well as rename buildings) should be in the hands of the communities that these monuments are in. While some monuments occupy space that is wider in scope (state grounds, federal land), most are under the purview of some localized power. But in any case, a monument's performative power is always and necessarily local in nature; it has to sit in some particular place and thus affect a particular community on a daily basis. As such, if a major segment of people in the community in which a monument sits wants it to come down, it should come down; the principle of subsidiarity should be in full effect.[18] For those who want Confederate monuments to be disrupted, this may seem to be a worrisome suggestion: if the majority of people in a community want a monument to stay up, does that make it right? Will this not lead to intransigent communities able to resist movements for justice in their local town? This worry is understandable—although it cannot be eliminated as a possibility, unless total coercion is brought to bear—but it is important to remember that, in the majority of cases, seizing control of such decisions from local polities has worked the opposite way. That is, in the face of very real threats by local communities to remove, cover, or vandalize Confederate monuments in their own jurisdictions, state legislatures have passed laws "protecting" monuments from local disdain. Laws of this sort are on the books throughout the South, including recently passed laws in North Carolina (2015), Tennessee (2016), and Alabama (2017). In the case of Virginia, a proposed law was rejected that would have returned this power (also banned) to local municipalities. The issues relating to monuments and power are on full display here, as these laws are clearly not neutral, but reflect and enforce an arrangement through purportedly neutral, legal means. Facing the collective past and undermining the power that has been used to reinforce particular narratives about the past involves ensuring the legal means for communities to make their own decisions about Confederate statues. As long as such laws remain on the books, there will be a continued legitimate place for people to tear down monuments in defiance of a power-laden process masked by procedure. Faced with this level of paternalism (such laws usually require requests for monument removal to be approved by a state-run commission), pulling down a statue is, at the very least, understandable. One can imagine a defense of yanking down Confederate statues that echoes Daniel Berrigan's comment about burning military files and draft cards: better monuments than people.[19]

Beyond Cheap Grace: Confession, Mourning, and Repentance

Removing Confederate monuments is the most fitting response in the majority of cases—the gold standard from which other forms of disruption derive their value. With that said, removal is not the only or even a sufficient response to Confederate monuments. Once one recognizes the deeper convictions that are at play in these statues, more (rather than less) might need to be done. But this statement requires explanation, as one may suspect that to advocate anything other than removal is simply a way to hedge one's bets, or is expressive of a misplaced discomfort at monumental disruption, or is even a covert plan to mitigate the disruption that Confederate monuments deserve. If removal is a necessary but not sufficient response to Confederate statues, what exactly should be done instead (or in addition)?

One strategy that could either accompany removal or be done in its stead—particularly if removal is not a live possibility—is to engage in a practice of lament and repentance. Whether a monument remains standing, is taken down, or is moved to a different location, a powerful means of disruption would be for communities to organize services that confess, mourn, and repent from what these monuments represent about their city and the way these narratives continue to structure American society.[20] A monument's meaning is ultimately re-funded by present communities, and so gathering people around monuments in order to initiate a more thorough process of storytelling about the feelings and memories Confederate monuments evoke would be a powerful way of altering their uptake in real time. Mourning, after all, is an activity of ethical imagination.[21] Through confession and lament, these public things could gather a people who develop the capacities required to see and hear one another, as well as the capacities needed to undermine the narratives that give these monuments their power. Confederate monuments have worked in this way throughout history, serving as transitional objects that gathered a people and then reinforced social bonds, particularly as objects at the center of civic rituals celebrating Lost Cause ideology. In their current form, Confederate monuments work in much the same way, although their power is subtler: they manifest a vision of the future and a narrative about the past that reinforces an imagined community shaped by these convictions in the present. Thus, the idea that Confederate monuments might serve to gather people, or be objects around which people organize, is completely in line with how they already function; this suggestion simply argues that they might be used to gather a different collection of people, engaging in a different set of practices, who thereby offer counter-narratives undermining the intended uptake of the very monuments around which they are gathered.

One can imagine several ways this work could be done. It is certainly possible to imagine grassroots organizing efforts that bring together a variety of people in and around the monument—even just the willingness to participate in such an activity would be a major step forward. But given the Christian themes that are embedded within Confederate monuments, one would hope that the (still largely segregated) churches that populate the American South would lead the way in this effort.[22] It is hard to imagine certain groups of people being willing to participate in a communal ritual in which sins both past and present are confessed, in which deep and generational pain is given voice, even if one is convinced that participating in such a ritual would be transformative. But it seems like Christians, at least, ought to be a people who are willing to say with Augustine: "See, I do not hide my wounds."[23] That is, Christians should know that facing even inherited wounds is a prerequisite to healing; that wounds cannot be erased or wished away; that mourning is a practice we can engage in even if other narratives about reality have broken down.[24] As such, is it so impossible to imagine churches using a local Confederate monument as a site around which they together participate in a service of prayer and repentance, in which participants together give voice to the pain, sin, and struggles of their foremothers and forefathers, celebrate their resilience, and lament the things that cannot be undone? Perhaps it is nearly impossible to imagine—as much of an indictment as that is on the American church—but if a service of corporate confession were done, it would serve as a powerful disruption to the monuments as they sit, without (necessarily) overturning a single stone.

In many cases the location of churches in relation to one another and Confederate monuments suggests how to begin such a process. For instance, the oldest Confederate monument on the state capitol grounds in Raleigh, North Carolina sits directly across the street from the mostly white First Baptist Church, founded in 1812. On the other side of the State Capitol is another First Baptist Church, founded in 1868 when black members left to form the "First Colored Baptist Church."[25] Several other churches are in the radius of this monument—some of which share a similar history with one another—but taking only these two, very close neighbors: What would happen if these churches committed to a series of services at the foot of the Confederate monument in which they named this legacy and prayed for healing, both among themselves and the country? The white churches that have historically wielded more power and privilege should be the ones to initiate such a process—or do the work in their own congregations that would lead to this outcome—seeking to confess the wrongdoing of one's own people rather than calling for the other's repentance as a prerequisite for gathering.[26] There is no doubt that engaging in this process would be difficult, but it could also create the space for deconstructing the narratives and histories that lay behind Confederate monuments. It is in this kind of imagined space that people could narrate and renarrate their story to one another, rather than allowing a monument to do all the work of narration and remembrance, which limits the ways one can imagine what is going on in the world today and in the past.[27] This kind of practice would be vital if the monument in Raleigh (for instance) was removed tomorrow—which it should be—as the wounds recalled by such monuments continue to be carried within people, even after the external reminders are gone.

Of course, people will list various reasons for refusing to participate in such a practice. Perhaps one thinks it would be uncomfortable. Perhaps one thinks it is inappropriate to confess or forgive matters that did not happen directly to oneself. Perhaps one thinks this is all overblown, and that harping on racial tensions from the past creates division where none existed. Or perhaps one thinks that the focus should be on fixing these problems in the present rather than wasting time and energy on mourning. People should strive to forget these wounds—whether they are actual or perceived—and foreswear most types of anger at injustices suffered or injustices done as barriers to building a better world.[28] The most likely reason a Christian would give to forego the practice of lament would be that Christians are supposed to be a people of forgiveness, not mourning. Christians are called to forgive unconditionally rather than dwell on wrongdoings, even when repentance is not offered by the offending parties or cannot be offered due to the passage of time. This insight might even be therapized, wherein one is assured that one cannot heal from past trauma unless one forgives the perpetrating party. To dwell on wrongdoing is psychologically and spiritually unhealthy.

To be sure, Christians care about forgiveness. Christians affirm that forgiveness is more fundamental to reality than violence, hatred, and sin—that forgiveness is central to reconciliation with one another and God. But not everything that is called forgiveness is worthy of the name. Christians must not countenance what Dietrich Bonhoeffer called cheap grace, which is forgiveness without repentance, or grace without the cross.[29] Forgiveness must not be used as a means to erase a complicated past, or dismiss someone's feelings of distress and anger as illegitimate, unchristian, and an impediment to true justice. Unfortunately, forgiveness-talk is often used in just these ways, putting undue burdens on those who are victims and eliding any need for repentance on the part of those who have done wrong. The problem with this is not only that it is simply unhelpful to ask people to mute their anger before getting on with the process of justice and reconciliation; it is also that repudiating negative emotions wholesale in favor of psychologized versions of forgiveness ignores the role that anger and resentment has played in creating social processes that eventually lead to forgiveness.[30] Even in the Gospels themselves, forgiveness is not spoken of as something that is done in a dispassionate or blind manner, but is consistently coupled with the importance of repentance on the part of the offending party and the creation of a bilateral process.[31] Forgiveness in Jesus' teaching is relational rather than individual and therapeutic.[32] In other words, forgiveness is not a dismissal or a forgetting of wrongs done, but a particular kind of remembrance under the aspect of one's place in the body of Christ.[33] By contrast, cheap grace is a way of hiding from one's sins; it is the opposite of apocalypse. In the reality constructed by cheap grace—in a church that holds correct doctrine but neglects the call of discipleship—"the world finds a cheap covering for its sins; no contrition is required, still less any real desire to be delivered from sin."[34]

In contrast to a cheap forgiveness that would avoid or dismiss the need for contemporary rituals of mourning, costly grace at once recognizes the importance of forgiveness without sacrificing the ongoing place of lament and confession—even if such a process will be painful or awkward. Costly grace seeks to create the space where stories can be shared, where it is safe for all parties to speak freely, and where forgiveness can be offered, if one chooses to give it. Cheap grace is accompanied by a form of politics marked by amnesia and a "covering" that would seek to move forward without justice—resurrection without a cross. It encourages people to get over wrongs done, and as such might better be called "dismissal." Conversely, a politics of true forgiveness will go through rather than around repentance and mourning, encouraging people to face one another in hope.[35] Its politics is one of mutual (though not equivalent) confession, as modeled in the Lord's Prayer.[36] To be sure, in the case of Confederate monuments, talk of repentance and confession is complicated by the obvious fact that these statues deal with things that happened in the past, and it is true that one cannot ask forgiveness or seek justice for people who are gone. Talk of repentance is further complicated by the fact that the primary institutions that are capable of structuring this kind of process (church, nation-state) were implicated in these very issues.[37] Nonetheless, people can mourn the events that have created the world today; people can hope for a time in the future when the process of lament is taken seriously; and people can confess and seek forgiveness for their own complicity in the narratives conjured by Confederate monuments, or their apathy in the face of deep structural evil. Focusing on an ongoing ritual of gathering and lament—irrespective of what has happened or will happen with the monuments themselves—enables one to connect the narratives of white supremacy and sacrifice implicit in the monuments to the ways these same narratives work in the world today, for which one *can* repent and *can* act. Such connections include the logic of Jim Crow embedded within U.S. prison policies, the unfortunate revival of race science that parallels nineteenth-century phrenology, the ongoing use of sacrificial rhetoric to sacralize state violence, and the still-present belief in Anglo-Saxon supremacy to justify contemporary policing practices and "stand your ground" laws.[38] Condemning Confederate monuments is easy. Calling for prison reform or working against school resegregation and gentrification is harder, as it moves one past a purely aesthetic preference for a cityscape devoid of Confederate iconography only to be palatable to corporate forces that continue to enervate the body politic.[39]

To imagine people willing to sit with their complicity (on the one hand) and with legacies of generational trauma and resilience (on the other) is to imagine a people willing to wrestle with the ways their present is shaped by the past.[40] For Christians, the Jesus who is present in and through processes of corporate disruption is Jesus the stumbling stone, the Jesus who is capable of offending, the Jesus who inaugurated a reign that achieves true justice and peace by going through rather than around mourning and repentance and confession.[41] To be sure, the practice of lament may rob people of the illusion that they know precisely what to do or how to proceed, as these scripts may be found to be far more embedded in American society than was previously realized. But it may also create the space whereby at the very least "they" become "us," and in ritual performances about an unjust past people both remember and protest, simultaneously calling to mind and declaring judgment over sins of the past.[42] That is, through the practice of mourning people might find the language to question how things are, lament what was, and reject that things must continue along this path.

Additive Iconoclasm: The Power of Contextualization

In seeking to disrupt the scripts that underlay Confederate monuments, removal and gathering together are two important (and not mutually exclusive) options for achieving this goal. Whichever is preferred, the goal in both cases should be to alter the cultural, political soil within which Confederate monuments thrive, and to avoid either historical erasure or a triumphalism built on self-deception. For different reasons, both are temptations born of the desire to narrate one's story in a way that is flattering, thus manifesting a penchant for self-deception that Nietzsche described well: "'I have done that,' says my memory. 'I cannot have done that,' says my pride, and remains inexorable. Eventually—memory yields."[43] Although they are not without risks themselves, both options are intuitive and thus recommended by people of a variety of backgrounds. The same cannot be said of a third option for disrupting Confederate monuments that may appear counterintuitive at first glance, and as such is less often considered in popular discourse: the strategy of adding statues and other aesthetic additions to Confederate monuments, using images that already exist to tell a more truthful story about the past and to foster a reckoning with who a people have been. Moving Confederate monuments to a museum is designed to do this work, as is placing a plaque next to a monument that attempts to more fully explain the monument's history, and both actions are good. But in the first case, the kind of visceral, visual disruption that happens with a public image is abandoned in favor of the sterile, detached, isolated halls of the modern museum, whose insights are only available to those who would visit (or pay to visit). And in the second case, adding plaques is at once overly didactic and overly subtle, only formative insofar as someone walks up and does a close reading of a monument. Adding images to the monuments while keeping them in public—whether these additions are temporary or permanent—seeks to do a similar form of contextualization and disruption by diverting the power of these images to a different end altogether. This work could (and should) be done elsewhere, of course—in museums and historic sites—but given the unfortunate fact that the narratives that underlay Confederate monuments continue to have public sway, and given that the United States is hardly past the historical moment that these monuments occupy, there is value in attempting this sort of disruption in public, altering their uptake as they sit and for all to see.

In part, this strategy is born of the conviction that images have a unique power to jar humans out of complacency and spur humans toward God, even as images also have the power to trap people in patterns of seeing, thinking, and desiring.[44] Whether one tends toward a general disposition of iconoclasm (the destruction of images) or iconophilia (the love of images) depends upon whether or not one thinks that images are prone to seizing one's ability to imagine a reality beyond what they signal. Christians have a word for an image or visual representation that takes the place of God: an idol. However, distinguishing an image from an idol is tricky, and must be done on a case-by-case basis. To call something an idol does not name qualities inherent to an image but rather describes the nature of a relationship between image and viewer that is always mediated by the communities, institutions, and histories in question. One group's image is another group's idol.[45] What distinguishes an image from an idol, according to theologian Natalie Carnes, is that an idol resists any form of self-negation, referring only and predominantly to itself. An image, on the other hand, points to (or does not occlude) a wider reality; it remains open to a presence beyond itself, and thus relativizes its own importance.[46] In the image, presence and absence interweave. The question is how to negotiate the relation between the two, rather than arguing wholesale either to remove or to keep all images.[47] As such, sharply differentiating between a love of images and the destruction of images turns out to be a false dichotomy. Instead, people should seek to foster modes of icon-oclasm that are faithful to God, and avoid modes of iconoclasm that fail to recognize images' inevitable power.[48] Applied to Confederate monuments, the implication is clear: the power of these images is to be expected. One should not try to avoid this reality, but should seek ways of inheriting or disrupting these particular images that inspire faithfulness to Christ, the Image of God.

There is no automatic, one-size-fits-all picture of what this looks like. There is only the (ongoing, shifting) challenge of having a right desire and relationship to particular images, which is itself a matter of ongoing discernment. Images that cause desire to stall out before it reaches its end in God are tempting (in the pejorative sense), whereas those that continue to spur people on toward this end are good.[49] One can think through how to respond to images and statues that already exist using this theological framework, and even assess the appropriateness of responses to particular monuments. Destroying an image is not out of the question, depending on the circumstances, but the aim of such an action (or else, the assessment of such an action even if done for other reasons) must be the "unsticking" of people's focus from the image itself. Other forms of disruption should have a similar goal. The response to idols must recognize the problem with them in the first place: not that they arouse people's love and adoration but that they stop and divert it from its path toward God. Idols promise a kind of satisfaction that they cannot fulfill, tricking people into thinking of them as a final source of fulfill-ment, inspiring in people a love that is too weak rather than too strong. As such, destroying an idol can be important in the process of reopening desires and imagination, providing a reprieve from being in the thrall of a particular image—but the reprieve is only temporary. After being rid of an idolatrous image, people are immediately vulnerable to being enthralled once more.[50] That is, pure iconoclasm is often necessary, but it is not a permanent solution to the problem of stuck or diverted desire. Humans will inevitably be shaped by images, and the purely destructive act on its own does not direct desire differently or better. Other responses to images—even problematic images—seem necessary to this latter goal.

With this in mind, the majority of Confederate monuments can be seen as attempting to seize and direct the desires of their audience to theological narratives about whiteness, sacrifice, and an era marked by Southern virtues of nobility and manliness.[51] Confederate monuments seek to direct one's desire both forward and backward, trapping people within its constructed present: backward, in a nostalgic pining for a lost golden age that never was (nor would have been "golden" for anyone besides landholding white men); and forward, toward a hoped-for future in which white maleness is again ascendant. Given the complex relationship between iconophilia and iconoclasm, it may be possible to subvert Confederate monuments by directing their power in a way that undermines their idolatrous functionality. Whereas simply removing Confederate monuments may do little to direct desires beyond the narratives they assume and reinforce, adding certain images around Confederate monuments might be shocking enough to jar someone out of a trance, such that one's desire is no longer wholly focused on the monuments themselves and what they represent. Other desires—for equity and justice, for neighborliness, for a public reckoning with a racist past, for the kingdom to be manifest on earth as it is in heaven—might begin to relativize and even override one's desire to maintain a statue.

The kind of additions that would truly be iconoclastic would need to be carefully and intentionally chosen, designed to subvert the theology conjured by Confederate monuments and to make the contradictions of the American story abundantly clear—the aesthetic equivalent to W. E. B. Du Bois' suggestion of a more truthful slogan to put on Confederate statues: "Sacred to the memory of those who fought to Perpetuate Human Slavery."[52] It is for this reason that adding lynching memorials in and around Confederate monuments carries such promise. Not only would these images drastically change the uptake of monuments that intend to valorize the Lost Cause, but they would also commemorate events that were born from and connect to the narratives carried forth by Confederate monuments themselves. That is, lynching memorials avoid an anemic form of aesthetic addition that taps into the myth of multicultural progressivism, wherein the story of the United States is seen as an upward, automatic, and nearly unbroken spiral toward greater inclusivity and justice. This is the flaw of the addition to Richmond's Monument Avenue that was agreed upon in the 1990s: the statue of Arthur Ashe at once leaves the underlying ideology of the other statues on the road undisturbed, as well as suggests a story of progress whereby these monuments are given a valid (rather than tragic) place in an ultimately triumphant tale.[53] Public monuments to and about lynching certainly avoid that temptation, bringing something to the fore that lies deep in the collective unconscious that is scandalous and ugly and that, once seen, alters the way one views Confederate monuments and the ideologies they represent. Memorializing lynching would not automatically alleviate this past or heal the rifts that are inherited from this moment, but it might help people face that past as a reality. Ironically, under a certain aspect, Confederate monuments accidentally signal the hidden truth about the United States as a nation marked by white supremacy. Surely this is why some celebrate Confederate monuments, but it is also for this reason that others wish for them to go away, as they are reminders of a truth about the United States that is not easy or comfortable. It is vital that Americans find ways to face rather than erase that history, and without celebrating it.[54] Insofar as Christ is uniquely present among the lynched, working to liberate the lynched from being lynched and the lynchers from the oppression of being lynchers, to face this reality will begin reshaping one's desires such that they are more truly directed toward Christ himself.

To be sure, monuments to lynching must not be the only disruptive additions to Confederate statues, as one must not fall into the trap of providing only negative or depressed representations of black folks in public, thus reinforcing the victim-victimizer dichotomy. Celebrations of black power and survival over time must also be included, here and throughout Southern cityscapes, as well as markers and celebrations of other people whose stories are often left unheard or minimized in official versions of history, particularly Southern history. But as important as such "positive" aesthetic additions would be, one must be careful that they do not fall into a kind of progressivism that would avoid facing or disrupting ingrained injustice by weaving these stories into an ultimately nice, triumphant story of steady progress, such that any anger or dissatisfaction with the present state of affairs is unreasonable. Critiques of this sort have been made about the monument to Martin Luther King Jr. on the National Mall in Washington, D.C., dedicated in 2012. In its design and placement around heroes of U.S. history, King is indeed celebrated, but it is not the King who was a threat to the American orthodoxies this monument serves to reinforce. Certainly this is not the King who declared "eternal hostility to poverty, racism, and militarism,"[55] and who died as a suspected enemy of the state for his criticism of American exceptionalism and the war in Vietnam. Whatever the intention of the monument's design, it is now drawn into a narrative about a post-racial society and the triumph over white supremacy—a claim that at this moment in U.S. history is laughable. To be sure, King's monument is not bad, but through a set of evasive aesthetic relations it may distort one's ability to see current material conditions clearly.[56] Even aesthetic creations originally designed to disrupt can be reincorporated into an official narrative about society, thus blunting their original intent. Something like this has happened with another structure on the National Mall, the Vietnam Veterans Memorial, which was specifically designed to interrupt the celebratory nature of its neighboring monuments but has now been engrafted into a narrative of progress, such that the Vietnam War is seen as an exception that nonetheless proves the rule of American greatness.[57]

Because even the most disruptive monument can be reincorporated into a narrative that tames its intended uptake, any strategy of additive disruption should include the creation of ongoing, shifting, impermanent images in and around Confederate monuments.[58] Art displays and other more temporary aesthetic additions can disrupt Confederate monuments as well as shift with the ongoing flow of time. One example includes the simple draping of a black cloak over the Confederate monuments in Charlottesville, Virginia, which for a period of time displayed both a community's dissatisfaction with the monument's continued presence as well as the impermanence of such a disruptive act—a kind of disruptive down payment on further disruptions to come.[59] Temporarily disrupting monuments in this way is a species of what Carnes calls "additive iconoclasm," meaning a strategy of disrupting images premised on the reality that pictures hold people captive—externally rather than in one's head—and that, as such, seeks to break open bewitched imaginations by adding images to an otherwise monolithic space.[60] Iconoclasm by way of addition—either permanent or temporary—may be able to disrupt in a way that few other things can, changing the aspect under which an image is viewed such that the whole is suddenly seen in a new light.[61]

Whether permanent or temporary, the idea of disrupting Confederate monuments through the creation of images dares to imagine a widespread network of symbols that bring the internal contradictions of this country to light. In making the tensions unavoidable, the hope is that something new might emerge in their wake, or that people might at least learn to leave the past contradictory rather than "fixing" it. To be sure, any addition will require ongoing and antecedent organizational work. Nothing of this sort will come to pass without political pressure and grassroots organizing, and as such the two strategies are interrelated. But both will share as a goal the disruption and ultimate elimination of Confederate monuments as people seek to re-member the past in such a way that traces of the end might be glimpsed in the present.[62] To imagine the kinds of monuments that would disrupt and replace those that currently dot the Southern landscape, and the kind of people who would be capable of constructing and countenancing this kind of narrative about itself, is to dare to imagine a radically different nation than the one that currently exists. Implementing these suggestions will be challenging. But God forbid that people give up working for a more just world because it will be difficult.

An Apocalyptic Moment: Contingency, Risk, and Living into the Future

Charlottesville was an unveiling. It pulled back the mask on what has been going on in the United States, and garnered forces that many hoped had been eliminated or marginalized. To be sure, this hope was always naive, but it was a hope born of good intentions. For some people, the violence and animosity conjured by the statue to Robert E. Lee revealed something about Confederate monuments that was previously obscured from view. For others, it merely confirmed what one already knew about these statues: that they are about something far deeper and more problematic than public history. In any case, the narratives behind these monuments were suddenly able to be seen in a different light—if only for a moment—as were the equivocations and defenses of Confederate monuments following the Unite the Right rally. After Charlottesville, stolid and civil debates about Confederate monuments seemed inappropriate, even nauseating. The only legitimate debate was how to respond to this revelation. Should things go back to the way they were? Should efforts be made to re-cover this shameful reality—both past and present—in the hopes that, in hiding it from sight, it might go away? Or should people find ways to face and undermine this sickness at its roots? Insofar as it leads people to take this latter option, the unveiling at Charlottesville is also an opportunity. With the mask having slipped, Americans have an opportunity to let it stay slipped, and to knock it from the hands of those who would attempt to raise it back up.

Simply put, Christians should lean into this apocalyptic moment rather than retreat to a cheap palliation or return to a false sense of normality or "civility" that was always illusory, and would (again) leave persons of color in a position of vulnerability and marginalization. Christians should be a people who are ready and willing to work for justice in the world, even if achieving this goal means condemning parts of one's own history, and in this way dying to oneself. Describing Confederate monuments in their theological dimensions is one way to understand both the power they wield in the world and the level at which they must be undermined: not just as objects of political power, but as idols. A few paths of disrupting Confederate monuments have been explored which would squarely face the crisis they represent. These suggestions are not meant to settle the conversation about how best to undermine Confederate monuments and all they represent—far from it. The hope is that describing Confederate monuments under a theological aspect might aid in a discernment process about how to proceed from this point. But doing the actual work of discerning how to practically respond to Confederate monuments cannot be done by a lone voice writing a book (let alone by one white man).

All responses to Confederate monuments will be marked by an irreducible level of contingency and risk, and no outcome is certain. Even the most well-intentioned strategy must be willing to shift and change, as white supremacy itself is an incredibly adaptive ideology. As such, one should be ready to admit that one's suggested means of disrupting a Confederate monument is risky and could backfire in unforeseen ways. There is no way it could be otherwise.[63] What one should be after is not the elimination of risk, but responses that have a reasonable chance of jarring people out of entrenched ways of seeing the world. Hopefully there will be more suggestions for disrupting Confederate monuments which consider the systematic and theological nature of the challenges they represent. Time does not heal, and the narratives behind Confederate monuments will not automatically be subverted. As such, to paraphrase a sentiment from Frederick Douglass: "Better to confront such a past . . . than to wait for its resurgence."[64]

Christians will have their own means of assessing responses to Confederate monuments, measuring paths of disruption in light of their capacity to prepare people to live in faithful anticipation of God's eschatological judgment. That is, analyzing Confederate monuments as theological objects should be done with the conviction that the future that God desires has been revealed and made present in Christ. If Christians compare the present to God's eschatological future and find the former wanting, the goal should be to reshape and even dismantle the present order of things in order to live faithfully into God's future. Christians should not want merely to inhabit the world as it is, but to transform it such that it is more in line with the reality proclaimed by Jesus—that God's will might be done on earth as it is in heaven. To echo James Baldwin, Christians should want this even if it means breaking up the world as constructed, even if it brings risk to security and identity, and knowing that the temptation will be strong to revert to what one previously knew (or thought one knew).[65] In this sense altering or removing Confederate monuments can only be an initial step in dismantling the wider network of white supremacy that is an affront to the kingdom of God inaugurated by Jesus. An initial step—but an important step, and one that is long overdue.

Notes

Preface

1 See the video of the event itself and Bree Newsome speaking at Vox, "Activist Bree Newsome takes down Confederate Flag at South Carolina Statehouse," June 27, 2015, YouTube video, 0:53, https://www.youtube.com/watch?v=LYgbwbmsHfw.

2 George Yancy, "Why White People Need Blackface," *New York Times*, March 4, 2019.

3 James Baldwin, "Notes for a Hypothetical Novel," in *Nobody Knows My Name* (1961; New York: First Vintage, 1993), 153.

4 This is a recurrent theme in the work of Michel Foucault. For a clear and readable articulation of this thesis, see Noam Chomsky and Michel Foucault, *The Chomsky-Foucault Debate: On Human Nature* (New York: New Press, 2006), 41.

Introduction

1 Audre Lorde, "Age, Race, Class, and Sex: Women Redefining Difference," in *Sister Outsider: Essays and Speeches* (1984; New York: Crossing, 2007), 123.

2 Joe Heim, "A stark contrast inside and outside a Charlottesville church during the torch march," *Washington Post*, August 19, 2017, https://www.washingtonpost.com/local/a-stark-contrast-inside-and-outside-a-charlottesville-church-during-the-torch-march/2017/08/

19/a2311a7a-847a-11e7-902a-2a9f2d808496_story.html?utm_term=
.afe8ebfef226.

3 Joe Heim, "Recounting a day of rage, hate, violence and death,"
Washington Post, August 14, 2017, https://www.washingtonpost
.com/graphics/2017/local/charlottesville-timeline/?utm_term=
.16da4a35c4f7.

4 This most prominent and immediate action in this regard was the
removal of the Confederate Battle Flag from the State Capitol in South
Carolina. Several monuments were taken down, and buildings, roads,
and parks renamed—including Emancipation Park in Charlottesville,
which was previously named Lee Park. See Brigit Katz, "At Least 110
Confederate Monuments and Symbols Have Been Removed Since
2015," *Smithsonian*, June 8, 2018, https://www.smithsonianmag.com/
smart-news/least-110-confederate-monuments-and-symbols-have
-been-removed-2015-180969254.

5 To date, the Southern Poverty Law Center has documented 1,747
such symbols to the Confederacy in the United States, including 772
monuments and statues across 23 states and the District of Columbia.
"Whose Heritage? Public Symbols of the Confederacy," February 1,
2019, https://www.splcenter.org/20190201/whose-heritage-public
-symbols-confederacy.

6 John C. Calhoun, "On Abolition Petitions," U.S. Senate, February 6,
1837, in *The Confederate and Neo-Confederate Reader: The "Great Truth"
about the "Lost Cause,"* ed. James W. Loewen and Edward H. Sebesta
(Oxford: University Press of Mississippi, 2010), 30–35. Calhoun was
featured on the Confederate one-cent stamp.

7 This sense of white grievance—what is often referred to in right wing
circles as "white genocide"—is a major ideological driver in Dylann
Roof's manifesto.

8 Javier Espinoza, "Cecil Rhodes statue to remain at Oxford University after alumni threaten to withdraw millions," *Telegraph*, January 29,
2016, https://www.telegraph.co.uk/education/universityeducation/
12128151/Cecil-Rhodes-statue-to-remain-at-Oxford-University
-after-alumni-threatens-to-withdraw-millions.html.

9 Norimitsu Onishi, "A Colonial-Era Wound Opens in Namibia," *New
York Times*, January 21, 2017, https://www.nytimes.com/2017/01/21/
world/africa/namibia-germany-colonial.html

10 Taiwan has taken a similar tact, placing over 200 statues to Chiang
Kai-shek in a designated park. Kai-shek was a leader who many Tai-
wanese people associate with Chinese overreach.

11 Maria Perez, "'Racist + Rapist' Spray Painted on Thomas Jefferson Statue at the University of Virginia," *Newsweek*, April 14, 2018, http://www.newsweek.com/thomas-jefferson-statue-vandalism-university-virginia-886233

12 A prominent example of this position can be found in the grassroots organization "Take 'Em Down NOLA," which widened their aim from Confederate monuments in New Orleans to symbols of any slave-holding person.

13 Indeed, at a basic level all historical sites are contested, involving clashes of interpretation about the past as well as concerns about present attitudes these interpretations serve to bolster. Cf. Teresa Bergman, *Exhibiting Patriotism: Creating and Contesting Interpretations of American Historic Sites* (Walnut Creek, Calif.: Left Coast, 2013), 16–17; and Joy Sather-Wagstaff, *Heritage That Hurts: Tourists in the Memoryscapes of September 11* (Walnut Creek, Calif.: Left Coast, 2011), 25–26.

14 Helpful studies of the interrelation between contested memory and memorialization, and how quickly such debates tend to emerge after traumatic events, include Andreas Huyssen, *Present Pasts: Urban Palimpsests and the Politics of Memory* (Stanford: Stanford University Press, 2003); Edward T. Linenthal, *The Unfinished Bombing: Oklahoma City in American Memory* (Oxford: Oxford University Press, 2001), ch. 5; Elizabeth Greenspan, *Battle for Ground Zero: Inside the Political Struggle to Rebuild the World Trade Center* (New York: St. Martin's Press, 2013); and James E. Young, *The Texture of Memory: Holocaust Memorials and Meaning* (New Haven: Yale University Press, 1993).

15 Claims of white genocide connected to Confederate monument removal can easily be found online. At the Unite the Right rally in Charlottesville, one group carried a banner that read, "'Diversity' = White Genocide," https://www.flickr.com/photos/rodneydunning/36401911981. For other examples of people making the connection between white genocide and monument removal, cf. Jaweed Kaleem, "After violence in Charlottesville, cities rush to take down monuments as white supremacists gear up to fight," *Los Angeles Times*, August 14, 2017, https://www.latimes.com/nation/la-na-charlottesville-causes-20170814-story.html; Abdul Aziz, "The Secret, All-White Committee Advising New Orleans' Black Woman Mayor on the Fate of Confederate Statues," *Splinter*, May 22, 2018, https://splinternews.com/the-secret-all-white-committee-advising-new-orleans-b-1826236431; Nicole Hemmer, "Charlottesville wasn't about Robert E. Lee, Mr. President. It was about racism," *CNN*, April 26, 2019, https://www.cnn.com/2019/04/26/opinions/trump-defends-charlottesville

-comments-after-biden-video-hemmer/index.html; and Katie Fretland, Ryan Poe, and Jennifer Pignolet, "Confederate groups rally in Memphis after monuments' removal from parks," *Commercial Appeal*, January 6, 2018, https://www.commercialappeal.com/story/news/government/city/2018/01/06/memphis-confederate-statue-protest-removal/1004853001.

16 One could add a fourth response: in the face of people calling for monuments to come down, one could go the other way and put monuments up to the person or event in question.

17 On the emotionally weighted nature of contemporary debates about memorials in the contemporary United States—let alone responses to already-standing monuments—see Erika Doss, *Memorial Mania: Public Feeling in America* (Chicago: University of Chicago Press, 2010).

18 For a helpful analysis of the varying responses to Confederate monuments today, taking one case study as an example, see Stephen McFarland, Samantha L. Bowden, and M. Martin Bosman, "'Take 'Em Down Hillsborough!': Race, Space, and the 2017 Struggle Over Confederate Iconography in Neoliberal Tampa," *Southeastern Geographer* 59, no. 2 (2019): 172–95.

19 Taking many of these concerns to heart, Pamela Klassen at the University of Toronto has conducted the "Religion and Public Memory Project" from 2015–2020. The project focused on how religion shapes, provokes, and complicates projects of public memory in multicultural societies.

20 Cf. Michelle Alexander, *The New Jim Crow: Mass Incarceration in the Age of Colorblindness* (New York: New Press, 2012).

21 I am reminded of these words from James Baldwin: "I know another Negro, a man very dear to me, who says, with conviction and with truth, 'The spirit of the South is the spirit of America.' He was born in the North and did his military training in the South. He did not, as far as I can gather, find the South 'worse'; he found it, if anything, all too familiar." James Baldwin, "Fifth Avenue, Uptown: A Letter from Harlem," in *Nobody Knows My Name*, 69.

22 Robert S. Nelson and Margaret Olin, "Introduction," in *Monuments and Memory, Made and Unmade*, ed. Robert S. Nelson and Margaret Olin (Chicago: University of Chicago Press, 2003), 6.

23 Ted Smith argues that ethical theories that proceed in this way assume an "intramundane account of the good." Ted A. Smith, *Weird John Brown: Divine Violence and the Limits of Ethics* (Stanford: Stanford University Press, 2015), 35.

1 • History

1 W. E. B. Du Bois, "The Perfect Vacation," in *The Crisis* 40, no. 8 (1931): 279. Cf. W. E. B. Du Bois, *Black Reconstruction in America: Toward a History of the Part Which Black Folk Played in the Attempt to Reconstruct Democracy in America, 1860–1880* (1935; New York: Free Press, 1998), 715–16.

2 I am paraphrasing nineteenth-century anthropologist John Lubbock: "What we do see depends mainly on what we look for. When we turn our eyes to the sky, it is in most cases merely to see whether it is likely to rain. In the same field the farmer will notice the crop, the geologists the fossils, botanists the flowers, artists the colouring, sportsmen the cover for game. Though we may all look at the same things, it does not at all follow that we should see them." *The Beauties of Nature and the Wonders of the World We Live In* (1892; New York: Macmillan, 1905), 3–4.

3 Daniel J. Simons and Christopher F. Chabris, "Gorillas in Our Midst: Sustained Inattentional Blindness for Dynamic Events," *Perception* 28, no. 9 (1999): 1059–74.

4 In Gaines M. Foster, *Ghosts of the Confederacy: Defeat, the Lost Cause, and the Emergence of the New South, 1865 to 1913* (New York: Oxford University Press, 1987), 125.

5 See Michel-Rolph Trouillot, *Silencing the Past: Power and the Production of History* (Boston: Beacon, 1995), 146. Laying a baseline historical understanding is important for analyzing all "media of memory," none of which drop from the sky but come into being through a complex interplay of various material, historical, and social factors. See Astrid Erll, *Memory in Culture*, trans. Sara B. Young (2005; New York: Palgrave Macmillan, 2011), 125. On the concept of thick description, see Clifford Geertz, "Thick Description: Toward an Interpretive Theory of Culture," in *The Interpretation of Cultures: Selected Essays* (New York: Basic, 1973).

6 Kirk Savage, *Standing Soldiers, Kneeling Slaves: Race, War, and Monument in Nineteenth-Century America* (Princeton: Princeton University Press, 1997), 166.

7 Foster, *Ghosts*, 41–42.

8 Cf. W. Fitzhugh Brundage, *The Southern Past: A Clash of Race and Memory* (Cambridge, Mass.: Belknap and Harvard University Press, 2005), ch. 1.

9 Foster, *Ghosts*, 38–39.

10 Foster, *Ghosts*, 40–41. Foster has an appendix that details Confederate monuments' design and placement, and how this changed over time; *Ghosts*, 273. Cf. David W. Blight, *Race and Reunion: The Civil War in American Memory* (Cambridge, Mass.: Belknap and Harvard University Press, 2001), 77.

11 Sanford Levinson, *Written in Stone: Public Monuments in Changing Societies* (Durham: Duke University Press, 1998), 5.

12 See Stephanie McCurry, *Confederate Reckoning: Power and Politics in the Civil War South* (Cambridge, Mass.: Harvard University Press, 2010). Slaves were also uncooperative (at best) in the Southern war effort.

13 Foster, *Ghosts*, 24–27.

14 Foster, *Ghosts*, 37.

15 Foster, *Ghosts*, 15–16, 26.

16 Foster, *Ghosts*, 42, 45.

17 Foster, *Ghosts*, 37. As Foster goes on to say, these ritual processes and the material symbols forged to remind Southerners of these rituals gave power and legitimacy to what he so aptly calls "the ghosts of the Confederacy."

18 I explicitly mean to evoke the sense of civil religion meant by Robert Bellah. See Robert N. Bellah, "Civil Religion in America," *Daedalus* 96, no. 1 (1967): 1–21.

19 Charles Reagan Wilson, *Baptized in Blood: The Religion of the Lost Cause, 1865–1920* (1980; Athens: University of Georgia Press, 2009), 28.

20 Wilson, *Baptized in Blood*, 35. W. Fitzhugh Brundage, "No Deed but Memory," in *Where These Memories Grow: History, Memory, and Southern Identity*, ed. W. Fitzhugh Brundage (Chapel Hill: University of North Carolina Press, 2015), 8.

21 Foster, *Ghosts*, 37.

22 Blight, *Race and Reunion*, 65.

23 Wilson, *Baptized in Blood*, xv.

24 A prominent early example is the decoration ritual that the black community performed in Charleston, South Carolina immediately following the war. See Blight, *Race and Reunion*, 66–68.

25 Blight, *Race and Reunion*, 70. William Blair shows just how contested these commemoration rituals became. What began as a way of reifying a particular vision of Southern identity, structured chiefly around the Lost Cause ideology, was soon a site of contestation over the meaning of the war and Reconstruction. See William A. Blair, *Cities of the Dead: Contesting the Memory of the Civil War in the South, 1865–1914* (Chapel Hill: University of North Carolina Press, 2004).

26 Blight, *Race and Reunion*, 22.

27 Blight, *Race and Reunion*, 101.

28 Blight, *Race and Reunion*, 107. That these concerns were written out of the popular narrative about the Civil War and its aftermath shows just how true it is that what is remembered about the past is largely determined by those in power, who shape what eventually gets passed on as history—and get to occlude the reality of the very contestations that they eventually win. See Brundage, *Southern Past*.

29 Blight, *Race and Reunion*, 113–14.

30 Blight, *Race and Reunion*, 117, 121–22.

31 As Gaines Foster puts it, invoking the unique problem of the malformed conscience: "Faced with defeat, they judged their actions against their consciences and ruled themselves righteous." Foster, *Ghosts*, 35.

32 As James Cone puts it, at this moment in history America is struggling to define itself as a white nation and black people as "child-like" and therefore "incapable of political and social equality." James H. Cone, *The Cross and the Lynching Tree* (Maryknoll, N.Y.: Orbis, 2011), 6. It is far from coincidental that the vast majority of Confederate monuments are constructed during this time.

33 Foster, *Ghosts*, 40.

34 Foster, *Ghosts*, 273.

35 As helpful as the differentiation remains between earlier and later commemoration, early commemoration was not necessarily innocent. Even the initial impetus for commemoration had roots in resistance to perceived northern slights, which ranged from disdain for the project of Reconstruction to the way resources for commemorating the dead were allocated. As such, even the earliest memorials cannot be seen as only about grief and sorrow; many also sprung from a desire to keep sectionalist identity alive and strong. Put simply, "Ensuring the immortality of the fallen and of their memory became a means of perpetuating southern resistance to northern domination and to the reconstruction of southern society." Drew Gilpin Faust, *This Republic of Suffering: Death and the American Civil War* (New York: Alfred A. Knopf, 2008), 243. Cf. Faust, *Republic of Suffering*, 238, 247.

36 David Blight does a good job documenting this shift. One of Blight's central theses is that the tension between healing and justice was early and ongoing up to and following the Civil War, and that it broadly represents the differences between black and white visions of American history. Blight, *Race and Reunion*, 3.

37 By referring to the Lost Cause tradition as a "myth," I mean to emphasize its power as an interpretive story, rather than to suggest that every

element of the tradition is made up from whole cloth. Some elements are total fiction while others have more basis in reality (Lee's military prowess), but what makes the narrative "mythology" is the way it makes sense of the world for people. In any case, even the elements that are truthful are propagandistic in that the narrative over-focuses on these details at the expense of others. The basic element of propaganda, after all, is not untruth but emphasis.

38 Wilson, *Baptized in Blood*, 77.

39 As the *Christian Index* (based in Macon, Ga.) wrote in 1866, "The victory over Southern arms is to be followed by a victory over Southern *opinions*," a victory they sought to forestall. Wilson, *Baptized in Blood*, 7. Emphasis in quotations is original to the source unless otherwise noted.

40 Wilson, *Baptized in Blood*, 1.

41 Wilson, *Baptized in Blood*, 7. Blight, *Race and Reunion*, 51. At this early stage, Pollard bluntly names the white supremacist motives behind this struggle over memory: "While the war decided the question of slavery and sectional reunion, the war did not decide Negro equality." That battle, Pollard saw, was ongoing.

42 This is well attested in primary documents and anti-abolitionist writing prior to 1861. Cf. Drew Gilpin Faust, ed., *The Ideology of Slavery: Proslavery Thought in the Antebellum South, 1830–1860* (Baton Rouge: Louisiana State University Press, 1981); Mark A. Noll, *The Civil War as a Theological Crisis* (Chapel Hill: University of North Carolina Press, 2006), ch. 3; and Loewen and Sebesta, *Confederate and Neo-Confederate Reader.*

43 "Whatever the extent of Union victory on the battlefield, the verdicts to be rendered in history and memory were not settled at Appomattox." Blight, *Race and Reunion*, 261.

44 Paul A. Shackel, *Memory in Black and White: Race, Commemoration, and the Post-Bellum Landscape* (Walnut Creek, Calif.: AltaMira, 2003), 26.

45 Shackel, *Memory*, 27; Foster, *Ghosts*, 51–52. Foster points out that Lee was ambivalent about the Lost Cause. On the one hand, he opposed monuments generally and supported sectional unity; on the other, he clearly believed the major tenets of the Lost Cause, especially regarding "overwhelming numbers" and the unique bravery of the Army of Northern Virginia. His concern seemed to be with a too-strident tone associated especially with men like Jubal Early, rather than any objection to the accuracy of the myth itself.

46 Foster, *Ghosts*, 52. Foster compares the fervor of dedication and hope for renewal among Lost Cause advocates to the millennial revitalization movements of the nineteenth century, particularly in the desire to manifest a new world out of the past and in service to the future. Cf.

Foster, *Ghosts*, 57; Shackel, *Memory*, 27. For this reason, it is odd that Foster takes umbrage with describing the Lost Cause as a civil religion, preferring to call it a "tradition." His own rhetoric here, and his own astute descriptions of the Lost Cause phenomenon, readily show its "religious" aspects, both in that it glommed onto existing religiosity in the South, and in that it was marked by beliefs, totems, rituals, practices, and even something like sacred texts. Foster mostly resists the term "civil religion" because it suggests that the Lost Cause became a permanent feature of Southern identity, a claim he wants to resist. But to me its ongoing power has only been revealed in the years since Foster wrote. Cf. Foster, *Ghosts*, 7–8.

47 Monument dedications were a central ritualized setting where the Lost Cause jeremiad against the emerging New South could be heard, along with veteran funerals, Confederate Memorial Days, fast and thanksgiving days, and meetings of local veterans' groups. Wilson, *Baptized in Blood*, 29, 82.

48 Foster, *Ghosts*, 61–62.

49 Foster, *Ghosts*, 95.

50 Wilson, *Baptized in Blood*, 19.

51 Quoted in Wilson, *Baptized in Blood*, 22.

52 Wilson, *Baptized in Blood*, 18.

53 Foster, *Ghosts*, 102.

54 Foster, *Ghosts*, 101–2.

55 Blight, *Race and Reunion*, 80. Thus does Brundage say that through these activities, participants became, "if only temporarily and symbolically, contemporaries with mythical events." Brundage, "No Deed but Memory," 9.

56 W. E. B. Du Bois, *The Souls of Black Folk* (1903; New York: Restless, 2017), 7.

57 Blight, *Race and Reunion*, 79.

58 Blight, *Race and Reunion*, 284–89. The needed funds were approved by the U.S. Senate, but failed in the House of Representatives. On the controversies concerning faithful slave monuments as well as the specific story behind the Hayward Shepherd Memorial at Harpers Ferry, see Shackel, *Memory*, ch. 3. For a theological engagement with the mammy as a cultural production, and with reference to the proposed mammy statue, see Emilie M. Townes, *Womanist Ethics and the Cultural Production of Evil* (New York: Palgrave Macmillan, 2006), ch. 3, esp. 35–36.

59 Examples include the Faithful Slaves Monument in Fort Mill, S.C. (1895); a line on the common soldier statue in Columbia, N.C. (1902);

and a marker near a more prominent Confederate monument in Madison, Fla. (1909).

60 Blight, *Race and Reunion*, 82–83. As Blight goes on to say, "In the long history of Lost Cause tradition, both got their wish."

61 Edward A. Pollard, "The Lost Cause Regained," in Loewen and Sebesta, *Confederate and Neo-Confederate Reader*, 250.

62 Blight, *Race and Reunion*, 42.

63 Blight, *Race and Reunion*, 110.

64 See Amy Louise Wood, *Lynching and Spectacle: Witnessing Racial Violence in America, 1890–1940* (Chapel Hill: University of North Carolina Press, 2009); and Angela D. Sims, *Lynched: The Power of Memory in a Culture of Terror* (Waco: Baylor University Press, 2016).

65 Wood, *Lynching and Spectacle*, 1.

66 In her detailed collection of oral histories of people who lived through the reality of lynching, Angela Sims shows that lynching functioned in precisely this way among black communities. See Sims, *Lynched*, xv, 10, 32, 107.

67 Focusing just on the context of North Carolina, see the incredibly helpful interactive map provided by the "Locating Lynching" project, http://lynching.web.unc.edu. North Carolina had fewer instances of lynching than other states, "only" lynching around one hundred people (that we know of) between 1880 and 1960.

68 Blight notes, for instance, that Walter White's *The Fire in the Flint* (New York: Alfred A. Knopf, 1924) ends with "a ritualized burning of a mutilated victim in the public square of a Southern town, in front of the local Confederate monument." Blight, *Race and Reunion*, 109. It reads: "In the open space before the Confederate Monument, wood and excelsior had been piled. Near by stood cans of kerosene. On the crude pyre they threw the body. Saturated it and the wood with oil. A match applied. In the early morning sunlight the fire leaped higher and higher. Mingled with the flames and smoke the exulting cries of those who had done their duty—they had avenged and upheld white civilization. . . ." White, *Fire in the Flint*, 236.

69 A sixteen-page assessment of this event is provided by Timothy B. Tyson, "The Ghosts of 1898: Wilmington's Race Riot and the Rise of White Supremacy," *News and Observer* (Raleigh, N.C.), November 17, 2006. Cf. H. Leon Prather, *We Have Taken a City: The Wilmington Racial Massacre and Coup of 1898* (1984; Wilmington, N.C.: Dram Tree, 2006).

70 Tyson, "Ghosts of 1898," 6.

71 Tyson, "Ghosts of 1898," 10.

72 Tyson, "Ghosts of 1898," 12. Cf. David Cunningham, *Klansville, U.S.A.: The Rise and Fall of the Civil Rights-Era Ku Klux Klan* (New York: Oxford University Press, 2013), 22; and David S. Cecelski and Timothy B. Tyson, eds., *Democracy Betrayed: The Wilmington Race Riot of 1898 and Its Legacy* (Chapel Hill: University of North Carolina Press, 1998).

73 I have in mind here Ted Smith's argument that this is the function of appeals to law in our time: they make orders founded on violence appear "neutral" and "objective," in supposed contrast to "religious" violence, which is somehow worse. Cf. Smith, *Weird John Brown*, 46–58, 64, 134–40. Thus does Smith describe law as reflective, "the means and medium by which the state reasons about its most basic questions"; *Weird John Brown*, 49.

74 Savage, *Standing Soldiers*, 151.

75 Blight, *Race and Reunion*, 198.

76 Conversely, as Tyson remarks, "No monument exists to the handful of visionaries who were able to imagine a better future, beyond the bounds of white supremacy." Tyson, "Ghosts of 1898," 3.

77 Blight, *Race and Reunion*, 46.

78 Wilson, *Baptized in Blood*, 73.

79 I am here paraphrasing a line by Charles Chesnutt, an African American author writing in 1901 about the Wilmington massacre. For Chesnutt, the weed of slavery had been clipped but "its roots remained, deeply imbedded in the soil, to spring up and trouble a new generation." Charles Chesnutt, *The Marrow of Tradition*; quoted in Blight, *Race and Reunion*, 344–45.

80 This period has been called the "commemorative age." Cf. John Bodnar, *Remaking America: Public Memory, Commemoration, and Patriotism in the Twentieth Century* (Princeton: Princeton University Press, 1992).

81 Cited in Shackel, *Memory*, 32. Shackel cites other black leaders condemning the coming "reunionist" wave in *Memory*, 32–34.

82 Blight, *Race and Reunion*, 129.

83 Blight, *Race and Reunion*, 89.

84 Shackel, *Memory*, 36. Cf. Stuart McConnell, *Glorious Contentment: The Grand Army of the Republic, 1865–1900* (Chapel Hill: University of North Carolina Press, 1992), 207, 213.

85 Du Bois, *Black Reconstruction*, 711–14.

86 Blight, *Race and Reunion*, 135.

87 Because historians across the United States served to bolster this historical effort, Du Bois argues that the victory of the Lost Cause narrative in service to the ends of sectional reunion was a part of a larger

whitewashing effort that he calls the "propaganda of history." Cf. Du Bois, *Black Reconstruction*, ch. 17.

88 Bodnar, *Remaking America*, 28–29.

89 Bodnar, *Remaking America*, 31. Bodnar goes on to say that it was important that reunification happened as quickly as possible, and that it be done in such a way that "regional pride" could be maintained.

90 Shackel, *Memory*, 28–31. Foster, *Ghosts*, 67–68. Foster notes that the only real way to promote reconciliation was to put forward the "sacrifice, resourcefulness, and bravery" on display even in one's foes—a goal that Confederate monuments absolutely helped promote. See Foster, *Ghosts*, 69.

91 J. L. M. Curry, a pastor, diplomat, and former officer in the Confederate Army, put the matter quite simply: "We live in the present and not in the dead past. . . . Let us live *in* the present and *for* the future, leaving the dead Past to take care of itself, drawing only profitable lessons from that and all history." Foster, *Ghosts*, 71. Of course, an important motive behind this kind of argument, from the perspective of a Southerner, would be to avoid recrimination and continued charges of treason.

92 Blight, *Race and Reunion*, 351–53.

93 Shackel argues that such matters were almost completely suppressed (at least among white America) from the time of Frederick Douglass' death and the Plessy v. Ferguson decision until the 1960s. Shackel, *Memory*, 16.

94 Blight, *Race and Reunion*, 129.

95 Shackel, *Memory*, 19, 179. As David Blight writes, "In the memorialization that swept over America in the decades after the war, no monuments ever commemorated the pitiful deaths of the Joseph and Willis Flints across the South. These stories and legacies, as much a part of the struggle over the meaning of the Civil War as Pickett's Charge or Sherman's March to the Sea, never found a place in the nation's epic." *Race and Reunion*, 119.

96 Frederick Douglass, "The Color Question," in Smith, *Weird John Brown*, 149.

97 Blight, *Race and Reunion*, 355.

98 Martin Luther King Jr., "Love, Law, and Civil Disobedience" (1961), in *A Testament of Hope: The Essential Writings and Speeches*, ed. James M. Washington (1986; New York: HarperOne, 2003), 50–51.

99 Blight, *Race and Reunion*, 389–90.

100 It was this very deficiency in white histories of Reconstruction—both North and South—that led Du Bois to write *Black Reconstruction*.

101 Savage, *Standing Soldiers*, 7–8.

102 Wilson, *Baptized in Blood*, 20.

103 Wilson, *Baptized in Blood*, 29.

104 Noll, *Civil War*, ch. 5.

105 Foster, *Ghosts*, 34–35; Wilson, *Baptized in Blood*, ch. 4.

106 Leon Festinger, Henry W. Riecken, and Stanley Schachter, *When Prophecy Fails: A Social and Psychological Study of a Modern Group That Predicted the Destruction of the World* (1956; London: Pinter & Martin, 2008). In this way, Foster's connection between the Lost Cause and (other) nineteenth-century religious movements, specifically "millennial vitalization movements" such as what led to the Great Disappointment, is particularly apt.

107 Cf. Murray A. Rae, *Architecture and Theology: The Art of Place* (Waco: Baylor University Press, 2017).

108 For an introduction to theopoetics, see L. Callid Keefe-Perry, *Way to Water: A Theopoetics Primer* (Eugene, Ore.: Cascade, 2014). For a classic treatment of the analysis of sacred symbols, see Geertz, *Interpretation of Cultures*, 126–41. In part, recognizing and analyzing the way objects "perform" is a species of speech-act theory, in that figures like J. L. Austin broaden our attention from just the way words "refer" to the way words are received by a hearer as well. It similarly draws on moves made by C. S. Peirce in semiotics. And in part it is a species of the hermeneutic turn, in which it is recognized that interpretation is both inevitable and already "baked in" to the way texts, and by extension other phenomena, are received. I discuss speech-act theory in more detail in chapter 2.

2 • Past

1 Jonathan Tran, *The Vietnam War and Theologies of Memory: Time and Eternity in the Far Country* (Chichester, UK: Wiley-Blackwell, 2010), 279.

2 Jefferson Davis, *The Rise and Fall of the Confederate Government, Volume 2* (New York: D. Appleton and Company, 1881), 192–93. See Blight, *Race and Reunion*, 259–60. Blight notes that the major defenders of the Lost Cause "could not develop their story of a heroic, victimized South without the images of faithful slaves and benevolent masters." If that story did not hold up, then the entire narrative of the Lost Cause quickly unraveled. As such, the goal in much critical race theory is not simply to "correct" for an imbalance—not simply to "elevate" the lower side of the grouping—but to undermine the entire Master-Slave, Lord-Servant, Black-White logic upon which such injustices are built.

See J. Kameron Carter, *Race: A Theological Account* (New York: Oxford University Press, 2008).

3 This is a paraphrase of the famous quip from Winston Churchill: "We shape our buildings, and afterwards our buildings shape us." For a theological defense of this notion, see Brad J. Kallenberg, *By Design: Ethics, Theology, and the Practice of Engineering* (Eugene, Ore.: Cascade, 2013).

4 Maurice Halbwachs, *The Collective Memory*, trans. Francis J. Ditter Jr. and Vida Yazdi Ditter (1925; New York: Harper & Row, 1980), ch. 2. Because of this, Halbwachs tends to emphasize group stability and continuity over disruption.

5 Erll, *Memory in Culture*, 15. On the idea that individuality necessarily emerges within sociality, see Alasdair MacIntyre, *Dependent Rational Animals* (Chicago: Open Court, 1999).

6 Halbwachs, *The Collective Memory*, 38.

7 Ludwig Wittgenstein, *On Certainty*, ed. G. E. M. Anscombe and G. H. von Wright, in *Major Works: Selected Philosophical Writings* (1969; New York: HarperCollins, 2009), §343.

8 See Paul Ricoeur, *Memory, History, Forgetting*, trans. Kathleen Blamey and David Pellauer (Chicago: University of Chicago Press, 2004), 122–24.

9 "There is no pre-cultural memory. But neither is there a 'Collective Memory' that is totally detached from individuals and embodied solely in media and institutions." Erll, *Memory in Culture*, 98. Even Halbwachs affirms that there is no collective without individuals, nor individuals divorced from community; cf. Maurice Halbwachs, *On Collective Memory* (Chicago: University of Chicago Press, 1992), 40.

10 Halbwachs, *On Collective Memory*, 9. Interestingly, Erll argues that media (such as monuments) serve as the "interface" or "switchboard" between individual and collective dimensions of remembering; Halbwachs, *On Collective Memory*, 113.

11 Halbwachs, *The Collective Memory*, 86. Cf. Erll, *Memory in Culture*, 17. On how this functions in Southern culture, which is much more multifaceted and contested than is sometimes suggested in popular uses of the phrase—which tend to conflate "southern," "white," and "Confederate"—see Brundage, *Southern Past*.

12 Bodnar, *Remaking America*, 13.

13 Erll, *Memory in Culture*, 28–29. Cf. Jan Assmann, *Das kulturelle Gedächtnis: Schrift, Erinnerung und politische Identität in frühen Hochkulturen* (Munich: Beck Press, 1992). Erll notes that official and vernacular memory could also be differentiated in terms of the latter resting on

everyday communication rather than official slogans, and is thus more individual and present focused.

14 Bodnar, *Remaking America*, 14. As Bodnar goes on to say, whichever interpretation emerges victorious becomes an ideology that does not need to be forced upon a populace, but is embraced as "obvious" and thus repeated of a people's own free will. *Remaking America*, 17, 19.

15 Erll, *Memory in Culture*, 109.

16 Erll, *Memory in Culture*, 23. Cf. Pierre Nora, *Rethinking France: Les Lieux De Memoire*, 4 vols., trans. David P. Jordan (Chicago: University of Chicago Press, 2001–2010).

17 On this Nora-influenced tripartite distinction, see Erll, *Memory in Culture*, 24.

18 Erll, *Memory in Culture*, 102–4. Erll is critiquing Halbwachs' tendency to reduce collective memory to nothing but the social dimension; scholars in the fields of art and literature to overemphasize the material dimension; and scholars interested in individual memory to deemphasize sociality and materiality. I take the recent work on the concept of "extended mind" to both confirm this insight regarding materiality and to cut through debates about whether collective memory is "in" monuments or merely projected "onto" monuments by people. Humans simply think with objects, from the "outside-in," as it were, such that we might say that societies remember not "in" monuments but inseparably *through* them. Cf. Andy Clark, *Supersizing the Mind: Embodiment, Action, and Cognitive Extension* (Oxford: Oxford University Press, 2008).

19 Erll, *Memory in Culture*, 113.

20 Erll, *Memory in Culture*, 100. It is at this point that collective memory might appear to be little more than an overextended analogy. Statues do not remember, after all, nor do they have the capacity for memory. Individuals remember; *perhaps* societies remember; to say anything more must be a metaphor, and a bad metaphor at that. See John R. Gillis, "Memory and Identity: The History of a Relationship," in *Commemorations: The Politics of National Identity*, ed. John R. Gillis (Princeton: Princeton University Press, 1991). Of course, collective memory is never fully or adequately contained by or "in" an object, and it is important to note the complex cultural processes that give rise to something like collective memory. It would be misleading to apply individual psychological phenomena to cultural processes in a simplistic manner, and dead statues do not remember, strictly speaking. Nonetheless, such warnings do not negate the more nuanced uses of "monuments remembering," which signal the way memory is

prompted by the relationship between humans and things. As Halb-wachs himself puts it, "Even if stones are moveable, relationships estab-lished between stones and men are not so easily altered. When a group has lived a long time in a place adapted to its habits, its thoughts as well as its movements are in turn ordered by the succession of images from these external objects." Halbwachs, *The Collective Memory*, 133.

21 Erll, *Memory in Culture*, 116, 131. This recalls Halbwachs' discussion of an individual "momentarily adopting" a collective "viewpoint" as he or she walks through a city. Such interfacing can only happen through media which shape individual remembrances of the past in the present; "media frameworks of remembering generate media-specific individ-ual memories." Cf. Halbwachs, *The Collective Memory*, 23–24, 64.

22 Erll, *Memory in Culture*, 104. As Nora puts it, memory is prompted by material objects and cannot occur entirely without such materiality; Pierre Nora, "Between Memory and History: *Les Lieux de Mémoire*," *Representations* 26 (Spring 1989): 13.

23 Erll, *Memory in Culture*, 99. In this I am rejecting the hard division between "memory" and "history" put forth by some theorists, chiefly Pierre Nora in "Between Memory and History," 8. History, historical consciousness, and memory should be distinguished, to be sure, but not neatly separated. Cf. Sather-Wagstaff, *Heritage That Hurts*, 40–41.

24 Erll, *Memory in Culture*, 101, 104. Many theorists who study collective memory connect their work to the field of semiotics, which is natural given the way sign-systems function within any act of remembering.

25 Consider, for instance, the difference between an open Bible at the front of a church and that same Bible under glass at the local museum.

26 Cf. J. L. Austin, *How to Do Things with Words*, 2nd ed., ed. J. O. Urmson and Marina Sbisà (1962; Cambridge, Mass.: Harvard University Press, 1975).

27 "If you look at a Pollock drip painting or at a canvas consisting of eight parallel stripes of paint, and what you are looking for is composition (matters of balance, form, reference among the parts, etc.), the result is absurdly trivial: a child could do it; I could do it. The question . . . must be: How is this to be seen? What is the painter doing? The prob-lem, one could say, is . . . determining how a man could be inspired to do *this*, why he feels *this* necessary or satisfactory, how he can *mean* this." Stanley Cavell, "Music Discomposed," in *The Cavell Reader*, ed. Stephen Mulhall (Cambridge, Mass.: Blackwell, 1996), 126.

28 On the social context of speech-acts, see Terrence W. Tilley, *The Evils of Theodicy* (Washington, D.C.: Georgetown University Press, 1991), 15–19.

29 Bodnar, *Remaking America*, 245. This is similar to Clifford Geertz's argument that multiple meanings of cultural objects are possible, even meanings that go beyond what was originally intended. Cf. Geertz, *Interpretation of Cultures*, 210–16.

30 On "stance taking" and speech-act theory, see James Wm. McClendon Jr. and James M. Smith, *Convictions: Defusing Religious Relativism* (Valley Forge, Pa.: Trinity Press International, 1994), 63.

31 Tilley, *Evils of Theodicy*, 21.

32 On essentially contested concepts, see W. B. Gallie, *Philosophy and the Historical Understanding* (London: Chatto and Windus, 1964); and William E. Connolly, "Essentially Contested Concepts," in *Democracy, Pluralism, and Political Theory*, ed. Samuel A. Chambers and Terrell Carver (New York: Routledge, 2008).

33 Frederick Douglass was chief among those who decried the false equivalence implied by this move, arguing as early as 1871 that it was impossible to equate the two sides in the name of "reconciliation," as one side expressly fought to maintain slavery. See Blight, *Race and Reunion*, 106.

34 See Harriet I. Flower, *The Dancing Lares and the Serpent in the Garden: Religion at the Roman Street Corner* (Princeton: Princeton University Press, 2017).

35 The Civil War seems to be the first time "that we discover language entering into political American discourse that compared the sacrifice of the soldier for his country to the sacrifice of Christ." Kelly Denton-Borhaug, *U.S. War-Culture, Sacrifice and Salvation* (Oakville, Conn.: Equinox, 2011), 132. Some even associate the rise of the rhetoric of sacrifice with the ascendance of "religious nationalism" in the United States. See Philip Gorski, *American Covenant: A History of Civil Religion from the Puritans to the Present* (Princeton: Princeton University Press, 2017), 20–21, 98–100. The point regarding Confederate monuments is that Christ's sacrifice came to be appropriated and even subtly conflated with soldiers' sacrifices, thus serving fundamentally idolatrous ends; I discuss this move in detail in chapter 3.

36 For instance, in 1860 between a third and two-fifths of Americans were formal members of churches, and the rate of Americans who regularly participated in church life but were not members was double that figure. See Noll, *Civil War*, 11.

37 Faust, *Republic of Suffering*, 190. Stanley Hauerwas explores these themes in *War and the American Difference: Theological Reflections on Violence and National Identity* (Grand Rapids: Baker Academic, 2011), 30–32.

38 Faust, *Republic of Suffering*, 5–6.

39 Faust, *Republic of Suffering*, 270. As Faust summarizes the point, "The very purposelessness of sacrifice created its purpose."

40 Noll, *Civil War*, 88–90. Noll points out that Lincoln was rather unique in asserting both the reality of providence and the near-impossibility for humans to know much about it.

41 Noll, *Civil War*, 75.

42 "Surrender made war's sacrifices seem purposeless; losses would remain unredeemed; southern fathers, brothers, and sons had not died that a nation might live." Faust, *Republic of Suffering*, 192.

43 Faust, *Republic of Suffering*, 248.

44 Jeffrey C. Alexander, "Toward a Theory of Cultural Trauma," in Jeffrey C. Alexander, Ron Eyerman, Bernhard Giesen, Neil J. Smelser, and Piotr Sztompka, *Cultural Trauma and Collective Identity* (Berkeley: University of California Press, 2004), 2–3. This phenomenon explains how the same event can traumatize one person but not another.

45 This is representative of a more general truth about collective memory and identity: "Identities are continuously constructed and secured not only by facing the present and the future but also by reconstructing the collectivity's earlier life." Alexander, "Toward a Theory," 22.

46 For one example of this, cf. Foster, *Ghosts*, 98–100.

47 This monument was removed by the city in August 2017, shortly after the Charlottesville riots, but the pedestal and inscription remain—frequently marked with alternative artwork, other statues (including a pregnant African American woman), and graffiti that has said "Black Lives Matter" and "Smash White Supremacy."

48 This analysis follows the relationship between incorporating and inscribing practices as described in Paul Connerton, *How Societies Remember* (Cambridge: Cambridge University Press, 1989).

49 See Michael Rothberg, *Multidirectional Memory: Remembering the Holocaust in the Age of Decolonization* (Stanford: Stanford University Press, 2009).

50 See Alexander, "Toward a Theory," 8–9. Of course, this imaginative work is always done with historical "data"; it is not imagined wholesale or from scratch.

51 This is true of history in general. "Silences are inherent in history because any single event enters history with some of its constituting parts missing. Something is always left out while something else is recorded. There is no perfect closure of any event, however one chooses to define the boundaries of that event. Thus whatever becomes fact does so with its own inborn absences, specific to its production." Trouillot, *Silencing the Past*, 49.

52 As Trouillot illustrates simply, "If the sportscaster told us every 'thing' that happened at each and every moment, we would not understand anything. If the account was indeed fully comprehensive of all facts it would be incomprehensible." Trouillot, *Silencing the Past*, 50.

53 Trouillot makes this point in relation to Disneyland representations of slavery; *Silencing the Past*, 148.

54 On a view of the past that avoids both "pure" constructivism as well as "historical positivism," see Trouillot, *Silencing the Past*, ch. 1.

55 Miroslav Volf, *The End of Memory: Remembering Rightly in a Violent World* (Grand Rapids: Eerdmans, 2006), 11. As Volf puts it, public remembering can form a "protective shield" around trauma, turning memory into "a vicious sword, and the just sword of memory often severs the very good it seeks to defend." See *End of Memory*, esp. 18, 31–33.

56 Volf, *End of Memory*, 41.

57 As Volf puts it, enemies should "remember together so as to reconcile," and "reconcile so as to remember together"; *End of Memory*, 35. Volf knows that calls for reconciliation can be problematic and must be made carefully. As Willie Jennings writes, reconciliation is only rightly imagined *after* one provides a clear-eyed assessment of the way identity and intimacy have been deformed in modernity; Willie James Jennings, *The Christian Imagination: Theology and the Origins of Race* (New Haven: Yale University Press, 2010), 9–10.

58 Volf, *End of Memory*, 22.

59 Volf, *End of Memory*, 33. To remember wrongdoing without healing is to relive injustice suffered, such that "the other is locked in unredemption and we are bound together in a relationship of nonreconciliation." Miroslav Volf, *Exclusion and Embrace: A Theological Exploration of Identity, Otherness, and Reconciliation* (Nashville: Abingdon, 1996), 133.

60 Volf, *End of Memory*, 11, 35.

61 Volf, *End of Memory*, 23.

62 Volf, *End of Memory*, 26.

63 Volf, *End of Memory*, chs. 7–8. In being clear that such forgetting need not and cannot happen until an eschatological transformation rather than in this life, Volf's argument differs from the one found in Martha C. Nussbaum, *Anger and Forgiveness: Resentment, Generosity, Justice* (New York: Oxford University Press, 2016).

64 Volf even applies this to the scars of Jesus himself. *End of Memory*, 190–91. This differs from Volf's thoughts on memory and the cross in *Exclusion and Embrace*, 139–40.

65 Volf, *Exclusion and Embrace*, 135–36. Cf. Volf, *End of Memory*, 210.

66 Insofar as human existence as such is marked by suffering and anxiety, one may wonder how much there would be left to remember if one completely forgot the bad.

67 Despite his critique of Volf, for instance, Jonathan Tran affirms the way Volf describes the complex connections between healing and memory, his distrust of theodicies that would "make sense" of evil suffered, and his recognition that all remembering involves elements of forgetting. Tran, *Vietnam War*, 129–30, 135, 163 n. 109, 204.

68 Tran, *Vietnam War*, 130–31, 133.

69 Volf, *Exclusion and Embrace*, 242; Volf, *End of Memory*, 49–50.

70 Tran, *Vietnam War*, 204–5.

71 Tran, *Vietnam War*, 133–36.

72 Tran, *Vietnam War*, 131, 136–38, 141–46. On this point, cf. Ricoeur, *Memory*.

73 This debate maps onto the choice often presented to historians: either positivism (affirm that history exists as is, with an absolute distinction between fact and narrative) or constructivism (whereby historical process and narratives completely overlap). As Trouillot notes, the way forward is not to "reconcile" these two positions or split the difference, but to reject the dichotomy altogether; see Trouillot, *Silencing the Past*, 4–16.

74 As Tran puts it, "The redemption made possible through Christ remembers the past, making history's suffering visible through Christ's sufferings *and* his glory, which in turn *temporally* animates reconciliation and *eternally* enlivens ever-lasting praise. Thus, right memory remembers doxologically." Tran, *Vietnam War*, 135. Note that Tran insists that Christological renarration is vital to remembering pleasures aright as well as pain.

75 Tran, *Vietnam War*, 129.

76 See Trouillot, *Silencing the Past*, 50.

77 Trouillot, *Silencing the Past*, 14–15.

78 Trouillot, *Silencing the Past*, 149. "Authenticity is required, lest the representation becomes a fake, a morally repugnant spectacle." Cf. Trouillot, *Silencing the Past*, 151–52.

79 Tran argues that the back and forth exchange of forgiveness anticipates an eschatological destiny that "engrafts sinners into the larger story of God's redemption of *all* things, giving new stories." Tran, *Vietnam War*, 159.

80 Tran, *Vietnam War*, 136.

81 Cf. Shelly Rambo, *Resurrecting Wounds: Living in the Afterlife of Trauma* (Waco: Baylor University Press, 2017); and Serene Jones, *Trauma and*

Grace: Theology in a Ruptured World, 2nd ed. (2009; Louisville: Westminster John Knox, 2019).

82 Tran, *Vietnam War*, 163.

83 Tran, *Vietnam War*, 203.

84 As Angela Sims puts it, to remain open to multiple, shared narratives "can be an invitation to participate in a collective process of truth telling in which space is created to hear, without a need to respond to another, and to engage simultaneously in a process of self-examination." *Lynched*, 55–56.

85 Sims, *Lynched*, 63.

86 On the ethics of "screwing with" structures of power from below—an ethics "para joder"—cf. Miguel A. De La Torre, *Latina/o Social Ethics: Moving Beyond Eurocentric Moral Thinking* (Waco: Baylor University Press, 2010), ch. 4; and *Embracing Hopelessness* (Minneapolis: Fortress, 2017).

87 As Trouillot writes, "We are never as steeped in history as when we pretend not to be, but if we stop pretending we may gain in understanding what we lose in false innocence." *Silencing the Past*, xix.

88 Nelson and Olin, *Monuments and Memory*, 4.

89 Luke Timothy Johnson, *The Writings of the New Testament: An Interpretation*, rev. ed. (London: SCM Press, 1999), 125–26. On the concept of typological identity between past and present, cf. James Wm. McClendon Jr., *Ethics: Systematic Theology, Volume 1*, rev. ed. (1986; Nashville: Abingdon, 2002), ch. 1. Tran refers to this phenomenon as "eucharistic re-membering." *Vietnam War*, ch. 7.

90 Flora A. Keshgegian, *Redeeming Memories: A Theology of Healing and Transformation* (Nashville: Abingdon, 2000), 134. Keshgegian is summarizing the work of Johann Baptist Metz.

91 William T. Cavanaugh, *Torture and Eucharist* (Malden, Mass.: Blackwell, 1998), 229.

92 Cavanaugh, *Torture*, 229–30, 234. As such, any entity that asks for its own form of sacrifice is competing with God.

93 Hauerwas, *War*, 57–70.

94 Cavanaugh, *Torture*, 232. Christians live into "the gathering of a new social body in which the only sacrifice is the mutual self-offering of Christian charity."

95 Put starkly, "God is not Moloch." Cf. Smith, *Weird John Brown*, 170.

96 Quoted in Wilson, *Baptized in Blood*, 154.

97 Wilson, *Baptized in Blood*, 29. Wilson notes explicit connections between Christ's sacrifice and the sacrifices of Confederate soldiers throughout his book; cf. *Baptized in Blood*, 24, 44–45, 72, 162.

98 See Orlando Patterson, *Rituals of Blood: The Consequences of Slavery in Two American Centuries* (New York: Basic, 1998), ch. 2; and Donald G. Mathews, "The Southern Rite of Human Sacrifice: Lynching and Religion in the South, 1875–1940," *Journal of Southern Religion* 3 (2000).

99 Cf. Denton-Borhaug, *U.S. War-Culture*, 73, 139–40, 244.

100 "Just as the commemoration of the Civil War established a foundational narrative of sectional division and reunion among whites while ignoring the underlying racial conflicts, the Ashe memorial is indicative of a common practice of commemorating the civil rights movement as a narrative of racial unity and harmony while ignoring the underlying economic inequalities that are Jim Crow's legacy." Matthew Mace Barbee, *Race and Masculinity in Southern Memory: History of Richmond, Virginia's Monument Avenue, 1948–1996* (Lanham, Md.: Lexington, 2014), 184.

101 "Jesus Christ is the Truth and thus stands in judgment over all statements about truth. But having said that, we must immediately balance it with another statement, without which the first statement falsifies what it intends to affirm. . . . There is no truth in Jesus Christ independent of the oppressed of the land—their history and culture. And in America, the oppressed are the people of color—black, yellow, red, and brown. Indeed it can be said that to know Jesus is to know him as revealed in the struggle of the oppressed for freedom." James H. Cone, *God of the Oppressed*, rev. ed. (1975; Maryknoll, N.Y.: Orbis, 1997), 31.

102 See Cone, *Cross*, xiv, 158. W. E. B. Du Bois also saw this clearly; see Cone, *Cross*, 102–3.

103 Cone, *Cross*, 158.

104 Cone, *Cross*, 160.

105 Sims, *Lynched*, 2.

106 Sims, *Lynched*, 42.

107 Sims, *Lynched*, 4.

108 Keshgegian, *Redeeming Memories*, 141.

109 Keshgegian, *Redeeming Memories*, 142. Keshgegian sees this as a feminist corrective to Metz's work.

110 As Cone writes, "What happened to the indifference among white liberal religious leaders that fostered silence in the face of the lynching industry? Where is that indifference today? Did the hate and indifference vanish so that we no longer have to be concerned about t̲ ⸺? What happened to the denial of whites who claimed that they'd not even known about lynching, even though many blacks were lynched during their adult years? Unless we confront these questions today, hate

and silence will continue to define our way of life in America." *Cross*, 164.

111 Sam Levin, "Lynching memorial leaves some quietly seething: 'Let sleeping dogs lie,'" *Guardian*, April 28, 2018, https://www.theguardian .com/us-news/2018/apr/28/lynching-memorial-backlash-montgomery -alabama. On the memorial itself, sponsored by the Equal Justice Initiative, see http://www.eji.org.

112 See Rambo, *Resurrecting Wounds*, 91.

113 Cf. Willie James Jennings, "Is America Willing to Be Freed from Its Demons?" *Religion Dispatches*, July 11, 2016, http://religiondispatches .org/is-america-willing-to-be-freed-from-its-demons.

114 Sims, *Lynched*, 22.

115 Given the self-perception of America being a city on a hill, it is not difficult to understand the tendency by many citizens to prefer "a form of historical amnesia" to an honest assessment of this past; Sims, *Lynched*, 29.

3 • Future

1 Justin Martyr, *1 Apol.* 6. Translation from Ante-Nicene Fathers.

2 Quoted in Levinson, *Written in Stone*, 45.

3 Levinson, *Written in Stone*, 48.

4 Landrieu also speaks of choosing a better future for New Orleans in his speech defending the removal of these monuments; cf. "Mitch Landrieu's Speech on the Removal of Confederate Monuments in New Orleans," *New York Times*, May 23, 2017, https://www.nytimes .com/2017/05/23/opinion/mitch-landrieus-speech-transcript.html.

5 Cf. Nelson and Olin, "Introduction," 6.

6 Erll, *Memory in Culture*, 29–30. Cf. David Glassberg, *American Historical Pageantry: The Uses of Tradition in the Early Twentieth Century* (Chapel Hill: University of North Carolina Press, 1990).

7 Paul Ricoeur, *Interpretation Theory: Discourse and the Surplus of Meaning* (Fort Worth: Texas Christian University Press, 1976). Cf. Dan Stiver, *Ricoeur and Theology* (London: Bloomsbury, 2012), 81–82.

8 Ludwig Wittgenstein, *Philosophical Investigations*, 4th ed., trans. G. E. M. Anscombe, P. M. S. Hacker, and Joachim Schulte (1953; Chichester, UK: Wiley-Blackwell, 2009), §610.

9 Stiver, *Ricoeur*, 30.

10 Ludwig Wittgenstein, *Remarks on the Philosophy of Psychology, Volume 2*, ed. G. H. von Wright and Heikki Nyman, trans. C. G. Luckhardt and A. E. Aue (Oxford: Blackwell, 1980), §629.

11 Ricoeur, *Interpretation Theory*, 58.

12 Jacques Rancière, *The Politics of Aesthetics: The Distribution of the Sensible* (2000; New York: Continuum, 2006). In this way are images positioned between that which is said and that which is symbolically and emotionally communicated. Indeed, "symbol" and "metaphor" are similar insofar as both are marked by double-meaning—what a signifier represents, what it implies, and the way in which the excess of signification has to be filled in by the viewer or hearer. Cf. Ricoeur, *Interpretation Theory*, 46, 55.

13 Rancière calls this the "imaging power of rupture"; his focus is on images in general rather than monuments. Jacques Rancière, *The Future of the Image*, trans. Gregory Elliott (2003; New York: Verso, 2007), 46.

14 This is a paraphrase of Jacques Rancière, who wrote that "by assembling words or forms, people define not merely various forms of art, but certain configurations of what can be seen and what can be thought, certain forms of inhabiting the material world." *Future*, 91.

15 I am drawing the insight regarding the relationship between aesthetics and ethics from Jennings, *Christian Imagination*, 274. The upshot is that before making pronouncements about how to theologically disrupt Confederate monuments, I want to take the advice of Wittgenstein: "Don't think, but look!" Wittgenstein, *Philosophical Investigations*, §66.

16 See Ricoeur, *Interpretation Theory*, 93–94. Ricoeur's use of horizons invokes the work of Hans-Georg Gadamer.

17 Savage, *Standing Soldiers*, 8.

18 Keefe-Perry, *Way to Water*, 205. This is based on a description of theopoetics provided by Catherine Keller.

19 Keefe-Perry, *Way to Water*, 206. This way of putting the matter dovetails with the analysis of white supremacy provided by Emilie Townes, who analyzes memory, history, and the power of images to describe what she calls the "fantastic hegemonic imagination." Cf. Townes, *Womanist Ethics*.

20 In speaking this way, I am evoking the idea that whiteness does not exist "out there" in some ephemeral imaginative world, nor only in the minds of individual actors, but also in space. Whiteness assumes physicality, such that one can say that race is spatialized as much as space is racialized. Cf. George Lipsitz, "The Racialization of Space and the Spatialization of Race: Theorizing the Hidden Architecture of Landscape," *Landscape Journal* 26, no. 1 (2007): 10–23. Of course, as Lipsitz makes clear, this spatialization goes well beyond the import of any monument, and involves myriad practices that spatialize race, from school district boundaries to police practices, zoning regulations to the

design of transit systems. Monuments are but a single marker of this wider spatialization process.

21 Savage, *Standing Soldiers*, 177. Savage calls this the duality between hero and servant.

22 See Wilson, *Baptized in Blood*, 19.

23 Foster, *Ghosts*, 40, 273. Cf. the helpful interactive map produced by the Southern Poverty Law Center: "Whose Heritage?"

24 Foster, *Ghosts*, 82.

25 Savage, *Standing Soldiers*, 166–67.

26 For the classic argument for the late arrival of Jim Crow (as opposed to the argument of some of its defenders that it was how things "always had been"), cf. C. Vann Woodward, *The Strange Career of Jim Crow* (1955; Oxford: Oxford University Press, 2002). Given the active construction of Jim Crow rule, monuments and the ceremonies that accompanied their dedication were crucial for inventing this tradition (to use Eric Hobsbawm's phrase).

27 Common soldier statues were typically constructed by one of only a few companies, who were not shy about advertising in cities and towns that lacked "their own" monument; Foster, *Ghosts*, 129–30.

28 Savage, *Standing Soldiers*, 164.

29 As Savage puts it: "Neither marked as transcendent and commanding, on the one hand, nor as bound and immobilized, on the other, the typical standing soldier offered an image of quiet self-discipline." *Standing Soldiers*, 176.

30 Savage, *Standing Soldiers*, 168.

31 Savage, *Standing Soldiers*, 162.

32 Shackel, *Memory*, 3–4.

33 Savage, *Standing Soldiers*, 176. Put differently, the body's meaning is fundamentally symbolic, "congealed through symbolic repetition and iteration that emits certain signs and presupposes certain norms." George Yancy, *Black Bodies, White Gazes: The Continuing Significance of Race in America*, 2nd ed. (Lanham, Md.: Rowman & Littlefield, 2017), xxxvi.

34 Savage, *Standing Soldiers*, 22–23.

35 Savage, *Standing Soldiers*, 66–67.

36 Savage, *Standing Soldiers*, 27–28.

37 Wilson, *Baptized in Blood*, 101.

38 Savage goes on to say of the monument that it is "most drastically a negation of the conventional markers of masculinity now monopolized by the white man above. Frozen forever in this unfortunate

juxtaposition, the monument is not really about emancipation but about its opposite—domination." *Standing Soldiers*, 90.

39 Savage, *Standing Soldiers*, 120. A monument that intended to celebrate emancipation still ended up suggesting that it only came through "the body of the white hero; the black body melted back into invisibility." *Standing Soldiers*, 88.

40 Savage, *Standing Soldiers*, 129–30. This was in direct opposition to the figure of Lincoln, who in his gangly stature and appearance was considered to be an aesthetic challenge, "the sculpturally impossible"; Savage, *Standing Soldiers*, 131–32.

41 Savage, *Standing Soldiers*, 134–35. Savage goes on: "The great power of this equestrian image was that it could bridge the old regime of slavery and the new regime of white rule without explicitly representing either; it helped legitimate the continuity between the two even as it disguised the physical and institutional forces that propped up both of them."

42 Savage, *Standing Soldiers*, 138.

43 Blight, *Race and Reunion*, 51.

44 Savage, *Standing Soldiers*, 149–50. Savage describes the intense fight over the design of the Lee monument, revealing that those involved knew the political stakes of getting the aesthetics exactly "right"; *Standing Soldiers*, 135–48.

45 Statues to Lee thus asserted a white ideal while also imagining an antebellum South that was basically free of slavery; Savage, *Standing Soldiers*, 150. Savage summarizes the dual effect regarding monuments well: while the winners of the war, through the Emancipation Monument, "were trying to rewrite the future into the past, the losers were trying to rewrite the past in order to change their future." *Standing Soldiers*, 18.

46 Savage, *Standing Soldiers*, 167, 181, 184.

47 Savage, *Standing Soldiers*, 210. The peak of Confederate monument construction and the common soldier statue, 1880–1920, correlates with the heyday of "muscular Christianity," which sought to "reclaim" the manliness of Jesus and the common man over against the purported "feminization" of American men. Cf. Kelly J. Baker, *Gospel According to the Klan: The KKK's Appeal to Protestant America, 1915–1930* (Lawrence: University Press of Kansas, 2011), 99–102.

48 Of course, concern with the "ideal" human form is common in white supremacist ideologies. One thinks of the Nazi obsession with celebrating the Aryan form—represented well in the 1938 propaganda film *Olympia: Festival of Beauty* about the 1936 Olympic games, which opens

with ten minutes of white athletes being positioned as statues. More recently, it was evident among the alt-right marchers in Charlottesville in 2017, who were instructed to be in good physical shape, well-dressed, sexy, and hip. In advance of the rally one organizer wrote: "It is very important to look good. . . . I cannot stress the point hard enough . . . we need to be extremely conscious of what we look like, and how we present ourselves. That matters more than our ideas. . . . If people see a bunch of mismatched overweight slobs, they are not going to care what they are saying." Jane Coaston, "What Sunday's Unite the Right 2 rally tells us about the state of the alt-right in America," *Vox*, August 12, 2018, https://www.vox.com/2018/8/12/17678974/alt-right-nazi-white-supremacy-rally-washington-august.

49 Eduardo Bonilla-Silva, *Racism without Racists: Color-Blind Racism and the Persistence of Racial Inequality in America*, 5th ed. (2003; Lanham, Md.: Rowman & Littlefield, 2018), 8.

50 Shackel, *Memory*, 3.

51 Shackel, *Memory*, 4.

52 Emilie Townes describes the phenomenon of white people not thinking of themselves as having a color in terms of "uninterrogated coloredness." *Womanist Ethics*, 57–78. On the way uninterrogated whiteness is revealed in Confederate monuments, see Karen V. Guth, "Sacred Emblems of Faith: Womanist Contributions to the Confederate Monument Debate," *Journal of the Society of Christian Ethics* 39, no. 2 (2019): 375–93. For a helpful analysis of this logic as it manifested among the Ku Klux Klan (at two different stages of its development), cf. Cunningham, *Klansville, U.S.A.*, and Baker, *Gospel According to the Klan*, 162–97.

53 Yancy, *Black Bodies, White Gazes*, 245. While this same logic applies to other groups as well (Asian, Native American, etc.), Yancy argues that black people have occupied a unique position: as the polar opposite of "white," black people were not simply "divergent" from the standard, but a different kind of person altogether; Yancy, *Black Bodies, White Gazes*, 37–38.

54 This notion of the white gaze, coined by George Yancy, recalls the notion of "double consciousness." Cf. Du Bois, *Souls*.

55 This is similar to Gramsci's understanding of hegemony as involving both coercion and consent. Regarding whiteness, this phenomenon is what leads Bonilla-Silva to refer to the "white habitus"; *Racism without Racists*, 121, 139–40.

56 Reestablishing this white common denominator was especially important at the turn of the twentieth century given the massive influx of European immigrants (more than twenty million people) coming to the

country between 1880 and 1920—coterminous with the peak of Confederate monument construction and the common soldier aesthetic. Cf. Baker, *Gospel According to the Klan*, 6, 44–45. Common soldier statues thus served to present an aesthetic North Star for not-yet-white immigrants, giving something these groups may potentially unite around or achieve over time. This assertion squares with the observation made by Eric Hobsbawm about monuments in Europe during a similar timeframe: they served to create and reinforce social cohesion, identity, and particularly structured social relations. Eric Hobsbawm, "Mass Producing Traditions: Europe, 1870–1914," in *The Invention of Tradition*, ed. Eric Hobsbawm and Terence Ranger (Cambridge: Cambridge University Press, 1983), 271–72.

57 "And because the group life of the various racially defined groups is based on hierarchy and domination, the ruling ideology expresses as 'common sense' the interests of the dominant race." Bonilla-Silva, *Racism without Racists*, 9.

58 Du Bois, *Black Reconstruction*, 708.

59 Blight, *Race and Reunion*, 107.

60 Cf. Shackel, *Memory*, 19.

61 Yancy, *Black Bodies, White Gazes*, 3.

62 As Yancy puts it, "Poor whites were fed on Jim Crow, even as their stomachs were empty." *Black Bodies, White Gazes*, 20.

63 One of the best explorations of the way black people can internalize white patterns of thought is the movie *Get Out* (2017). For his part, Yancy quotes a Congolese man who was receiving skin injections to make his skin lighter (a common practice throughout Africa, especially Nigeria and Togo): "'I pray every day and I ask God, "God why did you make me black? I don't like being black. I don't like black skin."'" To invoke the theological here implies a kind of cosmic punishment; that Blackness is a stain of sin, that which is to be mourned." Yancy notes that there is even a theodicy question invoked: Why would an omnibenevolent God inflict upon someone a dark epidermis, that which is symbolic of "evil," "inferiority," "ugliness"? *Black Bodies, White Gazes*, 169–70.

64 Yancy, *Black Bodies, White Gazes*, 176.

65 Yancy, *Black Bodies, White Gazes*, 180.

66 Yancy, *Black Bodies, White Gazes*, xv, 175.

67 Cf. Eric A. Weed, *The Religion of White Supremacy in the United States* (Lanham, Md.: Lexington, 2017).

68 Jennings, *Christian Imagination*, 78. This insight is similar to one made by James Baldwin: "The black man has functioned in the white man's

world as a fixed star, as an immovable pillar: and as he moves out of his place, heaven and earth are shaken to their foundations." James Baldwin, *The Fire Next Time* (New York: Dial, 1963), 23. Of course, as Wendell Berry notes, the irony is that this ties white and black people together, and that white racists *need* black people to maintain their sense of superiority. Cf. *The Hidden Wound* (1970; Berkeley: Counterpoint, 2010), 78.

69 Yancy, *Black Bodies, White Gazes*, 38.

70 Jennings, *Christian Imagination*, 258.

71 Jennings, *Christian Imagination*, 292. Cf. Willie James Jennings, *Acts* (Louisville: Westminster John Knox, 2017).

72 Jennings, *Christian Imagination*, 33.

73 Jennings, *Christian Imagination*, 254.

74 Jennings, *Christian Imagination*, 258.

75 Jennings, *Christian Imagination*, 36.

76 Jennings, *Christian Imagination*, 23–28.

77 Jennings, *Christian Imagination*, 63. Jennings shows that whiteness drove a wedge between people and the land itself, such that the development of whiteness and the alienation from the earth go hand in hand. *Christian Imagination*, 258, 262–63.

78 Jennings, *Christian Imagination*, 248.

79 Jennings, *Christian Imagination*, 292.

80 In its purest form, this view is expressed in claims—depressingly contemporary claims—that God is a racist. In 2018 Russell Walker ran for the state House of Representatives in North Carolina while claiming that God is a racist (literally) and that Jewish people "descend from Satan." He lost, but received around 37 percent of the vote. Cf. Abbie Bennett, "'God is racist,' Jewish people 'all descend from Satan,' NC candidate says," *News and Observer* (Raleigh, N.C.), June 27, 2018; "GOP to write more laws before grip loosens," *News and Observer*, November 8, 2018. For a classic reflection that takes this troubling conviction seriously as a prompt for black theodicy, cf. William R. Jones, *Is God a White Racist? A Preamble to Black Theology* (1973; Boston: Beacon, 1998).

81 Cf. Carter, *Race*, 91.

82 Jennings, *Christian Imagination*, 30–31, 78. "Instead, the body of another has remained at the center of our relational imagination, the body of a powerful, white, Western man, the image of self-sufficiency, social power, and self-determination." Jennings, *Christian Imagination*, 286.

83 Jennings, *Christian Imagination*, 60. The notion of whiteness, for Jennings, marks a purported category of people who relate to others and

the earth only as a teacher relates to a student. This, of course, directly contrasts with the figure of the "savage." Thus does Carter point to Kant's understanding of whiteness as a "race" that is not quite a race, or more than a race—a race that transcends race precisely because of its "developmental progress." *Race*, 88.

84 While this is beyond the purview of this book, these statues also map onto the assumed priority of (and a particular understanding of) masculinity over femininity, which was also a common concern at the time of their construction. Cf. Barbee, *Race and Masculinity*; and Foster, *Ghosts*, 124.

85 Jennings, *Christian Imagination*, 61.

86 I am here paraphrasing J. Kameron Carter: "The teleological end, which is the consummation of all things within the economic, political, and aesthetic—in short, within the structural—reality called 'whiteness,' is on the one hand made present and available now in white people and in white 'culture.' And on the other hand, it is through these white people and culture that the full reality of whiteness will globally expand to 'eschatologically' encompass all things and so bring the world to perfection." *Race*, 89.

87 The perfection of whiteness is here understood "in terms of an aesthetic (and thus an ethics) of balance over imbalance, of completeness over incompleteness." Carter, *Race*, 89.

88 Carter, *Race*, 90, 118.

89 Certain groups have always found themselves "in the middle" of this spectrum, between complete perfection and degradation. In particular, the Jews have frequently occupied a racially ambivalent position viz. whiteness, at least from the dominant European perspective. Cf. Carter, *Race*, 104–5.

90 Cf. Wilson, *Baptized in Blood*, 128–29.

91 On the mammy myth and the proposed mammy monument, see Townes, *Womanist Ethics*, 31–42.

92 This is an altered version of an argument made by J. Kameron Carter about critical treatments of race; *Race*, 40.

93 By saying that whiteness is not beautiful, I do not mean that lacking melanin is ugly or bad; by whiteness I mean the sense of Anglo-European supremacy that became associated with certain physical features, the inverse of what happened with blackness. I mean to say that Christians should resist "the white gaze," even—especially—if they are Anglo.

94 Of course, it is a basic tenet of speech-act theory that the meaning of an utterance is affected by the one doing the speaking. The same claim can mean completely different things depending on who says it, and when.

95 This kind of statement is ubiquitous in black liberation theology. Especially illuminating articulations of the differences between these visions of God—indeed, different understandings of Christ—are found in Reggie Williams, *Bonhoeffer's Black Jesus: Harlem Renaissance Theology and an Ethic of Resistance* (Waco: Baylor University Press, 2014); Kelly Brown Douglas, *The Black Christ* (Maryknoll, N.Y.: Orbis, 1994); Jacquelyn Grant, *White Women's Christ and Black Women's Jesus: Feminist Christology and Womanist Response* (Atlanta: Scholars Press, 1989); and James H. Cone, *A Black Theology of Liberation* (1970; Maryknoll, N.Y.: Orbis, 1986).

96 On idolatry and iconography, see Natalie Carnes, *Image and Presence: A Christological Reflection on Iconoclasm and Iconophilia* (Stanford: Stanford University Press, 2017).

97 Vincent W. Lloyd, *Religion of the Field Negro: On Black Secularism and Black Theology* (New York: Fordham University Press, 2018), 149–50.

98 Lloyd, *Religion*, 158–59.

99 Lloyd, *Religion*, 160.

100 Yancy, *Black Bodies, White Gazes*, 121.

101 Bruce T. Morrill, S.J., *Anamnesis as Dangerous Memory: Political and Liturgical Theology in Dialogue* (Collegeville, Minn.: Pueblo, 2000), 189. These thoughts echo the theology of Johann Baptist Metz.

102 It should thus be clear that I find laws making it impossible to remove Confederate monuments or change building names without the approval of the legislature to be egregious.

103 As Savage goes on: it would also involve, "at the very least, a reexamination of the myth of a united American people with equal representation in political and cultural domains." *Standing Soldiers*, 208, 191.

104 "If you are white, though, know that you are part of a system that would rather you live a lie than risk you seeing the truth. If you are white, you *must* face a certain kind of death—the death of your narrowness of vision, the death of your white narcissism, the death of your 'innocence,' the death of your neoliberal assumptions, the death of the metanarrative of meritocracy, the death of all of those things that underwrite your white gaze as the only way of seeing the world. This book asks that you die to such lies in order that you might truly live." Yancy, *Black Bodies, White Gazes*, xxii–xxiii.

105 Smith, *Weird John Brown*, 153–54.

4 • Present

1 James Baldwin, "Faulkner and Desegregation," in *Nobody Knows My Name*, 126.

2 "Exhibits that address class privilege and racial exploitation during the colonial and antebellum eras are now commonplace, but sites that delve into the political and economic underpinnings of white power during the era of Jim Crow remain rare. Apparently it is easier for museums to acknowledge the wealth and power that white slaveholders accrued than to address the benefits that whites in recent times received from the maintenance of white supremacy." Brundage, *Southern Past*, 318–19.

3 As Maurice Halbwachs puts it, "A 'current of social thought' is ordinarily as invisible as the atmosphere we breathe. In normal life its existence is recognized only when it is resisted." *The Collective Memory*, 38.

4 This is akin to what David Glassberg calls a "sense of history," a stance toward events from the past that were not experienced firsthand but give people a sense of place, locatedness, and belonging; it locates a people in time, such that they know *who* and *where* they are now, in the present. David Glassberg, *Sense of History: The Place of the Past in American Life* (Amherst: University of Massachusetts Press, 2001), 7.

5 Nelson and Olin, "Introduction," 7.

6 As Joy Sather-Wagstaff writes, commemorative sites are not automatically sacred or important, but imbued with meanings that are negotiated, constructed, and reconstructed through human action in the present. They are not static. See Sather-Wagstaff, *Heritage That Hurts*, 20.

7 "These officials saw the past as a device that could help them attain these goals and never tired of using commemoration to restate what they thought the social order and citizen behavior should be." Bodnar, *Remaking America*, 245.

8 What is more, the materials that are used to prompt memory are integral to the way the past gets constructed. "The materiality of the medium is every bit as much involved in these constructions as is the social dimension: The producers and recipients of a medium of memory actively perform the work of construction—both in the decision as to which phenomena will be ascribed the qualities of memory media, as well as in the encoding and coding of that which is (to be) remembered." Erll, *Memory in Culture*, 125–26. As John Gillis puts it, people's engagement with material objects in space and over time shapes the mediation and performance of memory. Put simply, "Identities and memories are not things we think *about*, but things we

think *with.* . . . We must take responsibility for their uses and abuses, recognizing that every assertion of identity involves a choice that affects not just ourselves but others." John R. Gillis, "Memory and Identity," 5.

9 Because the power struggles behind monuments are usually forgotten over time, studying the fights and struggles over monuments of more recent vintage is a fruitful exercise. See Dana Heller, *The Selling of 9/11: How a National Tragedy Became a Commodity* (New York: Palgrave Macmillan, 2005); Linenthal, *Unfinished Bombing*; Setha M. Low, "Lessons from Imagining the World Trade Center Site: An Examination of Public Space and Culture," *Anthropology and Education Quarterly* 33, no. 3 (2002): 395–405; and Yifat Gutman, "Where Do We Go from Here: The Pasts, Presents, and Futures of Ground Zero," *Memory Studies* 2, no. 1 (2009): 55–70.

10 The past is not ontologically past (any more than our time is ontologically present). Rather, "the past is only past because there is a present, just as I can point to something *over there* because I am *here*. But nothing is inherently over there or here." Trouillot, *Silencing the Past*, 15.

11 Nelson and Olin, "Introduction," 6.

12 "As these negotiations always take place in the present, memory is directed toward the future, not the past, and is thus a highly temporal, dynamic, and contingent act." Alfred Reichardt, "The Dangers of Remembering: Sites and Temporalities of Memory in William Faulkner's *Light in August*," in *Sites of Memory in American Literatures and Cultures*, ed. Udo J. Hebel (Heidelberg: Universitätsverlag C. Winter, 2003), 73.

13 This example and line of thought is from Trouillot, *Silencing the Past*, 114–15. Trouillot goes on to say that "many historical controversies boil down to who has the power to name what." Far from a quibble over semantics, "the power to decide what is trivial—and annoying—is also part of the power to decide how 'what happened' becomes 'that which is said to have happened.'"

14 James E. Young, *Stages of Memory: Reflections on Memorial Art, Loss, and the Spaces Between* (Amherst: University of Massachusetts Press, 2016), 16. The processes that give rise to monuments "might also be regarded as a never-to-be-completed process, animated (not disabled) by the forces of history that bring it into being." If this process is done well, the images, slogans, and rituals that surround a historical construction can even come to replace the more mundane and contested realities they seek to represent, and thus can come to "seem more authentic to the masses than the original events they mimic or celebrate." Trouillot, *Silencing the Past*, 137.

15 Erll, *Memory in Culture*, 124–25.

16 See Trouillot, *Silencing the Past*, 151. The form this popular "consent" takes, of course, goes well beyond the monument or site in question, and extends to the variety of constructed items and visits that can emerge around a momentous place or event—the way it is consumed by people, which always outstrips the intentions of any designer. Cf. Sather-Wagstaff, *Heritage That Hurts*, 30–34, 118–19; Marita Sturken, *Tourists of History: Memory, Kitsch, and Consumerism from Oklahoma City to Ground Zero* (Durham: Duke University Press, 2007).

17 Young, *Stages of Memory*, 7, 10. Young says this is particularly a temptation when it comes to monuments to historical atrocities like the Holocaust.

18 Young, *Stages of Memory*, 16.

19 Nelson and Olin, "Introduction," 6–7.

20 Cf. Bergman, *Exhibiting Patriotism*, ch. 4.

21 Trouillot, *Silencing the Past*, 148.

22 Trouillot, *Silencing the Past*, 150. Trouillot continues, "From that viewpoint, the collective guilt of some white liberals toward 'the slave past' of the United States, or the 'colonial past' of Europe can be both misplaced and inauthentic. As a response to current accusations, it is misplaced inasmuch as these individuals are not responsible for the actions of their chosen ancestors. As a self-inflicted wound, it is comfortable inasmuch as it protects *them* from a racist present."

23 James Young's classic study shows how Holocaust memorials are colored by the place and time in which they are located; they reveal as much about the societies that constructed them as they do of the past. Cf. Young, *Texture of Memory*.

24 For a reflection on this monument, see Alfred Frankowski, *The Post-Racial Limits of Memorialization: Toward a Political Sense of Mourning* (Lanham, Md.: Lexington, 2015), 25–27; and James Young, *At Memory's Edge: After-Images of the Holocaust in Contemporary Art and Architecture* (New Haven: Yale University Press, 2000).

25 Frankowski, *Post-Racial Limits*, 27.

26 Trouillot, *Silencing the Past*, xviii.

27 The "us" here is implied, which makes me think of the so-called Tonto principle associated with Stanley Hauerwas: "What do you mean 'we,' white man?" Interestingly, James Baldwin invoked this anecdote from the Lone Ranger to discuss the politics of the first-person plural, calling it a "Negro joke." Cf. "The White Problem," in *The Cross of Redemption: Uncollected Writings*, ed. Randall Kenan (New York: Pantheon, 2010), 93.

28 Indeed, after increased pressure and political mobilization following the events in Charlottesville, the monument was removed from its location in downtown Winston-Salem on March 12, 2019, with plans to put it up in Salem Cemetery. The United Daughters of the Confederacy attempted to block the statue's removal by suing the city and county, a complaint that was dismissed with prejudice.

29 See Levinson, *Written in Stone*, 25. I am also reminded of the celebration that happened when the statue of Saddam Hussein in Baghdad was toppled in 2003.

30 Erika Doss shows how the rapid construction of monuments and memorials in the contemporary United States reflects present-day anxieties and passions—anxieties surely manifest in the way Americans inherit already-standing monuments as well. That is, monuments reflect issues of contemporary political concern (rather than "just" matters of history), which is why debates surrounding them are so often heated. See Doss, *Memorial Mania*.

31 James Wm. McClendon Jr., *Doctrine: Systematic Theology, Volume 2* (Nashville: Abingdon, 1994), 466.

32 Cf. Edward W. Soja, *Postmodern Geographies: The Reassertion of Space in Critical Social Theory* (New York: Verso, 1989). Soja argues that critical analyses of space must be considered along with history and sociality, what he calls the "trialectics of being," and that spatiality includes what is perceived, conceived, and lived. In spaces of this sort, the divisions between these modes are problematized if not collapsed. Cf. Edward W. Soja, "Thirdspace: Expanding the Scope of the Geographical Imagination," in *Human Geography Today*, ed. Doreen Massey, John Allen, and Philip Sarre (Malden, Mass.: Polity, 1999), 260–78.

33 Cf. Mary Nickel, "A Sign among You: Mnemonic Monuments and Communal Remembering in the Fourth Chapter of Joshua" (unpublished paper, December 10, 2015), 8–11.

34 To say this community is imagined is not to say it is unimportant or unreal, but simply to point out that members "will never know most of their fellow-members, meet them, or even hear of them, yet in the minds of each lives the image of their communion." Benedict Anderson, *Imagined Communities: Reflections on the Origin and Spread of Nationalism*, rev. ed. (1983; New York: Verso, 2016), 6.

35 Alasdair MacIntyre, *After Virtue: A Study in Moral Theory*, 2nd ed. (1981; Notre Dame: University of Notre Dame Press, 1984), 216.

36 Nelson and Olin, "Introduction," 4.

37 On the nuances and extended uses of the word "space," cf. Henri Lefe-
    bvre, *The Production of Space*, trans. Donald Nicholson-Smith (1974;
    Oxford: Blackwell, 1991).

38 Bonnie Honig, *Public Things: Democracy in Disrepair* (New York: Ford-
    ham University Press, 2017), 13. Examples of such "things" include
    bridges, roads, and other components of infrastructure; parks and
    libraries; schools; and indeed, monuments.

39 Honig, *Public Things*, 4–5, 7.

40 Honig, *Public Things*, 17.

41 Honig, *Public Things*, 2, 36. Monuments can bring people together as
    well as tear them apart; "public things act on publics not only expres-
    sively but also disturbingly, in ways that bind and *un*bind us." Honig,
    Public Things, 7.

42 Honig chiefly has in mind contestations over public parks, schools, and
    pools, among other things.

43 Honig, *Public Things*, 24.

44 On being born into a world of things, cf. Honig, *Public Things*, 35.

45 Honig, *Public Things*, 38.

46 For a classic study on the importance of collective mourning, why it
    did not happen in Germany after the second World War, and the soci-
    etal consequences for neglecting this work, cf. Alexander Mitscherlich
    and Margarete Mitscherlich, *The Inability to Mourn* (1967; New York:
    Grove Press, 1975).

47 Cf. Sherrilyn A. Ifill, *On the Courthouse Lawn: Confronting the Legacy of
    Lynching in the Twenty-First Century* (Boston: Beacon, 2007).

48 Cf. Frankowski, *Post-Racial Limits*.

49 Cf. Kelly Brown Douglas, *Stand Your Ground: Black Bodies and the Justice
    of God* (Maryknoll, N.Y.: Orbis, 2015), 3–47; and Richard T. Hughes,
    *Myths America Lives By: White Supremacy and the Stories That Give Us
    Meaning* (Urbana: University of Illinois Press, 2003).

50 Bridgette Holley, "Sins of the Past," *News and Observer* (Raleigh,
    N.C.), January 13, 2016. The insistence on focusing on the interiority
    and intentions of individual actors is typical of evangelical piety, and a
    major reason they have trouble addressing structural sins like racism.
    Cf. Michael O. Emerson and Christian Smith, *Divided by Faith: Evan-
    gelical Religion and the Problem of Race in America* (New York: Oxford
    University Press, 2000).

51 Thinking of whiteness as a power that outstrips any individual actor
    evokes William Stringfellow, *My People Is the Enemy* (New York:
    Holt, Rinehart, and Winston, 1964); and Delores Williams' work
    on "demonarchy," by which she means white systems of power that
    control and dehumanize black women in particular; "The Color of

Feminism: or Speaking the Black Woman's Tongue," *Journal of Religious Thought* 43, no. 1 (1986): 52. While whiteness is a wound for the most unrepentant white supremacist, it is also true for those who wish it were otherwise but know they cannot opt out of their inheritance so easily.

52 Frankowski, *Post-Racial Limits*, 4–5.

53 Aleida Assmann, "Three Stabilizers of Memory: Affect–Symbol–Trauma," in Hebel, *Sites of Memory*, 29–30.

54 Cf. Sunder John Boopalan, *Memory, Grief, and Agency: A Political Theological Account of Wrongs and Rites* (New York: Palgrave Macmillan, 2017).

55 Cf. Jones, *Trauma and Grace*.

56 Rambo, *Resurrecting Wounds*, 29–30.

57 Rambo, *Resurrecting Wounds*, 32. I am again reminded of Miroslav Volf's reflections on Jesus' scars (eventually) going away in the eschaton; see Volf, *End of Memory*, 190–91. This is distinct from Augustine, who famously argued that some wounds will remain even in heaven. See also Boopalan, *Memory, Grief, and Agency*, ch. 4.

58 Rambo, *Resurrecting Wounds*, 36.

59 Rambo, *Resurrecting Wounds*, 4.

60 Rambo, *Resurrecting Wounds*, 5.

61 Rambo, *Resurrecting Wounds*, 64.

62 Rambo, *Resurrecting Wounds*, 42.

63 Rambo, *Resurrecting Wounds*, 150.

64 Rambo, *Resurrecting Wounds*, 14.

65 Rambo, *Resurrecting Wounds*, 72. Cf. Berry, *Hidden Wound*, 21.

66 Berry, *Hidden Wound*, 9.

67 Rambo, *Resurrecting Wounds*, 78–79.

68 Rambo, *Resurrecting Wounds*, 83–84.

69 Rambo, *Resurrecting Wounds*, 91.

70 Karl Barth, *Ethics*, ed. Dietrich Braun, trans. Geoffrey W. Bromiley (New York: Seabury Press, 1981), 508; cf. Victor Thasiah, "Second Realities: Karl Barth's Ethics and Socially Engaged Art" (unpublished paper, Pacific Society of Christian Ethics, February 10, 2012), 6–7. This sentiment is consonant with critical theory insofar as it looks for "a mode of discourse which projects normative possibilities unrealized but felt in a particular given social reality." Iris Marion Young, *Justice and the Politics of Difference* (1990; Princeton: Princeton University Press, 2011), 6.

71 One might say that Confederate monuments have slowly formed a kind of "heterotopic" space that is vaguely unsettling to those who are not inducted into its space and world. The path explored here is partly an

attempt to use Confederate monuments to recreate a heterotopia for people who are not unsettled by such monuments (but should be). This is not an impossible task given that Confederate monuments already open onto realities beyond those that are immediately evident. Cf. Michel Foucault, "Of Other Spaces," *Diacritics* 16, no. 1 (1986): 22–27.

72 Thasiah, "Second Realities"; cf. T. J. Gorringe, *Earthly Visions: Theology and the Challenges of Art* (New Haven: Yale University Press, 2011).

73 As Barth writes, "Sighing for redemption, dissatisfaction with self, questioning our present in light of our future . . . has to take form. We have to *breathe* in the atmosphere of the redemption hidden in the future. We have to *act* in the experience of the coming Redeemer. We are ordered to fight, to build, to work, to organize, to fashion things." *Ethics*, 490. Quoted in Thasiah, "Second Realities," 5.

74 I was not raised to revere Confederate monuments or the narratives the monuments conjure—quite the opposite—and I confess to finding them offensive and unappealing. I deeply understand the inclination to pull them all down, and perhaps even to eschew all forms of public visual expression as irredeemably problematic.

75 Americans do not tend to remember for the sake of justice or truth-telling, but rather remember in ways that reinforce our perceived innocence. As such, it is an open question how this museum will fare going forward. Sturken argues this is evident chiefly in the American response to national trauma through consumerism, sentimental kitsch, and tourism. Cf. Sturken, *Tourists of History*. Of course, the lynching museum may also manifest the opposite of sentimental kitsch, "dark tourism," which faces the horror of certain events but usually does not encourage making the kinds of connections that would do the work of justice in the present. Cf. John Lennon and Malcolm Foley, *Dark Tourism: The Attraction of Death and Disaster* (London: Continuum, 2000).

76 Rambo, *Resurrecting Wounds*, 150. For Rambo this includes confronting "the complexities of life beyond 'deaths,' whether literal or figurative."

77 See Julian Carr, "Unveiling of Confederate Monument at University," Chapel Hill, June 2, 1913, http://hgreen.people.ua.edu/transcription -carr-speech.html. Carr's evocation of the Anglo-Saxon myth again recalls Kelly Brown Douglas' analysis in *Stand Your Ground*, ch. 1.

78 These thoughts are informed by Pierre Nora's warnings about memory in "Between Memory and History."

79 Rambo, *Resurrecting Wounds*, ch. 4.

80 See Soja's collection of quotes from bell hooks in Soja, "Thirdspace," 270–72.

81 Rambo, *Resurrecting Wounds*, 95–96.

82 Cf. Tran, *Vietnam War.*

83 In pointing to the importance of something like receptive, multiethnic encounter in which difference is celebrated rather than subsumed into a wider universal, I have in mind Willie Jennings' reflections on Pentecost in *Christian Imagination*, 293.

84 Making these connections *well* takes nuance. Black communities tend to be better at recognizing ways the present typologically echoes the past and provides glimpses of what is to come. Sims, *Lynched*, 29.

85 Cf. Ifill, *On the Courthouse Lawn.*

86 Cf. Jonathan Lear, "Gettysburg Mourning," *Critical Inquiry* 45, no. 1 (2018): 97–121.

87 Young, *Stages of Memory*, 16.

88 Cone, *Oppressed*, 99.

5 • Apocalypse

1 Friedrich Nietzsche, *The Anti-Christ* (1895), in *The Portable Nietzsche*, trans. Walter Kaufman (New York: Viking, 1959), §55, 639–40.

2 Some examples include a monument erected to Confederate soldiers in 2018, placed in a privately owned park in Mobile, Alabama; another in Brantley, Alabama, erected in 2017; a "Confederate Memorial of the Wind," erected on private land in Orange, Texas but purposely visible from the interstate; and a common soldier statue erected in Chickamauga, Georgia, put up in 2016, which includes a quote from the Gospel of John at its base: "Greater love hath no man than this, that a man lay down his life for his friends."

3 "Jack Kershaw Is Dead at 96; Challenged Conviction in King's Death," *New York Times*, September 24, 2010, https://www.nytimes.com/2010/09/24/us/24kershaw.html.

4 "Sons of Confederate Veterans Plan More Flags along NC Interstates," *WRAL*, January 25, 2018, https://www.wral.com/sons-of-confederate-veterans-plan-more-flags-along-nc-interstates/17288896. For example, a Confederate "mega-flag" was raised along I-40 on December 6, 2018, to counter the removal of the common soldier statue from the University of North Carolina's campus, with accompanying yard signs that read: "Save Our Monuments, Preserve Our History." https://www.wral.com/confederate-mega-flag-raised-along-i-40-to-protest-silent-sam-removal/18044308.

5 The monument was dedicated by the SCV of Smithfield, the same town that until 1977 had a billboard featuring a Klansman and the slogan, "Join and Support the United Klans of America." On Klan activity in North Carolina, cf. Cunningham, *Klansville, U.S.A.*

6 For instance, Memphis briefly contemplated selling their own monument to Forrest to a community who wanted it. This did not end up happening due to public outcry. A community who succeeded in this process was the University of Louisville, who moved their Confederate monument to Brandenburg, Kentucky in 2016. Cf. "A 121-year-old Confederate monument was coming down. This Kentucky town put it back up," *Washington Post*, August 20, 2017.

7 I am here evoking Richard Hughes' unpacking of six myths that fund the contemporary American psyche, all of which conspicuously ignore the myth of white supremacy that underlies all the others. Cf. Hughes, *Myths America Lives By*.

8 I owe this recognition to Jeffrey P. Bishop, *The Anticipatory Corpse: Medicine, Power, and the Care of the Dying* (Notre Dame: University of Notre Dame Press, 2011), 18.

9 At their most extreme, palliative monuments evoke a story that is pure fiction—as in Donald Trump's construction of a monument to a nonexistent Civil War battle that he put up on his golf course in Sterling, Virginia. (When told by historians that no such battle happened at this site, Trump responded, "How would they know that? Were they there?") Joyce Chen, "Donald Trump's Golf Course Plaque Honors Fake Civil War Battle," *Rolling Stone*, August 17, 2017, https://www.rollingstone.com/politics/politics-news/donald-trumps-golf-course-plaque-honors-fake-civil-war-battle-253119/. But this is rare. Usually, palliative monuments conceal in the way they narrate the events they recall. The atomic particle of palliation is not fiction, but emphasis.

10 I have in mind Augustine's prayer in the *Confessions*: "You, O Lord, turned me back upon myself. You took me from behind my own back, where I had placed myself because I did not wish to look upon myself." *The Confessions of St. Augustine*, trans. John K. Ryan (New York: Doubleday, 1960), 8.7.

11 See Smith, *Weird John Brown*, esp. 153–55, 177.

12 To reiterate, this applies only and specifically to monuments. All Confederate flags should be permanently removed from public spaces and state seals. They signal current, active allegiance.

13 All responses to Confederate monuments require discernment. Not everything about the past should be remembered, nor everything forgotten. What is required is what Paul Ricoeur calls a "just allotment" of memory. Ricoeur, *Memory*, xv.

14 I am taking the sentiment of shifting from center to periphery from Karen Guth.

15 Cf. David Lowenthal, *The Past Is a Foreign Country—Revisited* (Cambridge: Cambridge University Press, 2015).

16 "If we are indeed suffering from a surfeit of memory, we do need to make the effort to distinguish usable pasts from disposable pasts. Discrimination and productive remembering are called for, and mass culture and the virtual media are not inherently irreconcilable with that purpose." Huyssen, *Present Pasts*, 29.

17 That is to say, a monument may *become* noticed and painful upon being slated for removal, or *become* an object of defense only because it is threatened. "Threats to destroy or alter monuments, destructive parodies, and actual destruction are all integral to monumental and memorial discourses, as are the signs of destruction themselves. Sometimes an object becomes a monument only when it is destroyed or altered." Jaś Elsner, "Iconoclasm and the Preservation of Memory," in Nelson and Olin, *Monuments and Memory, Made and Unmade*, 205.

18 The unwelcome presence of "Silent Sam," which previously sat on the campus of the University of North Carolina, manifested this challenge exactly. After years of back and forth with the North Carolina state legislature, the statue was finally yanked down by protesters. Shockingly, some efforts were made to put the monument back up, despite the fact that most people at UNC—and notably the black faculty who wrote an open letter to this effect—did not want it, contextualized or otherwise. That should settle the matter, it seems to me, but for many it did not.

19 Berrigan's exact statement for the Catonsville Nine was, "Our apologies, good friends, for the fracture of good order, the burning of paper instead of children, the angering of the orderlies in the front parlor of the charnel house." Daniel Berrigan, S.J., *The Trial of the Cantonsville Nine* (New York: Samuel French, 1971).

20 On the ways that mourning is a powerful means of fostering resistance born of theological resources, including by creating rites that create the conditions necessary for moral responsibility and agency, cf. Boopalan, *Memory, Grief, and Agency*, 185–226.

21 Jonathan Lear, "Gettysburg Mourning," 119. Lear notes that with regard to the Confederacy, the United States has been stuck in an "unhealthy cultural imaginary" in which we *either* remember through idealization *or* try to forget. "In the South, Confederate dead have been idealized and glorified; in the North, many arrogantly look down on the South as ignorant and bigoted—and use that trope to exculpate themselves of racism in their own eyes." Lear, "Gettysburg Mourning," 118. Lear sees possibilities in mourning versus suppression: "Trying to get rid of

memory by obliterating it tends not to work. The problems are driven underground and they emerge in some other form, still unresolved. We need to create imaginative routes of deglorification and de-idealization that nevertheless allow us to remember." "Gettysburg Mourning," 120–21.

22 I am grateful to Mikael Broadway for this suggestion.

23 *Confessions* 10.28, trans. Ryan.

24 I am reminded of the extended meditation on mourning and loss found in Jones, *Trauma and Grace*, 151–65. These words in particular are striking, quoting a Vietnam veteran: "The way forward is never straight, and there is no going back. Having lived in the land of the bizarre, all one can do is step forward into a future where that bizarre world continues to haunt you, but perhaps in a new way. A space is opened up for other kinds of knowing as well. But the two worlds continue to haunt one another." Jones, *Trauma and Grace*, 156.

25 The split between the two is said to have been amicable, although there was growing tension between black and white members of the church until the split. Cf. W. Glenn Jonas Jr., *Nurturing the Vision: First Baptist Church, Raleigh, 1812–2012* (Macon: Mercer University Press, 2012), 125–26, 134–35. Even today, in describing how their church was used as a Confederate hospital during the Civil War, First Baptist Church describes the conflict as "the war between the states," which is a euphemistic term for the war created and perpetuated by Lost Cause advocates. Cf. http://fbcraleigh.org/home/fbc-raleigh-history.

26 In this I am invoking the principles of just peacemaking as laid out by Glen Stassen, in particular the importance of honestly acknowledging wrongdoing and complicity. Glen H. Stassen, *Just Peacemaking: Transforming Initiatives for Justice and Peace* (Louisville: Westminster John Knox, 1992), 107–9. As Stassen writes, "Repentance does not lead nostalgically into the past but prophetically into the future." And again, quoting a West German book on reconciliation: "Repression holds up the process of redemption; to remember brings it closer." Stassen, *Just Peacemaking*, 108–9.

27 That is, this practice would open up the space for counter-memory in a way that is similar to what is advocated by Angela Sims and Emilie Townes. Cf. Sims, *Lynched*; and Townes, *Womanist Ethics*. See also Guth, "Sacred Emblems."

28 Cf. Nussbaum, *Anger and Forgiveness*. Nussbaum does hold a place for "transition-anger," a response that moves from outrage to working to right wrongs suffered. For a theological defense of the appropriateness of anger, cf. Michael P. Jaycox, "The Civic Virtues of Social Anger: A

Critically Reconstructed Normative Ethic for Public Life," *Journal of the Society of Christian Ethics* 36, no. 1 (2016): 123–43.

29 Dietrich Bonhoeffer, *The Cost of Discipleship* (1959; New York: Touchstone, 1995), 44–45.

30 Maria Mayo, *The Limits of Forgiveness: Case Studies in the Distortion of a Biblical Ideal* (Minneapolis: Fortress, 2015), 42. Mayo shows that the work of Desmond Tutu and the South African Truth and Reconciliation Committee served to do precisely this with anger and victims. Cf. *Limits of Forgiveness*, 40–42, 97–157. Put simply, "Forgiveness alone did not end apartheid; protest and anger and righteous indignation paved the way to the TRC. The biblical account does not preclude anger even as it calls for bilateral forgiveness." Mayo, *Limits of Forgiveness*, 42.

31 Mayo, *Limits of Forgiveness*, 1–37.

32 Mayo, *Limits of Forgiveness*, 7.

33 McClendon, *Ethics*, 228. McClendon goes on to write that forgiveness "makes the other's story a part of his or her own story, and by owning it destroys forever its power to divide forgiver and forgiven." To forgive is to "learn a new and truer story about myself by discovering how fully my life is bound up even with those whose sins are also sins against myself." As such, forgiving cannot be mere forgetting, "for we can repress the memory and still be at enmity with one another."

34 Bonhoeffer, *Cost of Discipleship*, 43.

35 These themes are well-explored in Jennifer W. McBride, *Radical Discipleship: A Liturgical Politics of the Gospel* (Minneapolis: Fortress, 2017).

36 Mayo, *Limits of Forgiveness*, 155–57.

37 Smith, *Weird John Brown*, 153.

38 Cf. Alexander, *New Jim Crow*; Kazuko Suzuki and Diego A. von Vacono, eds., *Reconsidering Race: Social Science Perspectives on Racial Categories in the Age of Genomics* (New York: Oxford University Press, 2018); Dorothy Roberts, *Fatal Invention: How Science, Politics, and Big Business Re-Create Race in the Twenty-First Century* (New York: New Press, 2011); Denton-Borhaug, *U.S. War-Culture*; Douglas, *Stand Your Ground*. The Equal Justice Initiative's lynching museum makes the same kind of connections between past and present practice.

39 If this path of disruption were pursued with regard to Confederate monuments, it may even minimize (but not eliminate) the importance of these symbols, occluded by the solidarity work happening around and in front of them. The image of a gathered people who minimize and then eclipse from view a monument that nonetheless gathers them together is inspired by Bonnie Honig's observations about the civil rights movement and the Lincoln Memorial; cf. *Public Things*, 84–88.

40 Marika Rose, "For Our Sins: Christianity, Complicity and the Racialized Construction of Innocence," in *Exploring Complicity: Concepts, Cases and Critique*, ed. Afxentis Afxentiou, Robin Dunford, and Michael Neu (London: Rowman and Littlefield International, 2017), 53–64.

41 On the image of Jesus as stumbling block as a helpful image in political theology, cf. Rose, "For Our Sins," 59.

42 Craig Hovey, "Defacement and Disappearance: The Practice of Mourning with the Church of the Benevolent Self," in *Practicing to Aim at Truth: Theological Engagements in Honor of Nancey Murphy*, ed. Ryan Andrew Newson and Brad J. Kallenberg (Eugene, Ore.: Cascade, 2015), 262. For an exploration of the political weightiness of mourning in a different register, cf. Bruce Rogers-Vaughn, "Blessed Are Those Who Mourn: Depression as Political Resistance," *Pastoral Psychology* 63 (2014): 503–22.

43 Friedrich Nietzsche, *Beyond Good and Evil: Prelude to a Philosophy of the Future*, trans. Walter Kaufman (1886; New York: Vintage, 1989), §68. Cf. Volf, *Exclusion and Embrace*, 247.

44 This fundamental ambivalence of images parallels a tendency in the field of visual studies to think of images either as mere tokens and therefore of no ultimate importance in and of themselves, or as inherently dangerous and even idolatrous, and thus to be avoided. Carnes, *Image and Presence*, xi.

45 Carnes, *Image and Presence*, 5.

46 Carnes, *Image and Presence*, 154. In this sense iconoclasm is inherent to imaging and is unavoidable.

47 Carnes, *Image and Presence*, 15. Carnes argues that the presence-absence dialectic in images echoes off of this same intertwined relationship in Christ himself, the image of the invisible God.

48 Carnes names these two options "iconoclasms of fidelity" and "iconoclasms of temptation." *Image and Presence*, 13.

49 Carnes, *Image and Presence*, 154.

50 Carnes, *Image and Presence*, 175.

51 Put differently, Confederate monuments attempt to hook people into the "white aesthetic regime" that baptizes people into viewing space, themselves, time, and beauty through its commitments and desires. See Willie James Jennings, "The Aesthetic Struggle and Ecclesial Vision," in *Black Practical Theology*, ed. Dale P. Andrews and Robert London Smith Jr. (Waco: Baylor University Press, 2015).

52 Du Bois, "Perfect Vacation," 279. Cf. Du Bois, *Black Reconstruction*, 715–16.

53 Cf. Barbee, *Race and Masculinity*, 184.

54 This recommendation maps onto debates surrounding the appropriateness and effectiveness of so-called "counter-monuments." Cf. Quentin Stevens, Karen A. Franck, and Ruth Fazakerley, "Counter-monuments: The Anti-monumental and the Dialogic," *Journal of Architecture* 17, no. 6 (2012): 951–72; and Natalia Krzyżanowska, "The Discourse of Counter-monuments: Semiotics of Material Commemoration in Contemporary Urban Spaces," *Social Semiotics* 26, no. 5 (2016): 465–85.

55 Martin Luther King Jr., "A Time to Break Silence" (1967), in *Testament of Hope*, 242.

56 Cf. Alfred Frankowski, *Post-Racial Limits*, 16. The monument also "requires the forgetting of a multiplicity of struggles, deaths, suffering, and ultimately a whole order of life to which white society had been un- and anti-empathetic to throughout its own formation and to which it remains un-empathetic today." Frankowski, *Post-Racial Limits*, 2–3.

57 Tran, *Vietnam War.*

58 This maps onto the growing construction of monuments that are "touch" sites—that incorporate an element of change within their design and encourage interactivity by those visiting them. Cf. Bergman, *Exhibiting Patriotism*, 21, 173–74.

59 Natalie Carnes, "Breaking the Power of Monuments," *Stanford University Press Blog*, August 29, 2017, http://stanfordpress.typepad.com/blog/2017/08/breaking-the-power-of-monuments.html.

60 Carnes also describes this as "Wittgensteinian iconoclasm" following Ludwig Wittgenstein's insight that a main cause of philosophical disease is a one-sided diet: "One nourishes one's thinking with only one kind of example." Carnes, *Image and Presence*, 157–58. See Wittgenstein, *Philosophical Investigations*, §593.

61 Another way to put this is that by aesthetic addition, Confederate monuments might become a different kind of heterotopia, particularly insofar as it is able to juxtapose "in a single real space several spaces, several sites that are in themselves incompatible." Michel Foucault, "Of Other Spaces," 25.

62 On strategies for disrupting the narratives that underlay Confederate monuments, cf. Ifill, *On the Courthouse Lawn.*

63 I am here reminded of these words from Edward Soja, summarizing Lefebvre: "There are no closures, no permanent structures of knowledge, no intrinsically privileged epistemologies. One must always be moving on, nomadically searching for new sources of practical knowledge, better approximations, carrying along only what was most usefully learned from earlier voyages." Soja, "Thirdspace," 269.

64 Blight, *Race and Reunion*, 316.

65 "Any real change implies the breakup of the world as one has always known it, the loss of all that gave one an identity, the end of safety. And at such a moment, unable to see and not daring to imagine what the future will now bring forth, one clings to what one knew, or thought one knew; to what one possessed or dreamed that one possessed. Yet, it is only when a man is able, without bitterness or self-pity, to surrender a dream he has long cherished or a privilege he has long possessed that he is set free—he has set himself free—for higher dreams, for greater privileges." Baldwin, "Faulkner and Desegregation," 117.

Bibliography

Alexander, Jeffrey C., Ron Eyerman, Bernhard Giesen, Neil J. Smelser, and Piotr Sztompka. *Cultural Trauma and Collective Identity*. Berkeley: University of California Press, 2004.

Alexander, Michelle. *The New Jim Crow: Mass Incarceration in the Age of Colorblindness*. New York: New Press, 2012.

Anderson, Benedict. *Imagined Communities: Reflections on the Origin and Spread of Nationalism*. 1983. Rev. ed. New York: Verso, 2006.

Andrews, Dale P., and Robert London Smith Jr., eds. *Black Practical Theology*. Waco: Baylor University Press, 2015.

Assmann, Jan. *Das kulturelle Gedächtnis: Schrift, Erinnerung und politische Identität in frühen Hochkulturen*. Munich: Beck Press, 1992.

Augustine. *The Confessions of St. Augustine*. Translated by John K. Ryan. New York: Doubleday, 1960.

Austin, J. L. *How to Do Things with Words*. 1962. 2nd ed. Edited by J. O. Urmson and Marina Sbisà. Cambridge, Mass.: Harvard University Press, 1975.

Baker, Kelly J. *Gospel According to the Klan: The KKK's Appeal to Protestant America, 1915–1930*. Lawrence: University Press of Kansas, 2011.

Baldwin, James. *The Cross of Redemption: Uncollected Writings*. Edited by Randall Kenan. New York: Pantheon, 2010.

———. *The Fire Next Time*. New York: Dial Press, 1963.

———. *Nobody Knows My Name*. 1961. New York: First Vintage, 1993.

Barbee, Matthew Mace. *Race and Masculinity in Southern Memory: History of Richmond, Virginia's Monument Avenue, 1948–1996*. Lanham, Md.: Lexington, 2014.

Barth, Karl. *Ethics*. Edited by Dietrich Braun, translated by Geoffrey W. Bromiley. New York: Seabury Press, 1981.

213

Bellah, Robert N. "Civil Religion in America." *Daedalus* 96, no. 1 (1967): 1–21.

Bergman, Teresa. *Exhibiting Patriotism: Creating and Contesting Interpretations of American Historic Sites.* Walnut Creek, Calif.: Left Coast, 2013.

Berrigan, Daniel, S.J. *The Trial of the Cantonsville Nine.* New York: Samuel French, 1971.

Berry, Wendell. *The Hidden Wound.* 1970. Berkeley: Counterpoint, 2010.

Bishop, Jeffrey P. *The Anticipatory Corpse: Medicine, Power, and the Care of the Dying.* Notre Dame: University of Notre Dame Press, 2011.

Blair, William A. *Cities of the Dead: Contesting the Memory of the Civil War in the South, 1865–1914.* Chapel Hill: University of North Carolina Press, 2004.

Blight, David W. *Race and Reunion: The Civil War in American Memory.* Cambridge, Mass.: Belknap and Harvard University Press, 2001.

Bodnar, John. *Remaking America: Public Memory, Commemoration, and Patriotism in the Twentieth Century.* Princeton: Princeton University Press, 1992.

Bonhoeffer, Dietrich. *The Cost of Discipleship.* 1959. New York: Touchstone, 1995.

Bonilla-Silva, Eduardo. *Racism without Racists: Color-Blind Racism and the Persistence of Racial Inequality in America.* 2003. 5th ed. Lanham, Md.: Rowman & Littlefield, 2018.

Boopalan, Sunder John. *Memory, Grief, and Agency: A Political Theological Account of Wrongs and Rites.* New York: Palgrave Macmillan, 2017.

Brundage, W. Fitzhugh. *The Southern Past: A Clash of Race and Memory.* Cambridge, Mass.: Belknap and Harvard University Press, 2005.

———, ed. *Where These Memories Grow: History, Memory, and Southern Identity.* Chapel Hill: University of North Carolina Press, 2015.

Carnes, Natalie. *Image and Presence: A Christological Reflection on Iconoclasm and Iconophilia.* Stanford: Stanford University Press, 2017.

Carter, J. Kameron. *Race: A Theological Account.* New York: Oxford University Press, 2008.

Cavanaugh, William T. *Torture and Eucharist.* Malden, Mass.: Blackwell, 1998.

Cavell, Stanley. *The Cavell Reader.* Edited by Stephen Mulhall. Cambridge, Mass.: Blackwell, 1996.

Cecelski, David S., and Timothy B. Tyson, eds. *Democracy Betrayed: The Wilmington Race Riot of 1898 and Its Legacy.* Chapel Hill: University of North Carolina Press, 1998.

Chomsky, Noam, and Michel Foucault. *The Chomsky-Foucault Debate: On Human Nature.* New York: New Press, 2006.

Clark, Andy. *Supersizing the Mind: Embodiment, Action, and Cognitive Extension.* Oxford: Oxford University Press, 2008.

Cone, James H. *A Black Theology of Liberation.* 1970. Maryknoll, N.Y.: Orbis, 1986.

————. *The Cross and the Lynching Tree.* Maryknoll, N.Y.: Orbis, 2011.

————. *God of the Oppressed.* 1975. Rev. ed. Maryknoll, N.Y.: Orbis, 1997.

Connerton, Paul. *How Societies Remember.* Cambridge: Cambridge University Press, 1989.

Connolly, William E. *Democracy, Pluralism, and Political Theory.* Edited by Samuel A. Chambers and Terrell Carver. New York: Routledge, 2008.

Cunningham, David. *Klansville, U.S.A.: The Rise and Fall of the Civil Rights-Era Ku Klux Klan.* New York: Oxford University Press, 2013.

Davis, Jefferson. *The Rise and Fall of the Confederate Government, Volume 2.* New York: D. Appleton and Company, 1881.

De La Torre, Miguel A. *Embracing Hopelessness.* Minneapolis: Fortress, 2017.

————. *Latina/o Social Ethics: Moving Beyond Eurocentric Moral Thinking.* Waco: Baylor University Press, 2010.

Denton-Borhaug, Kelly. *U.S. War-Culture, Sacrifice and Salvation.* Oakville, Conn.: Equinox, 2011.

Doss, Erika. *Memorial Mania: Public Feeling in America.* Chicago: University of Chicago Press, 2010.

Douglas, Kelly Brown. *The Black Christ.* Maryknoll, N.Y.: Orbis, 1994.

————. *Stand Your Ground: Black Bodies and the Justice of God.* Maryknoll, N.Y.: Orbis, 2015.

Du Bois, W. E. B. *Black Reconstruction in America: Toward a History of the Part Which Black Folk Played in the Attempt to Reconstruct Democracy in America, 1860–1880.* 1935. New York: Free Press, 1998.

————. "The Perfect Vacation." *The Crisis* 40, no. 8 (1931).

————. *The Souls of Black Folk.* 1903. New York: Restless, 2017.

Emerson, Michael O., and Christian Smith. *Divided by Faith: Evangelical Religion and the Problem of Race in America.* New York: Oxford University Press, 2000.

Erll, Astrid. *Memory in Culture.* 2005. Translated by Sara B. Young. New York: Palgrave Macmillan, 2011.

Faust, Drew Gilpin, ed. *The Ideology of Slavery: Proslavery Thought in the Antebellum South, 1830–1860.* Baton Rouge: Louisiana State University Press, 1981.

———. *This Republic of Suffering: Death and the American Civil War.* New York: Alfred A. Knopf, 2008.

Festinger, Leon, Henry W. Riecken, and Stanley Schachter. *When Prophecy Fails: A Social and Psychological Study of a Modern Group That Predicted the Destruction of the World.* 1956. London: Pinter & Martin, 2008.

Flower, Harriet I. *The Dancing Lares and the Serpent in the Garden: Religion at the Roman Street Corner.* Princeton: Princeton University Press, 2017.

Foster, Gaines M. *Ghosts of the Confederacy: Defeat, the Lost Cause, and the Emergence of the New South, 1865 to 1913.* New York: Oxford University Press, 1987.

Foucault, Michel. "Of Other Spaces." *Diacritics* 16, no. 1 (1986): 22–27.

Frankowski, Alfred. *The Post-Racial Limits of Memorialization: Toward a Political Sense of Mourning.* Lanham, Md.: Lexington, 2015.

Gallie, W. B. *Philosophy and the Historical Understanding.* London: Chatto and Windus, 1964.

Geertz, Clifford. *The Interpretation of Cultures: Selected Essays.* New York: Basic, 1973.

Gillis, John R., ed. *Commemorations: The Politics of National Identity.* Princeton: Princeton University Press, 1994.

Glassberg, David. *American Historical Pageantry: The Uses of Tradition in the Early Twentieth Century.* Chapel Hill: University of North Carolina Press, 1990.

———. *Sense of History: The Place of the Past in American Life.* Amherst: University of Massachusetts Press, 2001.

Gorringe, T. J. *Earthly Visions: Theology and the Challenges of Art.* New Haven: Yale University Press, 2011.

Gorski, Philip. *American Covenant: A History of Civil Religion from the Puritans to the Present.* Princeton: Princeton University Press, 2017.

Grant, Jacquelyn. *White Women's Christ and Black Women's Jesus: Feminist Christology and Womanist Response.* Atlanta: Scholars Press, 1989.

Greenspan, Elizabeth. *Battle for Ground Zero: Inside the Political Struggle to Rebuild the World Trade Center.* New York: St. Martin's, 2013.

Guth, Karen V. "Sacred Emblems of Faith: Womanist Contributions to the Confederate Monuments Debate." *Journal of the Society of Christian Ethics* 39, no. 2 (2019): 375–93.

Gutman, Yifat. "Where Do We Go from Here: The Pasts, Presents, and Futures of Ground Zero." *Memory Studies* 2, no. 1 (2009): 55–70.

Halbwachs, Maurice. *The Collective Memory.* 1925. Translated by Francis J. Ditter Jr. and Vida Yazdi Ditter. New York: Harper & Row, 1980.

———. *On Collective Memory.* Chicago: University of Chicago Press, 1992.

Hauerwas, Stanley. *War and the American Difference: Theological Reflections on Violence and National Identity.* Grand Rapids: Baker Academic, 2011.

Hebel, Udo J., ed. *Sites of Memory in American Literatures and Cultures.* Heidelberg: Universitätsverlag C. Winter, 2003.

Heller, Dana. *The Selling of 9/11: How a National Tragedy Became a Commodity.* New York: Palgrave Macmillan, 2005.

Hobsbawm, Eric. "Mass Producing Traditions: Europe, 1870–1914." In *The Invention of Tradition,* edited by Eric Hobsbawm and Terence Ranger, 263–308. Cambridge: Cambridge University Press, 1983.

Honig, Bonnie. *Public Things: Democracy in Disrepair.* New York: Fordham University Press, 2017.

Horton, James Oliver, and Lois E. Horton. *Slavery and Public History: The Tough Stuff of American Memory.* 2006. Chapel Hill: University of North Carolina Press, 2009.

Hovey, Craig. "Defacement and Disappearance: The Practice of Mourning with the Church of the Benevolent Self." In *Practicing to Aim at Truth: Theological Engagements in Honor of Nancey Murphy,* edited by Ryan Andrew Newson and Brad J. Kallenberg, 261–76. Eugene, Ore.: Cascade, 2015.

Hughes, Richard T. *Myths America Lives By: White Supremacy and the Stories That Give Us Meaning.* Urbana: University of Illinois Press, 2003.

Huyssen, Andreas. *Present Pasts: Urban Palimpsests and the Politics of Memory.* Stanford: Stanford University Press, 2003.

Ifill, Sherrilyn A. *On the Courthouse Lawn: Confronting the Legacy of Lynching in the Twenty-First Century.* Boston: Beacon, 2007.

Jaycox, Michael P. "The Civic Virtues of Social Anger: A Critically Reconstructed Normative Ethic for Public Life." *Journal of the Society of Christian Ethics* 36, no. 1 (2016): 123–43.

Jennings, Willie James. *Acts.* Louisville: Westminster John Knox, 2017.

———. *The Christian Imagination: Theology and the Origins of Race.* New Haven: Yale University Press, 2010.

Johnson, Luke Timothy. *The Writings of the New Testament: An Interpretation.* Rev. ed. London: SCM Press, 1999.

Jonas, W. Glenn, Jr. *Nurturing the Vision: First Baptist Church, Raleigh, 1812–2012*. Macon: Mercer University Press, 2012.

Jones, Serene. *Trauma and Grace: Theology in a Ruptured World*. 2009. 2nd ed. Louisville: Westminster John Knox, 2019.

Jones, William R. *Is God a White Racist? A Preamble to Black Theology*. 1973. Boston: Beacon, 1998.

Kallenberg, Brad J. *By Design: Ethics, Theology, and the Practice of Engineering*. Eugene, Ore.: Cascade, 2013.

Keefe-Perry, L. Callid. *Way to Water: A Theopoetics Primer*. Eugene, Ore.: Cascade, 2014.

Keshgegian, Flora A. *Redeeming Memories: A Theology of Healing and Transformation*. Nashville: Abingdon, 2000.

King, Martin Luther, Jr. *A Testament of Hope: The Essential Writings and Speeches*. 1986. Edited by James M. Washington. New York: HarperOne, 2003.

Krzyżanowska, Natalia. "The Discourse of Counter-monuments: Semiotics of Material Commemoration in Contemporary Urban Spaces." *Social Semiotics* 26, no. 5 (2016): 465–85.

Lear, Jonathan. "Gettysburg Mourning." *Critical Inquiry* 45, no. 1 (2018): 97–121.

Lefebvre, Henri. *The Production of Space*. 1974. Translated by Donald Nicholson-Smith. Oxford: Blackwell, 1991.

Lennon, John, and Malcolm Foley. *Dark Tourism: The Attraction of Death and Disaster*. London: Continuum, 2000.

Levinson, Sanford. *Written in Stone: Public Monuments in Changing Societies*. Durham: Duke University Press, 1998.

Linenthal, Edward T. *The Unfinished Bombing: Oklahoma City in American Memory*. Oxford: Oxford University Press, 2001.

Lipsitz, George. "The Racialization of Space and the Spatialization of Race: Theorizing the Hidden Architecture of Landscape." *Landscape Journal* 26, no. 1 (2007): 10–23.

Lloyd, Vincent W. *Religion of the Field Negro: On Black Secularism and Black Theology*. New York: Fordham University Press, 2018.

Loewen, James W., and Edward H. Sebesta, eds. *The Confederate and Neo-Confederate Reader: The "Great Truth" about the "Lost Cause."* Oxford: University Press of Mississippi, 2010.

Lorde, Audre. *Sister Outsider: Essays and Speeches*. 1984. New York: Crossing, 2007.

Low, Setha M. "Lessons from Imagining the World Trade Center Site: An Examination of Public Space and Culture." *Anthropology and Education Quarterly* 33, no. 3 (2002): 395–405.

Lowenthal, David. *The Past Is a Foreign Country—Revisited*. Cambridge: Cambridge University Press, 2015.

Lubbock, John. *The Beauties of Nature and the Wonders of the World We Live In*. 1892. New York: Macmillan, 1905.

MacIntyre, Alasdair. *After Virtue: A Study in Moral Theory*. 1981. 2nd ed. Notre Dame: University of Notre Dame Press, 1984.

———. *Dependent Rational Animals*. Chicago: Open Court, 1999.

Mathews, Donald G. "The Southern Rite of Human Sacrifice: Lynching and Religion in the South, 1875–1940." *Journal of Southern Religion* 3 (2000).

Mayo, Maria. *The Limits of Forgiveness: Case Studies in the Distortion of a Biblical Ideal*. Minneapolis: Fortress, 2015.

McBride, Jennifer W. *Radical Discipleship: A Liturgical Politics of the Gospel*. Minneapolis: Fortress, 2017.

McClendon, James Wm., Jr. *Doctrine: Systematic Theology, Volume 2*. Nashville: Abingdon, 1994.

———. *Ethics: Systematic Theology, Volume 1*. 1986. Rev. ed. Nashville: Abingdon, 2002.

McClendon, James Wm., Jr., and James M. Smith. *Convictions: Defusing Religious Relativism*. Valley Forge, Pa.: Trinity Press International, 1994.

McConnell, Stuart. *Glorious Contentment: The Grand Army of the Republic, 1865–1900*. Chapel Hill: University of North Carolina Press, 1992.

McCurry, Stephanie. *Confederate Reckoning: Power and Politics in the Civil War South*. Cambridge, Mass.: Harvard University Press, 2010.

McFarland, Stephen, Samantha L. Bowden, and M. Martin Bosman. "'Take 'Em Down Hillsborough!': Race, Space, and the 2017 Struggle Over Confederate Iconography in Neoliberal Tampa." *Southeastern Geographer* 59, no. 2 (2019): 172–95.

Mitscherlich, Alexander, and Margarete Mitscherlich. *The Inability to Mourn*. 1967. New York: Grove Press, 1975.

Morrill, Bruce T., S.J. *Anamnesis as Dangerous Memory: Political and Liturgical Theology in Dialogue*. Collegeville, Minn.: Pueblo, 2000.

Nelson, Robert S., and Margaret Olin, eds. *Monuments and Memory, Made and Unmade*. Chicago: University of Chicago Press, 2003.

Nietzsche, Friedrich. *Beyond Good and Evil: Prelude to a Philosophy of the Future*. Translated by Walter Kaufman. 1886. New York: Vintage, 1989.

———. *The Portable Nietzsche*. Translated by Walter Kaufman. New York: Viking, 1959.

Noll, Mark A. *The Civil War as a Theological Crisis.* Chapel Hill: University of North Carolina Press, 2006.

Nora, Pierre. "Between Memory and History: *Les Lieux de Mémoire.*" *Representations* 26 (Spring 1989): 7–24.

———. *Rethinking France: Les Lieux De Mémoire.* 4 vols. Translated by David P. Jordan. Chicago: University of Chicago Press, 2001–2010.

Nussbaum, Martha C. *Anger and Forgiveness: Resentment, Generosity, Justice.* New York: Oxford University Press, 2016.

Patterson, Orlando. *Rituals of Blood: The Consequences of Slavery in Two American Centuries.* New York: Basic, 1998.

Prather, H. Leon. *We Have Taken a City: The Wilmington Racial Massacre and Coup of 1898.* 1984. Wilmington, N.C.: Dram Tree, 2006.

Rae, Murray A. *Architecture and Theology: The Art of Place.* Waco: Baylor University Press, 2017.

Rambo, Shelly. *Resurrecting Wounds: Living in the Afterlife of Trauma.* Waco: Baylor University Press, 2017.

Rancière, Jacques. *The Future of the Image.* 2003. Translated by Gregory Elliott. New York: Verso, 2007.

———. *The Politics of Aesthetics: The Distribution of the Sensible.* 2000. Translated by Gabriel Rockhill. New York: Continuum, 2006.

Ricoeur, Paul. *Interpretation Theory: Discourse and the Surplus of Meaning.* Fort Worth: Texas Christian University Press, 1976.

———. *Memory, History, Forgetting.* Translated by Kathleen Blamey and David Pellauer. Chicago: University of Chicago Press, 2004.

Roberts, Dorothy. *Fatal Invention: How Science, Politics, and Big Business Re-Create Race in the Twenty-First Century.* New York: New Press, 2011.

Rogers-Vaughn, Bruce. "Blessed Are Those Who Mourn: Depression as Political Resistance." *Pastoral Psychology* 63 (2014): 503–22.

Rose, Marika. "For Our Sins: Christianity, Complicity and the Racialized Construction of Innocence." In *Exploring Complicity: Concepts, Cases and Critique,* edited by Afxentis Afxentiou, Robin Dunford, and Michael Neu, 53–64. London: Rowman and Littlefield International, 2017.

Rothberg, Michael. *Multidirectional Memory: Remembering the Holocaust in the Age of Decolonization.* Stanford: Stanford University Press, 2009.

Sather-Wagstaff, Joy. *Heritage That Hurts: Tourists in the Memoryscapes of September 11.* Walnut Creek, Calif.: Left Coast, 2011.

Savage, Kirk. *Standing Soldiers, Kneeling Slaves: Race, War, and Monument in Nineteenth-Century America.* Princeton: Princeton University Press, 1997.

Shackel, Paul A. *Memory in Black and White: Race, Commemoration, and the Post-Bellum Landscape.* Walnut Creek, Calif.: AltaMira, 2003.

Simons, Daniel J., and Christopher F. Chabris. "Gorillas in Our Midst: Sustained Inattentional Blindness for Dynamic Events." *Perception* 28, no. 9 (1999): 1059–74.

Sims, Angela D. *Lynched: The Power of Memory in a Culture of Terror.* Waco: Baylor University Press, 2016.

Smith, Ted A. *Weird John Brown: Divine Violence and the Limits of Ethics.* Stanford: Stanford University Press, 2015.

Soja, Edward W. *Postmodern Geographies: The Reassertion of Space in Critical Social Theory.* New York: Verso, 1989.

———. "Thirdspace: Expanding the Scope of the Geographical Imagination." In *Human Geography Today,* edited by Doreen Massey, John Allen, and Philip Sarre, 260–78. Malden, Mass.: Polity, 1999.

Stassen, Glen H. *Just Peacemaking: Transforming Initiatives for Justice and Peace.* Louisville: Westminster John Knox, 1992.

Stevens, Quentin, Karen A. Franck, and Ruth Fazakerley. "Countermonuments: The Anti-monumental and the Dialogic." *Journal of Architecture* 17, no. 6 (2012): 951–72.

Stiver, Dan. *Ricoeur and Theology.* London: Bloomsbury, 2012.

Stringfellow, William. *My People Is the Enemy.* New York: Holt, Rinehart, and Winston, 1964.

Sturken, Marita. *Tourists of History: Memory, Kitsch, and Consumerism from Oklahoma City to Ground Zero.* Durham: Duke University Press, 2007.

Suzuki, Kazuko, and Diego A. von Vacono, eds. *Reconsidering Race: Social Science Perspectives on Racial Categories in the Age of Genomics.* New York: Oxford University Press, 2018.

Tilley, Terrence W. *The Evils of Theodicy.* Washington, D.C.: Georgetown University Press, 1991.

Townes, Emilie M. *Womanist Ethics and the Cultural Production of Evil.* New York: Palgrave Macmillan, 2006.

Tran, Jonathan. *The Vietnam War and Theologies of Memory: Time and Eternity in the Far Country.* Chichester, UK: Wiley-Blackwell, 2010.

Trouillot, Michel-Rolph. *Silencing the Past: Power and the Production of History.* Boston: Beacon, 1995.

Tyson, Timothy B. "The Ghosts of 1898: Wilmington's Race Riot and the Rise of White Supremacy." *News and Observer* (Raleigh, N.C.), November 17, 2006.

Volf, Miroslav. *The End of Memory: Remembering Rightly in a Violent World.* Grand Rapids: Eerdmans, 2006.

————. *Exclusion and Embrace: A Theological Exploration of Identity, Otherness, and Reconciliation.* Nashville: Abingdon, 1996.

Weed, Eric A. *The Religion of White Supremacy in the United States.* Lanham, Md.: Lexington, 2017.

White, Walter F. *The Fire in the Flint.* New York: Alfred A. Knopf, 1924.

Williams, Delores. "The Color of Feminism: Or Speaking the Black Woman's Tongue." *Journal of Religious Thought* 43, no. 1 (1986): 42–58.

Williams, Reggie. *Bonhoeffer's Black Jesus: Harlem Renaissance Theology and an Ethic of Resistance.* Waco: Baylor University Press, 2014.

Wilson, Charles Reagan. *Baptized in Blood: The Religion of the Lost Cause, 1865–1920.* 1980. Athens: University of Georgia Press, 2009.

Wittgenstein, Ludwig. *On Certainty.* 1969. Edited by G. E. M. Anscombe and G. H. von Wright. In *Major Works: Selected Philosophical Writings.* New York: HarperCollins, 2009.

————. *Philosophical Investigations.* 1953. 4th ed. Translated by G. E. M. Anscombe, P. M. S. Hacker, and Joachim Schulte. Chichester, UK: Wiley-Blackwell, 2009.

————. *Remarks on the Philosophy of Psychology, Volume 2.* Edited by G. H. von Wright and Heikki Nyman. Translated by C. G. Luckhardt and A. E. Aue. Oxford: Blackwell, 1980.

Wood, Amy Louise. *Lynching and Spectacle: Witnessing Racial Violence in America, 1890–1940.* Chapel Hill: University of North Carolina Press, 2009.

Woodward, C. Vann. *The Strange Career of Jim Crow.* 1955. Oxford: Oxford University Press, 2002.

Yancy, George. *Black Bodies, White Gazes: The Continuing Significance of Race in America.* 2nd ed. Lanham, Md.: Rowman & Littlefield, 2017.

Young, Iris Marion. *Justice and the Politics of Difference.* 1990. Princeton: Princeton University Press, 2011.

Young, James E. *At Memory's Edge: After-Images of the Holocaust in Contemporary Art and Architecture.* New Haven: Yale University Press, 2000.

————. *The Stages of Memory: Reflections on Memorial Art, Loss, and the Spaces Between.* Amherst: University of Massachusetts Press, 2016.

————. *The Texture of Memory: Holocaust Memorials and Meaning.* New Haven: Yale University Press, 1993.

Index

Augustine, 60, 152–53, 203n57, 206n10

Baldwin, James, v, xiii–xiv, 103, 165, 170n21, 194n68, 200n27, 212n65
Barth, Karl, 127, 204n73
Berry, Wendell, 124, 195n68

Calhoun, John C., 3, 168n6
Carter, J. Kameron, 92, 179n2, 195n83, 196n86, 196n87, 196n89, 196n92
Charlottesville riots, 1–2, 4, 72, 163–64, 192n48
Christ: and dangerous memory, 42; as key to remembering well, 58–62, 144, 156–57, 186n74; as lynched, 65–67, 161; as truly Human One, 96, 147, 188n101; *see also* sacrifice
civil religion: *see* Lost Cause
Civil War, 15, 33, 36, 52
collective memory: *see* memory
common soldier statue, 26, 82–84, 94–95, 111, 193n56
Cone, James, 22, 65–66, 133, 188n101, 188n110
courage: *see* valor of fallen soldiers

Davis, Jefferson, 17, 39–41
defense of statues, 6, 139–40, 144–45; *see also* disrupting statues through addition; removal of statues
Deo Vindice, 35–36, 41
disrupting statues through addition, 97–100, 126–29, 132–33, 137–38, 157–63; *see also* defense of statues; removal of statues
Douglass, Frederick, 23, 32, 34, 85–86, 98, 165, 178n93, 183n33
Du Bois, W. E. B., 11, 27, 32, 89, 98, 160, 177n87, 178n100, 188n102, 193n54

emigration to Brazil, 17–18
eschatology, 37, 57–62, 92–94, 99–100, 101–2, 121–22, 165

faithful slave myth, 27, 175n58; *see also* mammy

flag, Confederate, xi, 3, 136, 168n4, 206n12
forgiveness, 60, 154–56, 209n30, 209n33
Foucault, Michel, 167n4, 204n71, 211n61
future: and monuments, 37, 74, 95–96; *see also* eschatology

grief: *see* lament; mourning

Halbwachs, Maurice, 43–46, 198n3
history: and God, 9; as objective, 56–57; limits of, 7–8; narrating, 55, 61–62, 108; significance of, 14
Honig, Bonnie, 115–17
honor, loss of, 17, 21, 24, 65
hope, 18, 20, 31, 35, 67, 99–100, 102, 124, 126

identity: construction of, 43–44,
idolatry, 9, 64–65, 74–75, 96–98, 100, 147, 158–60, 164

Jackson, Stonewall, 25, 52, 79; monument to, 25–26, 35, 54, 129
Jefferson, Thomas, 2, 5, 7
Jennings, Willie, 69, 91–93, 185n57, 190n15, 205n83, 210n51
Jim Crow, 30–31, 82, 156, 191n26

King, Martin Luther, 34, 93–94, 109; monument to, 162
Ku Klux Klan, 21, 26, 136, 193n52

lament, 19, 99, 151–52, 156; *see also* mourning
Lee, Robert E.: as idealized figure, 13, 24–25, 51, 64–65, 79, 86; monument to, 2, 4, 27, 30, 54, 85, 86–87, 150, 164, 192n45; thoughts on Lost Cause, 174n45
Lincoln, Abraham, 32, 52, 85, 184n40, 192n40
Lost Cause: civil religion, 18–19, 24, 35, 42, 51, 64–65, 172n18, 173n37, 175n46; interpretation of the Civil War, 13–14, 23–28, 32, 39–41, 52, 86, 130, 140, 174n45, 179n2

223